THE NEW CLARENDON SHAKESPEARE

HAMLET

Edited by

GEORGE RYLANDS
Fellow of King's College, Cambridge

OXFORD UNIVERSITY PRESS

Oxford University Press, Walton Street, Oxford OX2 6DP

OXFORD NEW YORK TORONTO
DELHI BOMBAY CALCUTTA MADRAS KARACHI
PETALING JAYA SINGAPORE HONG KONG TOKYO
NAIROBI DAR ES SALAAM CAPE TOWN
MELBOURNE AUCKLAND

and associated companies in
BERLIN IBADAN

Oxford is a trade mark of Oxford University Press

First edition 1947
Reprinted 1950, 1955, 1956, 1959, 1961, 1962, 1965,
1967, 1969, 1970, 1971, 1974, 1978, 1982, 1985, 1986 (twice)
1989

━━━

THE NEW CLARENDON SHAKESPEARE

Under the general editorship of R. E. C. HOUGHTON, M.A.

	Edited by
Antony and Cleopatra	R. E. C. Houghton
As You Like It	Isabel J. Bisson
Coriolanus	B. H. Kemball-Cook
Hamlet	George Rylands
Henry IV, Part I	Bertram Newman
Henry IV, Part II	William R. Rutland
Henry V	Ronald F. W. Fletcher
Julius Caesar	R. E. C. Houghton
King Lear	R. E. C. Houghton
Macbeth	Bernard Groom
Measure for Measure	R. E. C. Houghton
Merchant of Venice	Ronald F. W. Fletcher
Midsummer Night's Dream	F. C. Horwood
Much Ado about Nothing	Philip Wayne
Othello	F. C. Horwood and
	R. E. C. Houghton
Richard II	John M. Lothian
Richard III	R. E. C. Houghton
Romeo and Juliet	R. E. C. Houghton
The Tempest	J. R. Sutherland
The Winter's Tale	S. L. Bethell
Twelfth Night	J. C. Dent

━━━

Printed in Hong Kong

PREFACE

THE *New Clarendon* Shakespeare aims primarily at presenting the text in such a way that it can be easily read and understood. The language of Shakespeare presents considerable difficulties to the beginner, difficulties which are constantly overlooked by readers familiar with the plays. But the answers of examination candidates, even at the university stage, often reveal unexpected ignorance of common Elizabethan usage and vocabulary. In this edition, therefore, the main emphasis has been placed on the interpretation of words and phrases, rather than on such linguistic matter as received much space in the old Clarendon Press editions of Clark and Wright. The notes have been divided, short glosses being placed below the text, while the more difficult passages are reserved for the commentary at the end. The latter, in the introductions to each scene and in the notes on individual lines, also gives full attention to points of literary and dramatic interest which have rightly come to the fore in modern teaching of English literature. Discussion of the true text and a few other more difficult notes are printed in smaller type within square brackets. The commentary and the introduction are supplemented by a substantial selection from the best criticism of the play, both old and new: a feature in which this edition of Shakespeare follows the plan set by the Clarendon English series. Here some matter will be found suitable for more advanced students, and the inclusion of varying opinions will provide material for reflection and comparison. It is the belief of the General Editor that students can best be taught to criticize by the provision of material which they can use as a starting-point as well as a model.

ACKNOWLEDGEMENTS

THE British Council (*English Literature*, by B. Ifor Evans: British Life and Thought Series—Longmans Green, 1944); The Cambridge University Press *Hamlet* (The New Shakespeare, edited by J. Dover Wilson and C. F. E. Spurgeon, *Shakespeare's Imagery*); Messrs. William Heinemann, Ltd. (A. C. Swinburne: *A Study of Shakespeare*); Messrs. Macmillan & Co., Ltd. (Sir Walter Raleigh, *Shakespeare*, and A. C. Bradley, *Shakespearian Tragedy*); Messrs. Methuen & Co., Ltd. (A. C. Clutton Brock: *Hamlet*); Messrs. Sidgwick & Jackson, Ltd., and the late Mr. Granville-Barker (H. Granville-Barker: *Prefaces to Shakespeare*).

The text of Hamlet *here printed is free from omission or alteration.*

CONTENTS

INTRODUCTION ✓

'Any thing so o'erdone is from the purpose of playing, whose end both at the first, and now, was and is, to hold as 'twere the mirror up to nature, to show virtue her own feature, scorn her own image, and the very age and body of the time his form and pressure.'

Shakespeare himself speaks in the Prince's advice to the players and as he was both an actor and a dramatist we may extend the word 'playing' to mean also 'play-writing'. The purpose of dramatist and actor is the same, and, as Hamlet expresses it, it is a double purpose. 'He was not of an age but for all time', wrote Ben Jonson, and Shakespeare's masterpieces do two things. They hold up the mirror to nature and they reveal the form and pressure of the time. The Tragedy of Hamlet mirrors the Elizabethan age, with its courtiers and ambassadors and soldiers, its grave-diggers and travelling players; a King and Queen and Prime Minister; the family affection and private life of a noble youth and his sister. And as the first audience of the play at the Globe could see themselves, so we, reading the play nearly three hundred and fifty years later, can look back and see that audience. But at the same time, to balance his crowded, shifting, varied, realistic stage, Shakespeare throws into the scale a single figure, the observed of all observers, the Prince of Denmark. In so doing he held up a mirror, not to the age but to nature, and ever since then actors and audience, critics and professors, readers and writers have looked into the mirror and seen—themselves. 'We feel not only the virtues, but the weaknesses, of Hamlet as our own', writes an eighteenth-century novelist, and Coleridge confesses, 'I have a smack of Hamlet myself.' The first comment on the play was written about the year 1600, in the margin of a Chaucer folio by a Cambridge don: 'His *Lucrece* & his tragedie of *Hamlet, Prince of Denmarke,* haue it in them, to please the wiser sort.' Gabriel Harvey who made that note had no doubts that he himself was one of 'the wiser sort'. 'It is *we* who are Hamlet', writes William Hazlitt; and in our own time another novelist and another don say the same. Anatole France after a performance at the Comédie-Française wrote: 'Vous êtes de tous les temps et de tous les pays. . . . Nous vivons ensemble, prince Hamlet, et vous êtes ce que nous sommes, un homme au milieu du mal universel. . . . Qui de nous ne vous ressemble en quelque chose?' And Mr. C. S. Lewis reaches a similar conclusion: 'It is often cast in the teeth of the great critics that each in painting *Hamlet* has drawn a portrait of himself. How if they were right? I would go a long way to meet Beatrice or Falstaff. . . . I would not cross the road to meet Hamlet. It would never be necessary. He is always where I am.'

Hamlet then is both 'of the age' and 'for all time'. We must think of the tragedy in two ways: *Hamlet* the play and Hamlet the Prince. *Hamlet* without the Prince of Denmark has become a proverb but the Prince of Denmark without the play is a chimera.

HAMLET THE PLAY

✱ Starting from the axiom 'the play's the thing', we must remind ourselves what a play is and is not, and then consider the peculiar characteristics of this particular play. Now a play is not a novel and even when written in verse it is not a poem, although the dramatist will trespass upon those preserves. A play is an emotional experience— whether we laugh or cry or grip the arms of the seat— which lasts for two-and-a-half to three hours and in which we are led from one given point to another given point by direct or indirect ways. We are always on the move. There is no going back. Within the two given points the dramatist crowds all the variety and surprise and excitement of romantic drama or, if he belongs to the classical school, draws us with a single line which grows tauter and more tense. The two limiting points, of departure and destination, are indissolubly linked. If the tension slackens, if we sometimes seem to pause or step aside, it is for a purpose of which the dramatist is aware even though we are not. As Aristotle baldly puts it, a drama has a beginning, a middle and an end. And Aristotle, the first dramatic critic, in his analysis of tragedy, puts *plot* first as the soul of drama and character second.*The *plot* is the sequence of situations and actions which dovetail together and bring about the inevitable catastrophe.* The initial situation pressing upon a particular temperament or personality and bringing it into conflict with other personalities results in action, which in turn works upon character and produces further situations that find vent in further action. In a novel, on the other hand, plot as a rule is subservient to character; its function is to reveal character. There may be only a single situation and little or no action. Moreover we can turn back the page. In a play we know a character first and foremost by what he says, then by what he does, and thirdly by what the other persons say about him. The novelist, however, is at our elbow to analyse, comment, and explain. He supplies relevant information about times and places and events outside the immediate scope of the book. There is another essential difference. The dramatist so writes his 'parts' that they may be performed by the flesh and blood actor, by different actors at different times; and the flesh and blood actor gives to the character a peculiar reality which is denied to the novelist. Shakespeare's Hamlet is the Hamlet of the theatre who has been impersonated by Burbage and Garrick and Irving and Gielgud. A. C. Bradley's Hamlet is the Hamlet of the novelist.

Hamlet the play is a melodrama composed by a poet, who was a man of the theatre, for performance in the open air by actors whose talents and limitations he thoroughly understood, primarily with the purpose of entertaining the diverse elements which made up an Elizabethan audience. That audience numbered some two thousand persons—about thirteen per cent. of London went to the theatre every week—and was a cross-section of the public. There were the nobility and gentry, the officials and professional men, the merchants and shopkeepers, the craftsmen and artisans, the students of the Inns of Court, the apprentices, the peddlers, carriers, porters and 'penny stinkards'. Youth probably predominated over age, male over female, the worldly over the pious, the responsive over the slow-witted. It was a working-class audience with a good showing of the leisured classes. To read the critics we might suppose that the play is all compact of psychology and metaphysics, but Shakespeare provides the galleries and the groundlings with a ghost, a duel, a scuffle in an open grave, a play within a play; with the madness of Ophelia, the garrulity of Polonius, the affectation of Osric and the rusticities of the grave-diggers. The Ghost is at the same time the most effective of all stage spooks and a provocative subject of discussion for the Protestant, the intellectual, or the spiritualist, who had read Reginald Scot's *Discourse upon Divels and Spirits* or Ludwig Lavater's *Of Ghostes and Spirites walking by Nyght.*

But if *Hamlet* is a melodrama it is also a work of art; that is to say, it has form. We must ignore the divisions into Acts and Scenes—they are not Shakespeare's—and apprehend the play as a whole. It falls into three movements. The First Movement (which fills Act I) is an Act of Exposition. It leads to the words 'Murder' and 'Revenge'. It is the Ghost's Act. But at the same time it establishes Claudius as 'the mighty opposite' of Hamlet; it voices unforgettably the secondary theme, 'Frailty, thy name is woman', and it presents the domestic life of Polonius and his children, the intimate family life which reflects and contrasts with that of the Royal Family, and the fortunes of which are in due course to bring about the counter-movement. The First Movement ends with the Prince's double realization of his duty and his inadequacy:

> The time is out of joint. O cursèd spite,
> That ever I was born to set it right!

Similarly the Second Movement ends with the resolve:

> O from this time forth,
> My thoughts be bloody or be nothing worth!

This Second Movement which is the pith and marrow of the play is unusually long. It is devoted to creating 'in the round' the personality of the hero, to proving the King's guilt by the device of the Murder of Gonzago play, to the full expression of the secondary moral theme in the 'Nunnery Scene' before, and the Bedchamber scene after, the play within the play, and, as regards the main action, ✳ to the hero's two tragic errors, namely the failure to kill the King at his prayers and the murder of Polonius. The second of these two errors gives the King the whip hand and leads to Hamlet's exile.

The turning point of the whole action, as so often in Shakespearian tragedy, is at first sight undetected, apparently trivial. It lies in the line

> How now, a rat? dead for a ducat, dead!

'From now on', wrote a German critic, 'all hinges on this error. He *has* made the thrust at last,—and what is the consequence? What has he accomplished? He has committed a murder! Instead of being freed from the old burthen, he has brought upon his soul a new one; instead of accomplishing what he is bound to do, he has become guilty. Thus the error punishes itself.'

To this we may add that with that dramatic irony which is the essence of tragedy, Hamlet, although he has put himself at the King's mercy so that the 'antic disposition', the assumed madness, recoils upon his head, has in fact ignited the train of circumstance which will lead him through the revenge imposed upon Laertes to the revelation of the King's guilt before the whole court and to the actual killing of the king. Hamlet, the son who has to revenge a dear father murdered, has himself murdered a father and will fall by the vengeance of the son.

> Our wills and fates do so contrary run,
> That our devices still are overthrown:
> Our thoughts are ours, their ends none of our own.

The Third Movement is devoted to the counterplot. Ophelia's madness (in part an interlude of pathos like the Willow Song scene in *Othello*), stands in the same relation to Laertes and the murder of Polonius as the Ghost's revelations to Hamlet in the First Act. Shakespeare uses all his skill to present the temptation and corruption of Laertes by Claudius. Gertrude's incestuous and hasty marriage and his father's death left Hamlet soul-sick. Ophelia's madness and the murder of Polonius expose Laertes to temptation. 'By the image of my cause I see the portraiture of his', says Hamlet. To establish the parallel strongly, Shakespeare keeps Hamlet off the stage and thus incidentally allows his actor a breathing space. When the Prince returns he is a changed man, wiser and more mature with something of Horatio's 'philosophy'. After the lull of the grave-diggers and a cessation of action, the whole play leaps forward with Laertes' leap into the open grave. From that moment (except for the interlude of Osric) the pace accelerates. Hamlet must carry into scene iii of the Fifth Act the excitement of the scuffle in the grave, as he pours into Horatio's ear the story of his voyage and the pirate ship and the fate of his schoolfellows. To make up for the long delayed action of the play, Shakespeare, when the finale and consummation come, gives us rapid physical action. The catastrophe which leaves four corpses on the stage lasts for but seven or eight minutes in the theatre.

The play then is a play, obeying the laws and seeking the effects which are peculiar to such a literary form. It is an Elizabethan melodrama and it is a work of art. But in so far as it was an Elizabethan play written for performance before an Elizabethan audience, we must not forget that, as so often in Shakespeare, the play was not original; it was not his invention. For many members of the audience the salient features of the story—a revenge story of the sort which attracted many dramatists—were well known. We find the plot of the play in the third book of the Danish History of Saxo Grammaticus written in the twelfth century. The elements of *Hamlet* are there. The story was retold with additions by Belleforest in 1576 in his *Histoires Tragiques*. Two points in the tradition are of particular interest. First, that the Amleth of history feigned a foolish and grotesque madness and under his mad speech concealed an unfathomable cunning, mingling craft and candour. Thus our Hamlet's madness, over which critics (and doctors) have spilt much ink, was taken over by Shakespeare as part of the conception. It was a *genuine* pretence. Shakespeare improves upon this, sees deeper into it and naturalizes it, making it indeed a safety-valve for the prince's melancholy and hysteria. In the English translation of Belleforest of 1608 we read that 'Hamblet rent and tore his clothes, wallowing and lying in the durt and mire, his face all filthy and blacke, running through the streets like a man distraught'. It may be that this suggested to Shakespeare his dramatic conception of Edgar's disguise as a Bedlam beggar. In *King Lear* the madness of the King is set against the feigned madness of Edgar and

the craft and candour of the 'natural', the Fool. Simula-
tion and dissimulation are favourite dramatic devices—
'I will dissemble' mutters the Victorian villain—Iago warns
the audience at the outset, 'I am not what I am.' In the
same way Hamlet assumes an antic disposition; we must
not confuse it with the 'favour and the prettiness' of the
mad Ophelia deprived of her 'most ingenious sense'.

The second point of particular interest in Shakespeare's
source relates to Ophelia. In Saxo the King tries to pene-
trate Amleth's dissembling by means of a beautiful woman
thrown in his path to seduce him, and Belleforest improves
upon this by making her one who had always been in love
with the Prince. Shakespeare has it both ways, so to speak,
by making her the daughter of the Prime Minister, loving
and honourably loved by Hamlet, who finds herself dis-
honourably employed by her own father as a decoy—'I'll
loose my daughter to him'—and when the Prince suspects
the eavesdropping plot, he turns on her and rates her as if
she were indeed a prostitute. Moreover, Shakespeare
prepares for the scene with the following aside from the
King which recalls the original story:

> The harlot's cheek, beautied with plastering art,
> Is not more ugly to the thing that helps it,
> Than is my deed to my most painted word.

In his love-letter Hamlet had written 'the most beautified
Ophelia' and in a moment he is to say; 'I have heard of
your paintings too, well enough. God hath given you one
face and you make yourselves another.' Finally, when
Ophelia goes mad, she sings an improper ballad as if she
believed that she had indeed lost the honour which her
brother had warned her to preserve from the prince's
'unmastered importunity'. She sings it in the presence of
the Queen whom Claudius had seduced when her husband
was still living. Such is Shakespeare's exploitation of the
old story.

We sometimes find in Shakespeare's plays that a missing link or ambiguity can be solved if we know his sources, and, although Saxo and Belleforest throw light upon the tragedy, it might well be that we should see clearer if we possessed a copy of the *Tragedy of Hamlet* which according to the account book of Philip Henslowe, theatrical manager of the Admiral's Company, was being acted in 1594. It was not probably a new play then, for we have a reference to it by Thomas Nashe in his preface to a pastoral romance, *Menaphon* (1589), written by his friend Robert Greene, another of the University Wits, as they were called. Nashe writes enigmatically but it seems clear that the author of this earlier *Hamlet* was Thomas Kyd, famous for his rhetorical revenge play, *The Spanish Tragedy*. If we possessed Kyd's Senecan Hamlet with its 'handfuls of tragical speeches', some aspects of Shakespeare's play might take on a sharper focus and be more easily understood. ✳

Last of all, when we try to see the play in its own time, we must consider it from the dramatist's own point of view. Our knowledge of Shakespeare himself is scanty, and conjecture perilous; but we do know roughly the order in which his plays were composed, and we can and should ask the question: 'Where had Shakespeare got to when he wrote the tragedy of *Hamlet*?' Let us simplify the matter somewhat crudely by saying that Shakespeare's dramatic career covered about twenty-one years which can be divided into three periods of seven years. From 1591 to 1598 he was imitating, experimenting, and finding his feet. The first four years of this period of imitation and experiment led to three successes; a comedy, a tragedy, and a history; all three are as much *poems* as they are plays. Poetry is the natural speech of an Oberon, a Romeo, a Richard II. But when we come to *King John* we find that the hero, the Bastard, is ill at ease in blank verse—at any rate in the blank verse which Shakespeare was able to write at that stage—and antipathetic to poetry. The last three years of this first period produced the triumphant masterpiece, the *Henry IV–Henry V* trilogy. Here we meet the greatest of all Shakespeare's *prose* creations, Falstaff. Hotspur is an advance on the Bastard, and Prince Hal is a denizen of two distinct worlds; the prose world of East-cheap and the poetical-rhetorical world of Westminster. At Agincourt he can talk prose incognito with the common soldiers and his declamatory speech 'Once more into the breach, dear friends' has been called (a little unfairly) the high-water mark of football oratory. Henry is a hero but he is a man of action, efficient, and a worldly success. He is created in prose and in rhetoric. He is a tremendous advance on the Bastard. But for a poet, even for a drama-tist, such a one is not and can never be a satisfactory hero. What then was Shakespeare to do next? It was a critical moment in his development. He had recently shown in *The Merchant of Venice* that he could create a figure of tragic stature and in a third dimension, Shylock; and in the same play he achieved a lucid, flexible kind of verse which could if necessary do the work of prose. Poetry in the manner of Spenser and rhetoric in the manner of Marlowe and Kyd had ceased to be a temptation or a distraction.

There followed a second period of seven years, a period of incredible creative activity which includes three comedies (his greatest), three tragedies (*Hamlet* being one), and three problem comedies as they have been called, profound and baffling and rich in treasure for those who will dig and delve for it. The tragedies concern us here. For *Julius Caesar* Shakespeare had a vivid original in the translation of Plutarch's Lives of the Noble Grecians and Romans by Sir Thomas North and this helped him to discover a new sort of hero. Not the Colossus, Caesar, not the brilliant Antony—his turn was to come in ten years time—but the thinker, the idealist, the high-minded failure, Brutus. When Shakespeare passed from the Roman experiment of *Julius Caesar* whose taste is a little bitter and whose style is classical, chilly, and athletic, he returned to the warm bustling Elizabethan world about him. And his new hero has behind him Romeo and Richard II, Hotspur and Hal, and above all Brutus. Out of these (in a sense) Hamlet was created. After the classical economy of *Julius Caesar*, in *Hamlet* he 'spread himself', as we say. And then having written a play into which he put everything he could think of, he again tried the classical method and design and wrote *Othello*, from which he left out as much as he dared. The last seven-year period begins with *Macbeth* and *King Lear*, in which we find certain themes of guilt and expiation, of suffering and reconciliation, themes which (after another Roman interlude) are to find full expression in the final romances, and more especially in the last of them, *The Tempest*.

In *Hamlet* Shakespeare garnered the harvest of his dramatic apprenticeship. His hero, like Hal, has the bene-fit of prose no less than verse. He is at ease in either medium as is the contemporary creation, Rosalind. The play quite apart from any other element appeals to us because of the unusual variety of the style; richness of diction as well as simplicity; lyrical, rhetorical, colloquial by turns; abound-ing in metaphor, delighting in quibble, emphatic in mean-ing, musical in phrasing; now rapid, now sustained, now broken, now melodious, now mannered, now humdrum and workaday. And this chimes with the profusion of episodes and persons, with the transitions from emotion to thought, from gaiety to pathos, from irony to horror. This richness of style, diversity of characters, and alternation of moods, have the effect of mitigating the *tragic* suffering of the play just as the lyrical expression in *Romeo and Juliet* idealizes the theme and robs the bitter-sweetness of its edge. *Hamlet* is like *Antony and Cleopatra* in all this, and the two plays, combining at once fine writing and striking realism, hold the audience spell-bound but do not harrow us with the intensity of *Othello* or *King Lear*.

If we put ourselves in Shakespeare's place we shall approach the play as a play. We shall appreciate it as an entertainment to draw the pence from the pockets of Elizabethan London, as a rehandling of a play now lost and of traditional material, and as the sort of play which Shakespeare was able and fitted to write in the year 1599–1600 after eight years or so of training and experiment.

✳ HAMLET THE PRINCE

The Prince of Denmark is part of the play. The part cannot be greater than the whole. Shakespeare, it is true, in this tragedy alone, goes near to infringing the Aristotelian ✳axiom that plot comes first and character second. We think so at least when we read the critics. But then the critics have never acted the part or produced the play. A. C. Bradley's Hamlet, it has been wittily said, is a better Hamlet than Shakespeare's. The Professor explains what the dramatist has left in doubt. Every line, every word is sifted and found significant. Loose ends are knotted up, contradictions cease to contradict, theatrical effects are interpreted as proofs of psychological subtlety and insight, until at last the hero stands before us, *totus, teres atque rotundus*, fully motivated and foursquare, a complete, reasonable and very human being. Bradley is the greatest of all Shakespearian expositors—all succeeding critics have drawn water at his well—but he interpreted the tragedy with the nineteenth-century novel in his head. He explains the Prince of Denmark but something has been lost in the process. The high lights have been dimmed, the deep shadows have been softened, the chiaroscuro fades into the common light of day. We are convinced by the judge's summing up, but the poet's mystery and music have disappeared. Now we can, of course, isolate Hamlet and carry him about with us and see ourselves reflected in his mirror, but there must always be a gulf which divides the expectant hush of a crowded theatre from the solitude and silence of the scholar's study. The bare boards of the stage are Hamlet's kingdom.

How has Shakespeare created Hamlet? First, by presenting him in all sorts of company. We see him with the girl he loves and with the mother whom he had adored. We see him with his closest friend whose temperament is the complement of his, and we see him with his school-fellows as he once knew them and as he learns to know them. He is a very different person with Claudius, with Laertes, and with Polonius. We laugh with him at Osric, with him we hold our breath in the dread presence of the Ghost. Perhaps he charms us most when he is with the common people, with the players and with the grave-digger. Shakespeare does not employ this creative device elsewhere to the same degree. It is not thus that Othello and Macbeth and Lear are made known to us. And then above all we listen to Hamlet when he is alone. He confides to us his many moods. We know what others think of him, we know what he thinks of others, and we know also what he thinks of himself. It follows that he is the most many-sided of Shakespeare's creations and has come to have for all men in all ages an independent existence. Hamlet might indeed say with Walt Whitman:

> Do I contradict myself?
> Very well then I contradict myself,
> (I am large, I contain multitudes.)

He contains his critics, if once we lift him out of the play. Every reader turns him into food for his own imaginings and speculation. He is at once individual and universal and in this respect Shakespeare employs the traditional method of design of the old Morality plays. In these there is a central figure in which we see ourselves—his name may be Humanum Genus or Lusty Juventus or Everyman— and we follow their spiritual progress of temptation and error, compassed round with the Cardinal Virtues and the Seven Deadly Sins, until the final reckoning. Shakespeare in his Morality has gilded representative MAN with the tincture of the Renaissance. Hamlet is *Il Cortegiano*— courtier, soldier, scholar—the Elizabethan ideal which combined the chivalry of an older day with the intellectual curiosity of the age of Bacon and Montaigne. But he never ceases to be the son, the lover, the friend. He is (like Rosalind) Youth. His psychology (such as it is) owes something to the Elizabethan study of Melancholy and to the theatrical type-character of the Malcontent. But dramatists, especially dramatic poets, are concerned with more important matters than psychology. The fact that a particular actor of the part is of such or such a stature and complexion, that he has a voice of such or such a timbre and range, be it Garrick or Gielgud, will give to the part as a whole an illusion of consistency which the printed page, unaided by critical conjecture and motivation, cannot give. Shakespeare leaves his actors great freedom, but he never forgets that each of his dramatis personae is an instrument in the orchestra whose performances unite in a complex whole, the symphony. Every speaker, however apparently insignificant—First Lord or Second Citizen— contributes to the total effect. *Hamlet* differs from the other tragedies in that it is more like a concerto than a symphony. How cunningly the composer announces and develops the first theme of the Ghost with the playing of the minor characters, Francisco, Bernardo, Marcellus, and Horatio. Horatio is created in a single scene—there will be no time to create him later. The second theme follows:

Claudius, the usurper, diplomat and murderer, addressing his Privy Council from his throne of state. How powerful the contrast is between the darkness and cold of the battlements under the starry sky and the close warmth and wealth of a corrupt court! Claudius must be established as a cunning and worthy opposite of the Prince. Shakespeare gives him some sixty lines at once eloquent and formal, modulating into a silkier tone as he lingers over the repetition of Laertes' name—other instruments supporting him the while, the Ambassadors, Polonius, Laertes—until at long last comes the expected cue,

> But now my cousin Hamlet, and my son—

Then and only then—with two hundred and fifty lines behind us—the solo instrument in the concerto utters a single riddling phrase,

> A little more than kin and less than kind.

In that is distilled the enigma and the dilemma of the Prince. Even so, in the concert hall, after the brass, the woodwind and the strings, the conductor's baton may pause for a second and the pianoforte speaks a single phrase, the germ of the major theme. Hamlet's line is enigmatic, suggestive, and characteristic. When all is said and done, when Ophelia is in her grave, when poisoned cup and envenomed foil have done their work, when after three and a half hours the curtain falls and the rest is silence, should not the audience be left with a sense of mystery? Shakespeare has given his commentators fair warning:

> Why look you now, how unworthy a thing you would make of me! you would play upon me, you would seem to know my stops, you would pluck out the heart of my mystery, you would sound me from my lowest note to the top of my compass—and there is much music, excellent voice in this little organ, yet cannot you make it speak.

'The fact', says Mr. Lewis, 'that the critics can never

leave *Hamlet* alone, the continual groping, the sense, un-extinguished by over a century of failures, that we have here something of inestimable importance, is surely the best evidence that the real and lasting mystery of our human situation has been greatly depicted.'

Hamlet then is Amleth and Hamlet; Hamlet is Sir Philip Sidney and the Earl of Essex; Hamlet is Richard Burbage and Henry Irving. He is Goethe and Coleridge. He is you and I. He is William Shakespeare. There is in him an unresolved element, a margin of interpretation, an unknown quantity to 'shake our dispositions with thoughts beyond the reaches of our souls'. If this is too evasive an answer, too romantic and metaphysical a conclusion, then we can return to the point from which it is our business to start. Hamlet is a creation of the theatre, a figment of the footlights. We see him, we hear him; it is the tone and pace of his words, his puns and metaphors and mannerisms; it is the strange and unforgettable situations in which he finds himself: all these things create the portrait, a speaking portrait above all. He stands for all time with his inky cloak, with his doublet unbraced, with a skull or a rapier in his hand. He kneels in terror before his father's ghost, he listens enraptured to the strolling player, he mocks the pitiful weak hams of the Prime Minister, he tramples on his mother's locket, he leaps into an open grave, he snatches the poisoned cup from Horatio. These pictures 'flash upon that inward eye which is the bliss of solitude'. And the words which Shakespeare heard inside his own head hang for ever upon the air and vibrate in the memory. 'Ha, ha boy! Art thou there truepenny?'; 'What a piece of work is a man'; 'I am but mad north-north-west'; 'Thou wretched, rash, intruding fool, farewell!'; 'Alas, poor Yorick'; 'the readiness is all'. The schoolboy who said that *Hamlet* was made up of quotations spoke more wisely than he knew.

THE STYLE

Shakespeare wrote *Hamlet* at a turning-point in his dramatic career when he looked before and after. He exploits the devices which he had mastered in ten years of imitation and experiment as a man of the theatre. By the year 1600 he knew his actors and he knew what words to put into their mouths. *Hamlet* is written for the speaking voice. That is the secret of its success. The verse is freer than ever before, but it is never flabby. There is none of the clumsiness of some of the earlier plays and none of the knots and complexities of his later work. Just as the dramatis personæ include all sorts and conditions of men, so Shakespeare tries a diversity of styles, penny plain and twopence coloured, the lyrical and the rhetorical and the realistic: and as the groundlings could enjoy the melodramatic situations and theatrical surprises, while the courtiers in their turn could jot down in their 'tables' the verbal flourishes and moral truths that took their fancy, so also Shakespeare's vocabulary is now familiar, emphatic and direct, now pictorial and suggestive, fanciful and far-fetched. *But he never forgets the speaking voice.* Pace and pitch may vary to suit the speaker and the mood, but we hear it in

> What's Hecuba to him or he to Hecuba
> That he should weep for her?

and

> Come, come and sit you down, you shall not budge,
> You go not till I set you up a glass
> Where you may see the inmost part of you.

and

> Why, man, they did make love to this employment,
> They are not near my conscience.

We hear it in Claudius's part

> And now, Laertes, what's the news with you?
> You told us of some suit, what is 't, Laertes?

and

> What then? what rests?
> Try what repentance can—what can it not?
> Yet what can it, when one cannot repent?

With what seductive smoothness a longer passage will slip from the same tongue:

> If he be now returned,
> As checking at his voyage, and that he means
> No more to undertake it, I will work him
> To an exploit, now ripe in my device,
> Under the which he shall not choose but fall:
> And for his death no wind of blame shall breathe,
> But even his mother shall uncharge the practice,
> And call it accident.

Mark it again in such a rapid interchange as the following, where there are several voices:

Hamlet. Indeed, indeed, sirs, but this troubles me.
Hold you the watch tonight?
    All.   We do, my lord.
    Hamlet. Armed, say you?
    All. Armed, my lord.
    Hamlet. From top to toe?
    All.   My lord, from head to foot.
    Hamlet. Then saw you not his face?
    Horatio. O yes, my lord, he wore his beaver up.
    Hamlet. What! looked he frowningly?
    Horatio. A countenance more in sorrow than in anger.
    Hamlet. Pale or red?
    Horatio. Nay, very pale.
    Hamlet.   And fixed his eyes upon you?
    Horatio. Most constantly.
    Hamlet.   I would I had been there.

The verse form does not hamper the dialogue one jot.

As a last example we can enjoy the 'character' writing of Polonius. Shakespeare had made an experiment in this kind with Juliet's Nurse, but Polonius leaves her far

behind and expresses pompous garrulity in verse with the
same ease as Mr. Justice Shallow in prose.

> Madam, I swear I use no art at all.
> That he is mad, 'tis true; 'tis true, 'tis pity,
> And pity 'tis, 'tis true—a foolish figure,
> But farewell it, for I will use no art.
> Mad let us grant him then, and now remains
> That we find out the cause of this effect,
> Or rather say the cause of this defect,
> For this effect defective comes by cause:
> Thus it remains, and the remainder thus.
> Perpend.
> I have a daughter, have while she is mine,
> Who in her duty and obedience, mark,
> Hath given me this, now gather and surmise.

It is a gift to an actor.

The groundwork of the play then in versification and
diction is naturalistic and often the dividing line between
the verse and the prose is a hair's breadth. The second
significant characteristic of the play—one that distinguishes
it from all the other tragedies—is the frequent and abound-
ing use of prose. Shakespeare had perfected his prose in
the *Henry IV–Henry V* trilogy. Prose is by no means
confined to minor character or to 'low life'. Royalty and
the Court speak it as readily as the grave-diggers. Prose,
also, as is Shakespeare's custom, is employed in the mad
scenes. It is so used in *King Lear* and in Lady Macbeth's
sleep-walking to show derangement or loss of reason. The
prose in *Hamlet* is of more kinds than one. Shakespeare
parodies the affectations of court dialect in the Osric scene
and at the other end of the scale we have the slow-witted
reasoning of the rustic clown:

Here lies the water—good. Here stands the man—good. If
the man go to the water and drown himself, it is, will he nill he,
he goes, mark you that. But if the water come to him, and

drown him, he drowns not himself—argal, he that is not guilty
of his own life, shortens not his own death.

Yet Hamlet can take his cue from that without discomfort,
and rise gradually to

Here hung those lips that I have kissed I know not how oft.
Where be your gibes now? your gambols, your songs, your
flashes of merriment, that were wont to set the table in a roar?
not one now to mock your own grinning? quite chop-fallen?
Now get you to my lady's chamber, and tell her, let her paint
an inch thick, to this favour she must come.

The only love scene—if so it can be called—is written in
prose; and what passionate emphasis beats behind the
rhythms:

I am very proud, revengeful, ambitious, with more offences
at my beck than I have thoughts to put them in, imagination
to give them shape, or time to act them in: what should such
fellows as I do crawling between earth and heaven? we are
arrant knaves all, believe none of us.

Only a moment later, and in strong contrast to the broken
utterance, the fits and starts and climaxes of the Ophelia
scene, we hear the Prince giving his advice to the players
in rapid, easy-flowing, natural sentences. We seem to be
listening in to the Elizabethan voice as we do in the jesting
and intimacy of his first meeting with his schoolfellows.
Yet in the midst of that scene, the second scene in the
Second Act, the longest in the play and for the most part
composed in prose, Shakespeare can introduce what is
practically a soliloquy, comparable in quality and feeling
to 'To be or not to be'. How little divides the prose passage
beginning 'I have of late, but wherefore I know not, lost
all my mirth' down to 'And yet to me what is this quintessence of dust' from verse. And of the same kind—the
prose of a poet—is the deeply moving close which leads

us from the Osric scene to the gentleman's apology (in verse) as he takes the hand of Laertes:

There is special providence in the fall of a sparrow. If it be now, 'tis not to come—if it be not to come, it will be now—if it be not now, yet it will come—the readiness is all. Since no man has aught of what he leaves, what is't to leave betimes. Let be.

To sum up, the prose speeches and prose dialogues are as essential to the part of the Prince as the Prince himself is to the play. They give him a third dimension.

To return to the verse, to the poetry of the tragedy. As we have seen, the groundwork is remarkably natural. But on this groundwork which shows us the speakers 'in their habit as they lived', Shakespeare embroiders; for example such a passage as Gertrude's description of the drowning of Ophelia, which has the effect of an operatic *aria*. We find also lyrical touches which recall the earlier manner of *Romeo and Juliet*:

> But look, the morn in russet mantle clad
> Walks o'er the dew of yon high eastward hill.

A more mature poetry informs such a passage as

> Anon as patient as the female dove,
> When that her golden couplets are disclosed
> His silence will sit drooping

and

> O'er whom his very madness like some ore
> Among a mineral of metals base,
> Shows itself pure—a' weeps for what is done.

It is significant that both these are spoken by the Queen. They have an idealizing effect: they redeem her and anticipate the deliberate poetry in which she is to relate the drowning of Ophelia. A more formal effect is sought in that speech of Ophelia which is, in a sense, an epitaph on the Hamlet whom we have never known, the Hamlet

before the play begins, who lives in Fortinbras, the delicate
and tender Prince:

> O what a noble mind is here o'erthrown!
> The courtier's, soldier's, scholar's, eye, tongue, sword.

There are many passages, more closely knit, more meta-
phorical than the play's normal writing—notably Hamlet's
speeches to the Queen in the bedchamber scene; or this:

> Do not believe his vows, for they are brokers
> Not of that dye which their investments show,
> But mere implorators of unholy suits,
> Breathing like sanctified and pious bonds,
> The better to beguile.

And this:

> No, let the candied tongue lick absurd pomp
> And crook the pregnant hinges of the knee,
> Where thrift may follow fawning.

Against these—and other more extended reasoning of the
same kind—we can set for contrast the direct effect which
Shakespeare achieves now and again within a single line.

> To be or not to be that is the question

or

> Thus conscience does make cowards of us all

or

> And a man's life's no more than to say 'one'

or

> I will speak daggers to her but use none

or

> But soft, methinks I scent the morning air.

More adventurous experiments within the compass of a
line are to be heard in

> Unhouseled, disappointed, unaneled

and

> O horrible! O horrible! most horrible!

and

> Remorseless, treacherous, lecherous, kindless, villain!

and

> Woo't fight? woo't weep? woo't fast? woo't tear thyself?

Most memorable of all is the change from latinized diction in the grand style to a line of ten simple native mono-syllables which seem to mark the failing breath and ebbing life of the dying Prince:

> Absent thee from felicity awhile
> And in this harsh world draw thy breath in pain
> To tell my story.

Shakespeare makes use also of the rhymed couplet, not with the same frequency as in his earlier work but for a particular effect. It marks the inherited sententiousness of Laertes at the end of his advice to his sister:

> Be wary then—best safety lies in fear,
> Youth to itself rebels, though none else near.

The most familiar use (which Shakespeare never abandoned) seals the end of a scene or movement:

> The time is out of joint. O cursèd spite,
> That ever I was born to set it right!

More curious and interesting—a unique effect indeed—are the couplets with which the Prince concludes his moralizing over Yorick's skull:

> Imperious Caesar, dead and turned to clay,
> Might stop a hole to keep the wind away.
> O that that earth which kept the world in awe
> Should patch a wall t'expel the winter's flaw.

He seems consciously to improvise, and the familiar sententious use of the couplet is here given an ironical tone; but it serves a second purpose in that the couplets come between the prose and the blank verse; they lead us from the rusticity of the clowns to the ceremonial of the funeral.

Lastly we should note that the player king and queen speak couplets, archaic in manner, to distinguish the convention of 'the play within the play'.

Formality of a different kind—a certain deliberate consciousness of writing—is to be found elsewhere for a particular purpose, for example the last thirty lines of the first scene of the play, especially the speech of Marcellus:

> Some say that ever 'gainst that season comes,
> Wherein our Saviour's birth is celebrated,
> The bird of dawning singeth all night long . . .

This gives a classical quiet close and in the formal line upon line structure of the whole paragraph prepares harmoniously for the formality of the court scene. But the poetry of it is as different from the official eloquence of the King's 'speech from the throne' as woodwind is from the brass. Deliberate also in balance of structure and careful wording is the resolve of Laertes:

> I bought an unction of a mountebank,
> So mortal, that but dip a knife in it,
> Where it draws blood, no cataplasm so rare,
> Collected from all simples that have virtue
> Under the moon, can save the thing from death
> That is but scratched withal. I'll touch my point
> With this contagion, that if I gall him slightly,
> It may be death.

It leads up to the central phrase, mysterious in its effect, where the sense runs over the previous line, 'Under the moon': and then away from it to the final word 'death'. Such mystery and atmosphere are evoked on a grander scale in the great speeches of the Ghost. But compared with the passage just quoted there is in the Ghost's

speeches an antique quality: Shakespeare seems to give
the Ghost his own idiom as it were, a certain formality of
rhythm and of language, just as Claudius and Polonius
have from time to time (although not, of course, throughout)
their individual pace and tone. With the Ghost this is best
instanced by:

> I could a tale unfold whose lightest word
> Would harrow up thy soul, freeze thy young blood,
> Make thy two eyes like stars start from their spheres,
> Thy knotted and combinéd locks to part,
> And each particular hair to stand on end,
> Like quills upon the fretful porpentine.

The first twenty-four lines of the scene and the three
previous apparitions of the Ghost are all intended to lead
up to the word Murder, three times repeated:

> *Ghost.* Revenge his foul and most unnatural murder!
> *Hamlet.* Murder!
> *Ghost.* Murder most foul, as in the best it is,
> But this most foul, strange and unnatural.
> *Hamlet.* Haste me to know't, that I with wings as swift
> As meditation or the thoughts of love,
> May sweep to my revenge.

These lines are the keystone of the First Movement. The
two words Murder and Revenge are the climax towards
which every part and detail are directed. The delayed effect
is summed up in the Ghost's 'I could a tale unfold . . .'
In fact the Ghost is, as dramatic personages mostly are at
one time or another, *rhetorical*. Rhetoric is an art in which
we are not particularly interested. It is almost a lost art.
To the Elizabethans and Jacobeans it was a fascinating
study and an essential part of education: from the tragedies
of Marlowe down to the pamphleteering of Milton, poets
and preachers, dramatists and story-tellers exercise all the
tricks of the trade—for in some ways it is more a trade than
an art. The power of persuading is a professional asset.

The Greeks, with their love of debate, political and legal, may be said to have invented it and Aristotle as usual tells us how the thing is done. The Romans (also as usual) borrowed from the Greeks, and Roman drama which was recited and read is rhetorical to excess. But the Elizabethans loved words and they loved excess. They were more used to listening than to reading, and rhetoric supposes an audience to be persuaded either by reason or by emotion or by both. A theatre audience has to be persuaded from the stage just as much as other audiences from the pulpit or the political platform, and in consequence the poetic drama of Shakespeare's age is immensely rhetorical. Although at first the rhetoric was crude, it was always supported by various figures or 'tropes' which were recognized with pleasure in those days but pass us by to-day. Shakespeare in the three parts of *Henry VI*, in *Titus Andronicus*, and in *Richard III* followed Marlowe (whose rhetoric is shot with poetry) and the Senecan school of Thomas Kyd. But his development was rapid; he soon began to put rhetoric to his own uses and to distinguish between the true and the false. Antony's speech over the dead body of Caesar is a masterpiece of professional public-speaking.

In *Hamlet* Shakespeare gives a taste of the Marlowe-Kyd style in the Pyrrhus speech, for which the Prince and perhaps Shakespeare show a nostalgic tenderness, and, as if Hamlet himself were inspired or infected by Shakespeare's dramatic predecessors, he closes the scene of 'the play within the play' with a short soliloquy which is quite different from anything else in the Prince's part:

'Tis now the very witching time of night,
When churchyards yawn, and hell itself breathes out
Contagion to the world: now could I drink hot blood,
And do such bitter business as the day
Would quake to look on.

This is more archaic than anything in the Ghost's part and very different from the effect of 'atmosphere' in Laertes's mountebank speech. Is Shakespeare playing to the ground-lings or is he bringing the rapid verbal fence of the preceding moments with Rosencrantz and Guildenstern and Polonius, the hysteria which follows the break-up of the play, to a deliberate stop? Is he focusing a spotlight on the Prince at the critical moment before he finds the King at prayers and passes him by to speak daggers to his mother? Is he forcing himself back into the framework of the traditional revenge melodrama? When Shakespeare came to write such a speech a few years later he condensed it into a few phrases of much greater potency:

> Come, seeling night,
> Scarf up the tender eye of pitiful day,
> And with thy bloody and invisible hand
> Cancel and tear to pieces that great bond
> Which keeps me pale! Light thickens, and the crow
> Makes wing to the rooky wood.

The Prince is rhetorical enough in the first half of the play and he criticizes himself for it in the 'O what a rogue and peasant slave am I' soliloquy. When, in the graveyard scene, Laertes speaks the same sort of language, his rhetoric strikes falsely on Hamlet's ear. 'What is he whose grief bears such an emphasis?' He eases his pent-up feeling in sardonic parody and deliberate rant:

> Be buried quick with her, and so will I.
> And if thou prate of mountains, let them throw
> Millions of acres on us, till our ground,
> Singeing his pate against the burning zone,
> Make Ossa like a wart! Nay, an thou'lt mouth,
> I'll rant as well as thou.

As then there are many scenes, episodes, and surprises, and all sorts and conditions of men among the characters,

B

even so (rightly and inevitably) there is a diversity of styles. In the scene in the Queen's closet Hamlet balances on a precipice edge between true rhetoric and rant, but the realism and even coarseness of some of his words and imagery, combined with the driving force given by touches of direct simplicity, preserve him. But the actor will find the richness of metaphor works against the acceleration of pace and that to carry the crescendo of the scene to the climax of the Ghost's entry is a strain. Shakespeare seldom, if ever again in his plays, makes such a demand upon his tragic hero. When we turn from scenes and speeches to the detail of words and phrases we find the same variety and range, the same 'reconciliation of opposites'. There is metaphor in plenty. Sometimes it is artificial and suggests that the speaker is not at his ease, for example in the King's speech to Laertes (IV. vii. 17) where he is feeling his way, and in much that follows, until at last he strikes home with a single memorable phrase: 'But to the quick o'th'ulcer.' Elsewhere metaphor translates a simple thought into the grand style, as in

> When sorrows come, they come not single spies
> But in battalions

or

> Had I but time, as this fell sergeant, death,
> Is strict in his arrest

or in the blended images of

> And I, of ladies most deject and wretched,
> That suck'd the honey of his music vows,
> Now see that noble and most sovereign reason,
> Like sweet bells jangled, out of tune and harsh;
> That unmatch'd form and feature of blown youth
> Blasted with ecstasy.

But just as the foppery of Osric is set against the honest fustian of the grave-diggers, and the garrulity of Polonius

against the laconic honesty of Horatio, so in the language
the embroidered phrases, the fine writing, the occasional
artifice and curiosity of expression are leavened by homeli-
ness of analogy and colloquial intimacy. The humblest
words and phrases stick in our memory: 'ay, there's the
rub'; 'tweaks me by the nose'; 'popped in between the
election and my hopes'; 'why, what an ass am I'; 'now
might I do it pat'; 'even for an eggshell'; 'or ere those
shoes were old'; 'with a bare bodkin'; 'I'll lug the guts
into the neighbour room'; 'the cat will mew and dog will
have his day'. It is significant that all these occur in the
hero's part.

In the writing of *Hamlet* then—apart from the handling
of the plot, the creation of character, the sense of the
theatre, the profounder expression of ideas—Shakespeare
gathered up the harvest of all that he had already attempted
or achieved, and in so doing he put the past behind him
and made a spectacular advance. A French critic once
said, 'Shakespeare tried all styles except simplicity'.
Hamlet alone, as previous quotations show, disproves that
reservation. In the plays that followed he abandoned some
of his devices and tried new ones, for as poet as well as
playwright, he never stood still. Indeed in the expansive
design of *Hamlet* we can detect and enjoy in embryo or
fully grown the comprehensive range, the extremes of his
verbal manipulation. We can forget the play and the
prince, and see the powers of the greatest and most reckless of verbal artists stretched to their utmost at a critical
moment in the very middle of his professional career.

✳ THE PLOT

I. i. The play opens at midnight on the Castle battlements at Elsinore when the sentry is being relieved.
Marcellus brings the sceptical Horatio to witness the
apparition of the late King which has twice been seen.

The Ghost duly appears but stalks away when questioned. Horatio tells Marcellus that young Fortinbras of Norway, son of the Fortinbras slain by old Hamlet, is threatening war to recover the lands lost by his father. The Ghost reappears but vanishes on the crowing of the cock. Horatio decides to impart what they have seen to the Prince.

I. ii. Claudius in full Council sends Ambassadors to Norway, Uncle of Fortinbras, to suppress the threat of war. He gives permission to Laertes to return to France and then turns to the silent and melancholy Hamlet. With the Queen's aid he persuades him not to return to the University of Wittenberg. The Council breaks up and Hamlet is left alone. In his first soliloquy he expresses his disgust at his mother's hasty and adulterous marriage to his father's brother. Horatio enters and tells him what they have seen on the battlements. Hamlet decides to keep watch himself that very night.

I. iii. Laertes bids farewell to his sister and Polonius speeds him on his way with further advice and then warns Ophelia, as her brother had done, to distrust Hamlet's love-making and to keep him at a distance.

I. iv and v. Hamlet watches for the Ghost with Marcellus and Horatio, and, despite their entreaties, follows him to a more removed ground alone. The Ghost divulges that Claudius, after seducing Gertrude, had murdered him by pouring poison in his ear. Hamlet swears revenge and, when the Ghost has vanished and his companions return, he makes them swear an oath of secrecy. He warns them that he may perchance thereafter 'put an antic disposition on' and begs them not to show any consciousness of the cause. They swear a third time and Hamlet bids the Ghost rest in peace. (This is the end of the First Movement.)

II. i. Polonius dispatches the old servant, Reynaldo, to Paris to see how Laertes is behaving himself. Ophelia enters, deeply agitated, and tells her father that Hamlet had come to her, dishevelled and pale and to all appearance out of his wits, as if to take a long and silent farewell of her. Polonius believes that neglected love has driven him mad and hastens to inform the King.

II. ii. Claudius and Gertrude welcome Hamlet's school-fellows, Rosencrantz and Guildenstern, and entreat them to discover what is amiss with the Prince. The Ambassadors return from Norway with the good news that Fortinbras, rebuked by old Norway, has agreed to keep the peace with Denmark and to lead his levies against Poland, requesting at the same time leave to pass through Claudius's dominions. Polonius expounds to the King and Queen his theory that Hamlet's madness comes from neglected love, showing them a letter from the Prince to Ophelia. They decide to put this to the proof by arranging an encounter which they can observe unseen from behind the arras. Hamlet enters and Polonius dismisses the King and Queen so that he may accost him; but the Prince assuming his antic disposition outwits him. To Rosencrantz and Guildenstern, who enter as Polonius leaves, Hamlet only reveals a deep-seated melancholy, which they are inclined to ascribe to dis-appointed ambition. They speak to him of the arrival of the travelling players who enter soon after. At Hamlet's request the first player recites a speech from an old play in which Aeneas speaks of the fall of Troy, the murder of Priam and the grief of Hecuba, 'the mobled queen'. The player is so carried away that the tears stand in his eyes. In the soliloquy which closes the scene Hamlet meditates on the fictive passion of the player and his own failure to feel and act in the face of a terrible reality. He resolves to test the King's guilt by the public performance of a play whose plot is something like the murder of his father.

III. i. Rosencrantz and Guildenstern report that they cannot discover the cause of Hamlet's melancholic mad-ness and tell the King and Queen of his excitement over the arrival of the players and of his desire for them to perform before the court. Polonius and the King then put their eavesdropping plot into effect and direct Ophelia to walk in the hall reading on a book of devotion. Polonius's remark that thus men often sugar over evil with pious action is as a lash to the King's guilty conscience. When the stage is empty Hamlet enters and meditates on suicide and the after-life. Ophelia enters and asks Hamlet to take back his love-tokens. He denies ever having loved her and bids her forget him. Suddenly he guesses that they are being spied upon and he bursts out into a passionate railing against her and womankind, ordering her to renounce the world and go into a nunnery. When he rushes from her, the King and Polonius come from behind the arras. Claudius realizes that the cause of his madness lies deeper than love and resolves to send him to England on a mission. Polonius advises that Gertrude should send for Hamlet after the play and entreat him to show his cause of grief while he once more plays the eavesdropper. The King agrees.

III. ii. Hamlet advises the players on the art of acting, commending naturalness and restraint. They go to make ready for the play. Hamlet calls Horatio and expresses his trust in his firm character and equable temper. The court enter for the play. Hamlet again assumes his antic disposition and jests coarsely and cruelly at Ophelia's expense. The Dumb Show takes place in which a King and Queen enter very lovingly. The King lies down to sleep. A man enters, takes off the crown, kisses it, and pours poison into the King's ear. The Queen returns and is wooed by the poisoner. She accepts his love. Claudius is talking with the Queen and misses the significance of the Dumb Show. The play is then performed, but when Claudius sees the player king poisoned he realises that Hamlet has discovered his crime. He rises and the play abruptly ends. Hamlet and Horatio are left alone. But before Hamlet can confide in Horatio, Rosencrantz and Guildenstern return and say that the Queen 'in most great affliction of spirit' has sent for him. Hamlet shows that he knows them for the spies and flunkies which they are. Polonius also summons him to his mother and receives short shrift from Hamlet who when he is left alone steels himself 'to speak daggers' to his mother 'but use none'.

III. iii.   Claudius, fearing for his safety, orders Rosencrantz and Guildenstern to get ready to take Hamlet to England. Left alone he tries to repent but he knows that prayer alone will not bring God's forgiveness. As he kneels in prayer Hamlet enters on his way to his mother's chamber. He draws his sword to avenge murder with murder, but forbears lest Claudius's soul may be saved if he is slain at his prayers: he would thus be baulked of his revenge. He spares him. Claudius's words as he rises from his knees show that his prayers have been in vain.

III. iv.   Polonius hides behind the arras in the Queen's bedchamber and Gertrude receives her son. She starts to rate him, but when he forces her into a chair she cries for help and the cry is taken up by Polonius. Hamlet makes a rapid pass through the arras and slays Polonius, thinking for a moment that it is the King. He is unmoved by the murder he has committed and accuses Gertrude in burning words of sexual depravity, forcing her to realize her shamelessness and inconstancy. The Ghost enters and briefly warns Hamlet not to forget his vow of vengeance still unperformed. Gertrude neither sees nor hears the Ghost and when he has vanished she snatches for a moment at the hope that Hamlet's accusation has been but the ravings of a madman. He convinces her of his sanity and her guilt, makes her promise secrecy and reveals that he is aware that Rosencrantz and Guildenstern will carry sealed letters with them when they accompany him in virtual banishment to England. With a last good-night he drags the body of Polonius from the room.

IV. i. Gertrude tells the King of the murder of Polonius. He calls for Rosencrantz and Guildenstern and tells them to bring Hamlet before him and to carry the body into the chapel. They must take ship for England that very night.

IV. ii. Hamlet baits his schoolfellows and runs from them in a sort of fantastic hide and seek.

IV. iii. Hamlet is brought guarded before the King and bids him a sardonic farewell. Claudius in a final soliloquy reveals that he has appealed to England to put Hamlet to death.

IV. iv. Fortinbras and his army pass over the stage. Hamlet catches a glimpse of them and asks a Captain what their purpose is. When he learns that twenty thousand men are making war for a little patch of Polish ground that 'hath in it no profit but the name', he meditates in soliloquy on his own failure to act and to revenge his father's murder and his mother's dishonour. He vows that henceforth he will be bloody in action. (With this vow the Second Movement closes.)

IV. v. Hamlet's murder of Polonius has driven Ophelia out of her mind and stirred up a rebellious spirit among the people of which Laertes takes advantage. He breaks into the palace demanding justice and revenge. Claudius faces him courageously and protests his own innocence. Ophelia enters with flowers which she gives to her brother and to the King and Queen, imagining them to be mourners with her at her father's grave. The King draws away Laertes to 'commune with his grief' and suppress the seeds of rebellion.

IV. vi. Sailors have brought letters to Horatio and to the King from Hamlet. We learn from Horatio's reading of his letter that in a grapple with a pirate ship Hamlet got clear of the vessel taking him to England and that his schoolfellows, of whom he has much to relate, have continued their voyage without him.

IV. vii. Claudius returns with Laertes and begins to poison his mind against Hamlet when a Messenger brings Hamlet's letter announcing his return. Claudius proposes his plot: Hamlet, emulous of Laertes's reputation as a duellist, shall be challenged to a rapier match, in which Laertes by using an unbaited foil may requite his father. Laertes decides to touch his rapier's point with poison, and, to make assurance doubly sure, Claudius will have a poisoned cup ready when the Prince in the heat of the action calls for drink. As their guilty plot is concluded, Gertrude enters with news of the drowning of Ophelia.

V. i. The grave-diggers are digging the grave of Ophelia, who is to be buried in consecrated ground, although she is thought to have taken her own life. Hamlet and Horatio enter and watch the grave-digger throwing up old skulls. One of these is the skull of Yorick, the jester, who carried Hamlet on his back as a child. The funeral procession approaches and Hamlet retires. When the body has been laid in the earth, Laertes, in an agony of grief, leaps in after it, calling for vengeance upon the Prince. Hamlet comes forward to answer the charge and leaps into the grave himself where they grapple together until the attendants separate them. Hamlet protests his love for Ophelia with a scathing outburst against Laertes which as quickly gives way to words of kindness. He hurries from the grave-yard followed by Horatio.

V. ii. Hamlet tells Horatio of his unsealing of the secret commission carried by Rosencrantz and Guildenstern, in which Claudius conjured the King of England to put him to death, and how he has replaced it with a death warrant upon the pair of them. A court fop enters and invites Hamlet to fight a wager with Laertes. Hamlet accepts the conditions and after a moment of misgiving shows himself resigned to whatever providence may have ordained. On the entry of the full court he makes a formal apology to Laertes and the duel begins. In the first bout Hamlet scores a hit. Claudius calls for drink and then puts the poison in the cup and offers it to Hamlet. He puts it by, and scores a hit in the second bout. Gertrude offers him the cup which he again refuses, and she herself drinks of it although Claudius forbids her. The third bout is a draw, but when Hamlet is off his guard Laertes wounds him. There is a scuffle and they exchange rapiers. Hamlet wounds Laertes deeply and the Queen as she falls cries out that she has been poisoned. Laertes reveals the plot upon Hamlet's life. Hamlet stabs Claudius and forces him to drink the poisoned cup, but he is himself mortally wounded. He prevents Horatio drinking of the cup and Osric announces the warlike approach of Fortinbras coming in conquest from Poland. The drum is heard and, as Hamlet dies, Fortinbras and the English Ambassadors enter. Rosencrantz and Guildenstern are dead by Hamlet's commandment. Fortinbras will succeed to the throne of Denmark, first learning from Horatio the details of the tragic story. Four captains bear off Hamlet like a soldier and guns fire a salute.

THE PLAY ON THE SHAKESPEARIAN STAGE

The Globe Playhouse was built in 1599. Details of its structure and its dramatic potentialities and conventions have recently been clarified by the comprehensive researches and lively imagination of an American scholar, John Cranford Adams. The Globe was a three-storied octagonal building which surrounded an interior yard 58 feet across and accommodated some two thousand spectators. From the point of view of playwright and player, the theatre consisted of five component parts. Chief of these was the platform stage which jutted out into the centre of the yard, tapering from a width of 43 feet at the scenic wall to 24 feet at the front. This platform, raised about 4 feet from the ground and enclosed by a low balustrade was strewn with rushes. In the centre of it a large 'trap' was situated for the admission of Ghosts and Apparitions and there were in addition several smaller traps. Twelve feet or so from the front rose two great posts, 24 feet apart. These held up the stage canopy known as the 'heavens' which could open for the descent of Jove upon his eagle or of a goddess in a triumphal car. The two columns served also as tree trunks in forest scenes and they doubtless were put to other uses. The main action of the play took place upon this unlocalized apron stage. Next in importance was the inner stage or 'study' at the rear of it. This corresponded to our modern 'picture-stage' in that it was concealed by curtains, so that an interior scene could be set, unseen by the spectators, and figures could be discovered in council, at a banquet, or in a cave. The side walls slanted obliquely to the back and were hung with arras while the back wall might contain a door and window, or a central gateway, or be enclosed with hangings also. As the width of the inner stage was 23 feet, the height 12 feet, and the depth from 7 to 8 feet, this unit of the Globe Playhouse by itself compares not unfavourably in size with many amateur stages of to-day. Above the 'study' was the upper stage, a double unit consisting of a narrow balcony projecting some 3 feet over the platform and known as the 'tarras', and secondly of the 'chamber' behind the 'tarras', curtained like the 'study' below and of roughly the same dimensions. Thus at the back of the platform stage there stood a two-floor house with the front missing. To these three main units of the Globe, namely the platform, the study, and the chamber, we must add the 'cellarage' or 'Hell' excavated beneath the platform and, lastly, the structure crowning the whole building, known as the 'huts' where thunder and other sound effects were contrived and where the cannon and ordnance were shot off. At the level of the third spectators' gallery, that is, immediately below the canopy of the 'heavens' and placed above the 'chamber' was a gallery for musicians. Descending to ground level, we should also note that at the back of the platform two side entrances with doors were placed obliquely one on each side of the 23-foot opening of the 'study', and that above these, on a level with the 'tarras', were projecting 'window stages', as was common enough above an Elizabethan street door.

It is clear therefore that Shakespeare's stage, although improvised from the Elizabethan Inn Yard, was not such a rough-and-ready piece of make-believe as has usually been supposed. Its strength lay in the fact that it combined two opposed methods of dramatic presentation: of conscientious realism, which fetters the modern playwright, on the one hand, and the ready acceptance of elementary conventions and nursery symbolism on the other. The costumes were elaborate, the stage machinery was highly ingenious, but a notice board could suffice on occasion to indicate Alexandria or Rome, and the audience achieved spontaneously 'that willing suspension of disbelief for the moment which constitutes poetic faith'.

In *Hamlet* the inner stage would be employed for the discovery of the King in Council as soon as Horatio and Marcellus leave the stage at the end of the first scene in the play. Claudius and Polonius can conceal themselves behind the curtains (or behind the hangings within the study itself), when they spy upon the Prince and Ophelia. Again, in the play-scene (III. ii), the inner stage will serve either for the presentation of the dumb show, or to set the thrones from which the King and Queen watch the players perform the Murder of Gonzago between the columns on

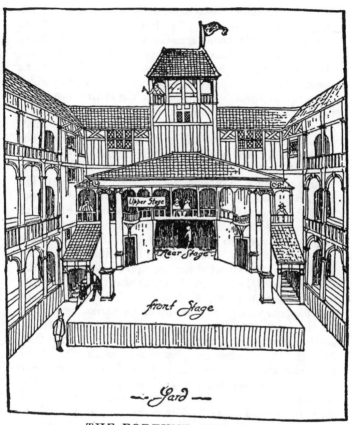

Upper Stage

Rear Stage

front Stage

~ Yard ~

THE FORTUNE THEATRE

A reconstruction by Mr. W. H. Godfrey from the builder's contract, which has survived. The theatre was built in 1600, two years later than the Globe, at which most of Shakespeare's plays were performed, and burnt down in 1621.

the platform stage. Each of these two methods of presenting 'the play within the play' has its drawbacks and its
advantages. If Ophelia's scene of madness (IV. v) is played
on the full stage, Claudius can be discovered within the
study in scene vii, deep in his persuasions of Laertes and
the hatching of his plot. The grave of Ophelia into which
Hamlet and Laertes leap (V. i) was the centre trap in the
inner stage, so that, at the close, as the curtains draw,
Hamlet can re-enter with Horatio at a side-entrance
already embarked upon the story of his adventures. The
curtains will open once more to discover the Court and the
preparations for the duel, the flagons and the foils. When
Claudius kneels in prayer within the 'study' (III. iii),
Hamlet passes him by and mounts off-stage to the upper
'chamber' where the Queen awaits him and where Polonius
has concealed himself behind the hangings. This upper
stage will serve also for the more intimate scenes in the
house of Polonius (I. iii and II. i). It is possible that Hamlet
watches for the Ghost upon the upper stage (I. iv) and
follows him to the platform below to hear the revelation of
Claudius's crime (I. v). Fortinbras and the Ambassadors
could appear with great effect upon the 'tarras' or balcony
for the finale of the tragedy when the main stage will be
cumbered with the living and the dead. Cannon are fired
from the 'huts' when the play is done as they had been
earlier for the King's carouse (I. iv) and in the duel scene
(V. ii). The Ghost appears and disappears through the
trap-doors in the platform and inner stage in Act I, and
shifts his ground in the 'cellarage' for the swearing of the
oath of secrecy. From these indications we realise that the
Globe Playhouse allowed not only of great variety and
spaciousness, but also of that continuity between scene
and scene with which we are more familiar in the cinema
than in the modern theatre, where the rise and fall of the
front curtains divide the drama into slices,—continuity and

speed which are essential in a play of such length. The Elizabethan Playhouse had this similarity also to the technique of the cinema. 'Close-ups' alternate with 'Long Shots'. Hamlet can soliloquize at the very front of the apron stage with the spectators behind him and at his elbow; but such a scene as that with his mother (III. iv) or the burial of Ophelia (v. i) is 'distanced'. In the same way Shakespeare alternates dialogues of two or three persons with full-stage effects which employ his whole company of players.

THE TEXT

The first collected edition of Shakespeare's plays was published in 1623, seven years after his death. It is known as the First Folio and it was reprinted three times in the seventeenth century. In 1709 Nicholas Rowe brought out the first 'modern edition'—that is to say, one with critical introduction, Act and Scene divisions and emendations of the text. But before 1623 sixteen of the plays had been printed singly. These editions of single plays are known as the Quartos and we have a Quarto of *Titus Andronicus* as early as 1594 and one of *Othello* printed in 1622, only a year before the First Folio. In the case of a popular play the first edition or First Quarto was reprinted, sometimes more than once: for instance *Richard II* was first printed in 1597 (Q 1), twice in 1598 (Q 2 and Q 3), again in 1608 (Q 4) and in 1615 (Q 5).

The two men who provided the material for the printers of the First Folio and saw it through the press were John Heminges and Henrie Condell who had been partners with Shakespeare in the dramatic company of the Lord Chamberlain's Men, known after the accession of James I as the King's Men. Heminges and Condell prefixed to their collected edition of the plays an address 'To the great Variety of Readers' in which they tell us something of Shakespeare's manuscript and of his ease in composing:

'His mind and hand went together: And what he thought, he vttered with that easinesse, that wee haue scarse receiued from him a blot in his papers.'

They also warn their readers against certain single editions of the plays which had already been printed:

'as where (before) you were abus'd with diuerse stolne, and surreptitious copies, maimed, and deformed by the frauds and stealthes of injurious impostors, that expos'd them: euen those, are now offer'd to your view cur'd, and perfect of their limbes; and all the rest, absolute in their numbers, as he conceiued them.'

Until a few years ago scholars and editors believed that Heminges and Condell were condemning with these words *all* the Quarto editions of Shakespeare's plays, but expert investigation of the evidence has now shown that they were discriminating between what have come to be called 'Good Quartos' and 'Bad Quartos'. The Bad Quartos, or 'stolne and surreptitious copies', are comparatively few. The most certain and the most notable of them are the *Romeo and Juliet* of 1597, the *Henry V* of 1600, the *Merry Wives of Windsor* of 1602, and the *Hamlet* of 1603. The Bad Quarto of *Hamlet*, which was superseded a year later by a Good Quarto (Q 2, 1604), gives us a text of the play which appears to have been pieced together from memory by the actor who played Marcellus and (perhaps) the Second Player; it is patched with passages of indifferent blank verse of his own composition or that of a collaborator—blank verse which incorporates echoes and reminiscences from various parts of the play, mixed with quotations from other plays, including very possibly the pre-Shakespearian version of *Hamlet* attributed to Thomas Kyd. This make-shift and illicit version was botched up for performances of the play

by a provincial touring company. Its value for us lies in
the fact that it contains certain stage-directions which may
reveal the 'business' of the London production. It also on
occasion assists an editor to choose between variant read-
ings of the Folio and the Good Quarto. There are three
peculiar points about it. One is that Polonius is called
Corambis, and another is the placing of the soliloquy, 'To
be or not to be', and the 'Nunnery' scene which follows it,
earlier in the play, immediately after the eavesdropping
has been planned by Corambis and the King. Thirdly, the
Grave-digger says of Yorick's skull: 'Look you, heres a
scull hath bin here this dozen yeare'. The good texts read
'three and twenty years'. It may well be that, in the
original performance, the Prince's age was nineteen and
not thirty, as we calculate it to be from the dialogue with
the Grave-digger. Perhaps the alteration was made when
Richard Burbage grew too old to give the impression of
adolescence which the Prince's part undoubtedly suggests.

We have then the Folio of 1623 and the Good Quarto.
The Quarto began to be printed at the end of the year 1604
and consequently some title-pages have the date 1604 and
some 1605. Q 2 is the fuller version and is longer than the
Folio by over 200 lines, but it omits some 85 lines found in
the Folio. The text of the Quarto is more erratic than that
of the Folio. There are plenty of misprints, unusual spell-
ings, and missing letters; but Professor Dover Wilson
concludes that it was set up in the printing house from
Shakespeare's own manuscript. The Folio editors on the
other hand, in Professor Wilson's opinion, gave the printers
a transcribed copy of the prompt book used at the Globe
Theatre, and that prompt book was itself a copy transcribed
from Shakespeare's manuscript. Thus, in the case of the
Folio, two copyists and their mistakes intervene between
the composer and the compositor.

DRAMATIS PERSONÆ

CLAUDIUS, King of Denmark.

HAMLET, Son to the late, and Nephew to the present, King.

FORTINBRAS, Prince of Norway.

HORATIO, Friend to Hamlet.

POLONIUS, Principal Secretary of State.

LAERTES, his Son.

VOLTIMAND ⎱
CORNELIUS ⎰ Ambassadors to Norway.

ROSENCRANTZ ⎱
GUILDENSTERN ⎰ formerly Fellow Students with Hamlet.

OSRIC, a Fop.

A Gentleman.

A Priest.

MARCELLUS ⎱
BERNARDO ⎰ Officers.

FRANCISCO, a Soldier.

REYNALDO, Servant to Polonius.

A Captain.

English Ambassadors.

Players. Two Clowns, Grave-diggers.

GERTRUDE, Queen of Denmark and Mother to Hamlet.

OPHELIA, Daughter to Polonius.

Lords, Ladies, Officers, Soldiers, Sailors, Messengers, and Attendants.

Ghost of Hamlet's Father.

SCENE. *Elsinore.*

HAMLET
PRINCE OF DENMARK

ACT I

Scene I. ELSINORE. A PLATFORM BEFORE THE CASTLE

FRANCISCO *at his post. Enter to him* BERNARDO.

Bernardo. Who's there?
Francisco. Nay, answer me. Stand and unfold yourself.
Bernardo. Long live the king!
Francisco. Bernardo?
Bernardo. He.   5
Francisco. You come most carefully upon your hour.
Ber. 'Tis now struck twelve; get thee to bed, Francisco.
Francisco. For this relief much thanks; 'tis bitter cold,
And I am sick at heart.
  Bernardo. Have you had quiet guard?
  Francisco.   Not a mouse stirring.   10
  Bernardo. Well, good-night.
If you do meet Horatio and Marcellus,
The rivals of my watch, bid them make haste.
  Fran. I think I hear them. Stand, ho! Who is there?

Enter HORATIO *and* MARCELLUS.

Horatio. Friends to this ground.
  Marcellus.   And liegemen to the Dane.   15
Francisco. Give you good-night.
  Marcellus.   O! farewell, honest soldier:
Who hath reliev'd you?
  Francisco.   Bernardo has my place.
Give you good-night.   [*Exit.*

13 **rivals:** partners.

Marcellus.   Holla! Bernardo!
Bernardo.   Say,
What! is Horatio there?
  Horatio.   A piece of him.   19
  Bernardo. Welcome, Horatio; welcome, good Marcellus.
  Horatio. What! has this thing appear'd again to-night?
  Bernardo. I have seen nothing.
  Marcellus. Horatio says 'tis but our fantasy,
And will not let belief take hold of him
Touching this dreaded sight twice seen of us: 25
Therefore I have entreated him along
With us to watch the minutes of this night;
That if again this apparition come,
He may approve our eyes and speak to it.
  Horatio. Tush, tush! 'twill not appear.
  Bernardo.   Sit down awhile,   30
And let us once again assail your ears,
That are so fortified against our story,
What we two nights have seen.
  Horatio.   Well, sit we down,
And let us hear Bernardo speak of this.
  Bernardo. Last night of all,   35
When yond same star that's westward from the pole
Had made his course to illume that part of heaven
Where now it burns, Marcellus and myself,
The bell then beating one,—

Enter GHOST.

  Mar. Peace! break thee off; look, where it comes again!
  Bernardo. In the same figure like the king that's dead. 41
  Marcellus. Thou art a scholar; speak to it, Horatio.
  Bernardo. Looks it not like the king? mark it, Horatio.

---

  23 **fantasy**: imagination.   29 **approve our eyes**: confirm what
we have seen.   35 **last night of all**: only last night.

Horatio. Most like: it harrows me with fear and wonder.

Bernardo. It would be spoke to.

Marcellus.   Question it, Horatio. 45

Horatio. What art thou that usurp'st this time of night,
Together with that fair and war-like form
In which the majesty of buried Denmark
Did sometimes march? by heaven I charge thee, speak!

Marcellus. It is offended.

Bernardo.   See! it stalks away.   50

Horatio. Stay! speak, speak! I charge thee, speak!

                              [*Exit* GHOST.

Marcellus. 'Tis gone, and will not answer.

Bernardo. How now, Horatio! you tremble and look pale:
Is not this something more than fantasy?
What think you on 't?   55

Horatio. Before my God, I might not this believe
Without the sensible and true avouch
Of mine own eyes.

Marcellus.   Is it not like the king?

Horatio. As thou art to thyself:
Such was the very armour he had on   60
When he the ambitious Norway combated;
So frown'd he once, when in an angry parle
He smote the sledded Polacks on the ice.
'Tis strange.

Marcellus. Thus twice before, and jump at this dead
        hour,   65
With martial stalk hath he gone by our watch.

Horatio. In what particular thought to work I know not;
But in the gross and scope of my opinion,

---

49 **sometimes:** formerly.   57 **sensible and true avouch:**
the positive evidence of my senses.   61 **Norway:** i.e. the King
of Norway.   62 **parle:** parley.   63 **sledded Polacks:** the
Poles who travel on sledges.   65 **jump:** exactly.   68 **gross
and scope of my opinion:** my own general view.

This bodes some strange eruption to our state.

   Mar. Good now, sit down, and tell me, he that knows,   **70**
Why this same strict and most observant watch
So nightly toils the subject of the land,
And why such daily cast of brazen cannon,
And foreign mart for implements of war,
Why such impress of shipwrights, whose sore task   **75**
Does not divide the Sunday from the week,
What might be toward, that this sweaty haste
Doth make the night joint-labourer with the day:
Who is't that can inform me?

   Horatio.   That can I;
At least, the whisper goes so. Our last king,   **80**
Whose image even but now appear'd to us,
Was, as you know, by Fortinbras of Norway,
Thereto prick'd on by a most emulate pride,
Dar'd to the combat; in which our valiant Hamlet—
For so this side of our known world esteem'd him—   **85**
Did slay this Fortinbras; who, by a seal'd compact,
Well ratified by law and heraldry,
Did forfeit with his life all those his lands
Which he stood seiz'd of, to the conqueror;
Against the which, a moiety competent   **90**
Was gagéd by our king; which had return'd
To the inheritance of Fortinbras,
Had he been vanquisher; as, by the same co-mart,

---

   70 Good now: if you please.   **72 So nightly toils the
subject of the land:** causes the people to labour night by night.
73 cast: casting.   **74 foreign mart:** purchase of war material
from abroad.   **75 impress:** compulsory service.   **77 toward:**
imminent.   **83 emulate pride:** determined rivalry.   **85 our
valiant Hamlet:** i.e. Hamlet's father, the late king.   **87 ratified
by law and heraldry:** legalized by covenant and obligations of
honour in the law of arms.   **89 seiz'd of:** possessed of.   **90
moiety competent:** equivalent amount.   **92 inheritance:**
possession.   **93 co-mart:** joint bargain.

And carriage of the article design'd,
His fell to Hamlet. Now, sir, young Fortinbras,   95
Of unimprovéd mettle hot and full,
Hath in the skirts of Norway here and there
Shark'd up a list of lawless resolutes
For food and diet to some enterprise
That hath a stomach in 't; which is no other—   100
As it doth well appear unto our state—
But to recover of us, by strong hand
And terms compulsative, those foresaid lands
So by his father lost. And this, I take it,
Is the main motive of our preparations,   105
The source of this our watch and the chief head
Of this post-haste and romage in the land.
 Bernardo. I think it be no other but e'en so;
Well may it sort that this portentous figure
Comes arméd through our watch, so like the king   110
That was and is the question of these wars.
 Horatio. A mote it is to trouble the mind's eye.
In the most high and palmy state of Rome,
A little ere the mightiest Julius fell,
The graves stood tenantless, and the sheeted dead   115
Did squeak and gibber in the Roman streets;
As stars with trains of fire and dews of blood,
Disasters in the sun; and the moist star
Upon whose influence Neptune's empire stands
Was sick almost to doomsday with eclipse;   120
And even the like precurse of fierce events,

94 **carriage of the article design'd**: the meaning of the relevant clause.   96 **unimprovéd**: untutored, inexpert.   98 **shark'd up**: swept up indiscriminately.   **lawless resolutes**: reckless outlaws.   100 **a stomach in 't**: a spice of adventure.   106 **head**: occasion.   107 **romage**: rummage, bustle.   109 **sort**: agree with this account.   111 **question**: subject.   112 **mote**: speck of dust, mere nothing.   118 **the moist star**: the moon. 121 **precurse**: fore-showing.

As harbingers preceding still the fates
And prologue to the omen coming on,
Have heaven and earth together demonstrated
Unto our climatures and countrymen.   125

Re-enter GHOST.

But, soft! behold! lo! where it comes again.
I'll cross it, though it blast me. Stay, illusion!
If thou hast any sound, or use of voice,
Speak to me:
If there be any good thing to be done,   130
That may to thee do ease and grace to me,
Speak to me:
If thou art privy to thy country's fate,
Which happily foreknowing may avoid,
O! speak!   135
Or if thou hast uphoarded in thy life
Extorted treasure in the womb of earth,
For which, they say, you spirits oft walk in death,
Speak of it: stay, and speak! [*Cock crows.*] Stop it,
    Marcellus.
Marcellus. Shall I strike at it with my partisan?   140
Horatio. Do, if it will not stand.
Bernardo.   'Tis here!
Horatio.   'Tis here! [*Exit* GHOST.
Marcellus. 'Tis gone!
We do it wrong, being so majestical,
To offer it the show of violence;
For it is, as the air, invulnerable,   145

---

122 **harbingers**: forerunners.   123 **omen coming on**: portended calamity.   125 **climatures**: regions.   134 **happily**: perchance.   137 **extorted**: i.e. which should therefore be restored.   140 **partisan**: spear with a broad head.

And our vain blows malicious mockery.

  Bernardo. It was about to speak when the cock crew.

  Horatio. And then it started like a guilty thing
Upon a fearful summons. I have heard,
The cock, that is the trumpet to the morn,   150
Doth with his lofty and shrill-sounding throat
Awake the god of day; and at his warning,
Whether in sea or fire, in earth or air,
Th' extravagant and erring spirit hies
To his confine; and of the truth herein   155
This present object made probation.

  Marcellus. It faded on the crowing of the cock.
Some say that ever 'gainst that season comes
Wherein our Saviour's birth is celebrated,
The bird of dawning singeth all night long;   160
And then, they say, no spirit dare stir abroad;
The nights are wholesome; then no planets strike,
No fairy takes, nor witch hath power to charm,
So hallow'd and so gracious is that time.

  Horatio. So have I heard and do in part believe it.   165
But look, the morn in russet mantle clad
Walks o'er the dew of yon high eastern hill;
Break we our watch up; and by my advice
Let us impart what we have seen to-night
Unto young Hamlet; for, upon my life,   170
This spirit, dumb to us, will speak to him.
Do you consent we shall acquaint him with it,
As needful in our loves, fitting our duty?

  Marcellus. Let's do 't, I pray; and I this morning know
Where we shall find him most conveniently.   [*Exeunt.*

---

150 **trumpet:** trumpeter.   154 **extravagant and erring:**
wandering and roaming (in literal sense).   156 **probation:** proof.
162 **strike:** affect with evil influence.   163 **takes:** strikes, blasts.
166 **russet:** homespun cloth, reddish or grey in colour.

Scene II. The Council Chamber

Enter CLAUDIUS, *King of Denmark,* GERTRUDE, *the Queen,*
  Councillors, POLONIUS *and his son* LAERTES, VOLTI-
  MAND *and* CORNELIUS, HAMLET *and* Attendants.

King. Though yet of Hamlet our dear brother's death
The memory be green, and that it us befitted
To bear our hearts in grief, and our whole kingdom
To be contracted in one brow of woe,
Yet so far hath discretion fought with nature   5
That we with wisest sorrow think on him,
Together with remembrance of ourselves.
Therefore our sometime sister, now our queen,
Th' imperial jointress to this war-like state,
Have we, as 'twere with a defeated joy,   10
With one auspicious and one dropping eye,
With mirth in funeral and with dirge in marriage,
In equal scale weighing delight and dole,
Taken to wife: nor have we herein barr'd
Your better wisdoms, which have freely gone   15
With this affair along: for all, our thanks.
Now follows, that you know, young Fortinbras,
Holding a weak supposal of our worth,
Or thinking by our late dear brother's death
Our state to be disjoint and out of frame,   20
Colleaguéd with the dream of his advantage,
He hath not fail'd to pester us with message,
Importing the surrender of those lands
Lost by his father, with all bands of law,
To our most valiant brother. So much for him.   25

9 **jointress:** a widow who holds a jointure or life-interest, partner
in.   11 **one auspicious and one dropping eye:** at once
rejoicing and sorrowing.   13 **dole:** grief.   14 **barr'd:**
excluded.   18 **supposal:** estimate.   21 **colleaguéd with
the dream of his advantage:** backed by his own imagined
superiority.   23 **importing:** concerning.

Now for ourself and for this time of meeting.
Thus much the business is: we have here writ
To Norway, uncle of young Fortinbras,
Who, impotent and bed-rid, scarcely hears
Of this his nephew's purpose, to suppress   30
His further gait herein; in that the levies,
The lists and full proportions, are all made
Out of his subject; and we here dispatch
You, good Cornelius, and you, Voltimand,
For bearers of this greeting to old Norway,   35
Giving to you no further personal power
To business with the king more than the scope
Of these delated articles allow.
Farewell and let your haste commend your duty.

  Cor.⎫
  Vol.⎭ In that and all things will we show our duty.   **40**

  King. We doubt it nothing: heartily farewell.
                       [*Exeunt* VOLTIMAND *and* CORNELIUS.
And now, Laertes, what's the news with you?
You told us of some suit; what is't, Laertes?
You cannot speak of reason to the Dane,
And lose your voice; what wouldst thou beg, Laertes, 45
That shall not be my offer, not thy asking?
The head is not more native to the heart,
The hand more instrumental to the mouth,
Than is the throne of Denmark to thy father.
What wouldst thou have, Laertes?

  Laertes.   Dread my lord,   **50**
Your leave and favour to return to France;
From whence though willingly I came to Denmark,
To show my duty in your coronation,

---

  31 **gait**: progress.   32 **lists and full proportions**: requisite
enlistment.   33 **subject**: subjects, people (cf. l. 72 of sc. i).
38 **delated articles**: detailed provisions.   46 i.e. that I am not
ready to give unasked.   49 **the throne**: i.e. the king.

Yet now, I must confess, that duty done,
My thoughts and wishes bend again toward France   55
And bow them to your gracious leave and pardon.

  King. Have you your father's leave? What says
    Polonius?

  Polonius. He hath, my lord, wrung from me my slow
    leave
By laboursome petition, and at last
Upon his will I seal'd my hard consent: 60
I do beseech you, give him leave to go.

  King. Take thy fair hour, Laertes; time be thine,
And thy best graces spend it at thy will.
But now, my cousin Hamlet, and my son,—

  Hamlet. [*Aside.*] A little more than kin, and less than
    kind.   65

  King. How is it that the clouds still hang on you?

  Hamlet. Not so, my lord; I am too much i' the sun.

  Queen. Good Hamlet, cast thy nighted colour off,
And let thine eye look like a friend on Denmark.
Do not for ever with thy vailéd lids   70
Seek for thy noble father in the dust:
Thou know'st 'tis common; all that live must die,
Passing through nature to eternity.

  Hamlet. Ay, madam, it is common.

  Queen.   If it be,
Why seems it so particular with thee?   75

  Hamlet. Seems, madam! Nay, it is; I know not 'seems'.
'Tis not alone my inky cloak, good mother,
Nor customary suits of solemn black,
Nor windy suspiration of forc'd breath,
No, nor the fruitful river in the eye,   80
Nor the dejected haviour of the visage,

---

  56 pardon: permission.   **68 nighted:** black, gloomy.   69
Denmark: i.e. the king.   **70 vailéd:** lowered, downcast.   75
particular: a subject of special concern.

Together with all forms, modes, shows of grief,
That can denote me truly; these indeed seem,
For they are actions that a man might play:
But I have that within which passeth show;   85
These but the trappings and the suits of woe.

   King. 'Tis sweet and commendable in your nature, Hamlet,
To give these mourning duties to your father:
But, you must know, your father lost a father;
That father lost, lost his; and the survivor bound   90
In filial obligation for some term
To do obsequious sorrow; but to persever
In obstinate condolement is a course
Of impious stubbornness; 'tis unmanly grief:
It shows a will most incorrect to heaven,   95
A heart unfortified, a mind impatient,
An understanding simple and unschool'd:
For what we know must be and is as common
As any the most vulgar thing to sense,
Why should we in our peevish opposition   100
Take it to heart? Fie! 'tis a fault to heaven,
A fault against the dead, a fault to nature,
To reason most absurd, whose common theme
Is death of fathers, and who still hath cried,
From the first corse till he that died to-day,   105
'This must be so.' We pray you, throw to earth
This unprevailing woe, and think of us
As of a father; for let the world take note,
You are the most immediate to our throne;
And with no less nobility of love   110
Than that which dearest father bears his son

---

83 **seem:** are mere appearances.   92 **obsequious:** connected
with obsequies: i.e. mourning.   98–9 **as common . . . to
sense:** as familiar as anything perceptible to our senses.   107
unprevailing: ineffective.   109 **most immediate:** nearest.

Do I impart toward you. For your intent
In going back to school in Wittenberg,
It is most retrograde to our desire;
And we beseech you, bend you to remain   115
Here, in the cheer and comfort of our eye,
Our chiefest courtier, cousin, and our son.

   Queen. Let not thy mother lose her prayers, Hamlet:
I pray thee, stay with us; go not to Wittenberg.

   Hamlet. I shall in all my best obey you, madam.   120

   King. Why, 'tis a loving and a fair reply:
Be as ourself in Denmark. Madam, come;
This gentle and unforc'd accord of Hamlet
Sits smiling to my heart; in grace whereof,
No jocund health that Denmark drinks to-day,   125
But the great cannon to the clouds shall tell,
And the king's rouse the heavens shall bruit again,
Re-speaking earthly thunder. Come away.

                      [Exeunt all except HAMLET.

   Hamlet. O! that this too too solid flesh would melt,
Thaw and resolve itself into a dew;   130
Or that the Everlasting had not fix'd
His canon 'gainst self-slaughter! O God! God!
How weary, stale, flat, and unprofitable
Seem to me all the uses of this world.
Fie on 't! Ah fie! 'tis an unweeded garden,   135
That grows to seed; things rank and gross in nature
Possess it merely. That it should come to this!
But two months dead: nay, not so much, not two:
So excellent a king; that was, to this,

---

112 **impart:** behave, make myself known ('myself' is understood).
114 **retrograde:** opposed.   127 **rouse:** a bumper. **bruit:**
noise abroad.   130 **resolve:** dissolve.   132 **canon 'gainst
self-slaughter:** i.e. the Sixth Commandment.   134 **uses:**
customs and employments.   137 **merely:** utterly.   139 **to this:**
compared to this.

Hyperion to a satyr; so loving to my mother   140
That he might not beteem the winds of heaven
Visit her face too roughly. Heaven and earth!
Must I remember? why, she would hang on him,
As if increase of appetite had grown
By what it fed on; and yet, within a month,   145
Let me not think on't: Frailty, thy name is woman!
A little month; or ere those shoes were old
With which she follow'd my poor father's body,
Like Niobe, all tears; why she, even she,—
O God! a beast, that wants discourse of reason,   150
Would have mourn'd longer,—married with mine uncle,
My father's brother, but no more like my father
Than I to Hercules: within a month,
Ere yet the salt of most unrighteous tears
Had left the flushing in her gallèd eyes,   155
She married. O! most wicked speed, to post
With such dexterity to incestuous sheets.
It is not nor it cannot come to good;
But break, my heart, for I must hold my tongue!

Enter HORATIO, MARCELLUS, *and* BERNARDO.

Horatio. Hail to your lordship!
Hamlet.   I am glad to see you well: 160
Horatio, or I do forget myself.
Horatio. The same, my lord, and your poor servant ever.
Hamlet. Sir, my good friend; I'll change that name with
    you.
And what make you from Wittenberg, Horatio?
Marcellus?   165
Marcellus. My good lord,—

---

141 **beteem:** permit.   150 **discourse of reason:** rational
faculties.   154 **unrighteous:** insincere.   155 **left the flushing
in her gallèd eyes:** had ceased turning her sore eyes red.   163
change: exchange the name of friend.

Hamlet. I am very glad to see you. [*To* BERNARDO.]
　　Good even, sir.
But what, in faith, make you from Wittenberg?
　Horatio. A truant disposition, good my lord.
　Hamlet. I would not hear your enemy say so,   170
Nor shall you do mine ear that violence,
To make it truster of your own report
Against yourself; I know you are no truant.
But what is your affair in Elsinore?
We'll teach you to drink deep ere you depart.   175
　Horatio. My lord, I came to see your father's funeral.
　Hamlet. I pray thee, do not mock me, fellow-student;
I think it was to see my mother's wedding.
　Horatio. Indeed, my lord, it follow'd hard upon.
　Ham. Thrift, thrift, Horatio! the funeral bak'd meats 180
Did coldly furnish forth the marriage tables.
Would I had met my dearest foe in heaven
Or ever I had seen that day, Horatio!
My father, methinks I see my father.
　Horatio. O! where, my lord?
　Hamlet.　　　　　　　　In my mind's eye, Horatio.   185
　Horatio. I saw him once; he was a goodly king.
　Hamlet. He was a man, take him for all in all,
I shall not look upon his like again.
　Horatio. My lord, I think I saw him yesternight.
　Hamlet. Saw who?   190
　Horatio. My lord, the king your father.
　Hamlet.　　　　　　　　　The king, my father!
　Horatio. Season your admiration for a while
With an attent ear, till I may deliver,
Upon the witness of these gentlemen,
This marvel to you.

168 **make you from:** are you doing away from.   182 **dearest
foe:** closest, i.e. bitterest, enemy.   192 **season your admiration:** moderate your amazement.

Hamlet.   For God's love, let me hear.   195
  Horatio. Two nights together had these gentlemen,
Marcellus and Bernardo, on their watch,
In the dead vast and middle of the night,
Been thus encounter'd: a figure like your father,
Arméd at point exactly, cap-a-pe,   200
Appears before them, and with solemn march
Goes slow and stately by them: thrice he walk'd
By their oppress'd and fear-surpriséd eyes,
Within his truncheon's length; whilst they, distill'd
Almost to jelly with the act of fear,   205
Stand dumb and speak not to him. This to me
In dreadful secrecy impart they did,
And I with them the third night kept the watch;
Where, as they had deliver'd, both in time,
Form of the thing, each word made true and good,   210
The apparition comes. I knew your father;
These hands are not more like.
  Hamlet.   But where was this?
  Marcellus. My lord, upon the platform where we watch'd.
  Hamlet. Did you not speak to it?
  Horatio.   My lord, I did;
But answer made it none; yet once methought   215
It lifted up it head and did address
Itself to motion, like as it would speak;
But even then the morning cock crew loud,
And at the sound it shrunk in haste away
And vanish'd from our sight.
  Hamlet.   'Tis very strange.   220

---

198 **vast**: emptiness, waste.   200 **arméd at point**: fully
armed and ready. **cap-a-pe**: *de cap à pied* (old French), head to
foot.   204 **truncheon**: field-marshal's baton. **distill'd**:
melted.   205 **act**: effect.   209 **deliver'd**: reported.   212
these hands are not more like: i.e. than your father and the
apparition.   216 **it**: old genitive for 'its'.

C

Horatio. As I do live, my honour'd lord, 'tis true;
And we did think it writ down in our duty
To let you know of it.

Hamlet. Indeed, indeed, sirs, but this troubles me.
Hold you the watch to-night?

Marcellus.
Bernardo. }   We do, my lord.   225

Hamlet. Arm'd, say you?

Marcellus.
Bernardo. }   Arm'd, my lord.

Hamlet.   From top to toe?

Marcellus.
Bernardo. } My lord, from head to foot.

Hamlet. Then saw you not his face?

Horatio. O yes! my lord; he wore his beaver up.

Hamlet. What! look'd he frowningly?   230

Horatio. A countenance more in sorrow than in anger.

Hamlet. Pale or red?

Horatio. Nay, very pale.

Hamlet.   And fix'd his eyes upon you?

Horatio. Most constantly.

Hamlet.   I would I had been there.

Horatio. It would have much amaz'd you.   235

Hamlet. Very like, very like. Stay'd it long?

Horatio. While one with moderate haste might tell a
    hundred.

Marcellus.
Bernardo. } Longer, longer.

Horatio. Not when I saw it.

Hamlet.   His beard was grizzled, no?

Horatio. It was, as I have seen it in his life,   240
A sable silver'd.

---

229 **beaver:** the visor of the helmet.   237 **tell:** count.
241 **a sable silver'd:** dark fur streaked with silver.

Hamlet.   I will watch to-night;
Perchance 'twill walk again.
    Horatio.   I warrant it will.
    Hamlet. If it assume my noble father's person,
I'll speak to it, though hell itself should gape
And bid me hold my peace. I pray you all,   245
If you have hitherto conceal'd this sight,
Let it be tenable in your silence still;
And whatsoever else shall hap to-night,
Give it an understanding, but no tongue:
I will requite your loves. So, fare you well.   250
Upon the platform, 'twixt eleven and twelve,
I'll visit you.
    All.   Our duty to your honour.
    Hamlet. Your loves, as mine to you. Farewell.
           [*Exeunt* HORATIO, MARCELLUS, *and* BERNARDO.
My father's spirit (in arms!) all is not well;
I doubt some foul play: would the night were come!   255
Till then sit still, my soul: foul deeds will rise,
Though all the earth o'erwhelm them, to men's eyes. [*Exit.*

Scene III. A Room in Polonius' House

Enter LAERTES *and* OPHELIA.

    Laertes. My necessaries are embark'd; farewell:
And, sister, as the winds give benefit
And convoy is assistant, do not sleep,
But let me hear from you.
    Ophelia.   Do you doubt that?
    Laertes. For Hamlet, and the trifling of his favour,   5
Hold it a fashion and a toy in blood,
A violet in the youth of primy nature,

---

247 **tenable in your silence:** kept secret.   **3 convoy is assistant:**
a means of conveyance offers itself.   **6 a toy in blood:** a freak of
the passions, a mere impulse.   **7 primy:** in its prime or springtime.

Forward, not permanent, sweet, not lasting,
The perfume and suppliance of a minute;
No more.
   Ophelia.   No more but so?
   Laertes.   Think it no more: 10
For nature, crescent, does not grow alone
In thews and bulk; but, as this temple waxes,
The inward service of the mind and soul
Grows wide withal. Perhaps he loves you now,
And now no soil nor cautel doth besmirch   15
The virtue of his will; but you must fear,
His greatness weigh'd, his will is not his own,
For he himself is subject to his birth;
He may not, as unvalu'd persons do,
Carve for himself, for on his choice depends   20
The safety and the health of the whole state;
And therefore must his choice be circumscrib'd
Unto the voice and yielding of that body
Whereof he is the head. Then if he says he loves you,
It fits your wisdom so far to believe it   25
As he in his particular act and place
May give his saying deed; which is no further
Than the main voice of Denmark goes withal.
Then weigh what loss your honour may sustain,
If with too credent ear you list his songs,   30
Or lose your heart, or your chaste treasure open
To his unmaster'd importunity.

11–14 i.e. as the body, which is the temple of the soul, grows in
muscular strength, so the inner spirit develops and expands with it.
crescent: growing (Lat. *crescens*).   **15 cautel:** craft.   **16
the virtue of his will:** the honour of his passion.   **17 his greatness weigh'd:** allowing for his high position.   **19 unvalu'd:**
of no account.   **20 carve for himself:** pick and choose,
help himself.   **23 voice and yielding:** approval and acquies-
cence.   **32 unmaster'd importunity:** uncontrolled and determined wooing.

Fear it, Ophelia, fear it, my dear sister;
And keep you in the rear of your affection,
Out of the shot and danger of desire.   85
The chariest maid is prodigal enough
If she unmask her beauty to the moon;
Virtue herself 'scapes not calumnious strokes;
The canker galls the infants of the spring
Too oft before their buttons be disclos'd,   40
And in the morn and liquid dew of youth
Contagious blastments are most imminent.
Be wary then; best safety lies in fear:
Youth to itself rebels, though none else near.
  Ophelia. I shall th' effect of this good lesson keep,   45
As watchman to my heart. But, good my brother,
Do not, as some ungracious pastors do,
Show me the steep and thorny way to heaven,
Whiles, like a puff'd and reckless libertine,
Himself the primrose path of dalliance treads,   50
And recks not his own rede.
  Laertes.   O! fear me not.
I stay too long; but here my father comes.

Enter POLONIUS.

A double blessing is a double grace;
Occasion smiles upon a second leave.
  Pol. Yet here, Laertes! aboard, aboard, for shame!   55
The wind sits in the shoulder of your sail,
And you are stay'd for. There, my blessing with thee!
And these few precepts in thy memory

---

34 i.e. do not let your affection run away with you.   **36 chariest:**
most fastidious and modest.   **39 canker:** canker-worm.   40
buttons be disclos'd: their buds open.   **47 ungracious pastors:** clergy without grace.   49–51 i.e. while he himself, like
a bloated and careless trifler, treads the primrose path of pleasure
and disregards his own counsel.   **54 leave:** leave-taking.

Look thou character. Give thy thoughts no tongue,
Nor any unproportion'd thought his act.   60
Be thou familiar, but by no means vulgar;
The friends thou hast, and their adoption tried,
Grapple them to thy soul with hoops of steel;
But do not dull thy palm with entertainment
Of each new-hatch'd, unfledg'd comrade. Beware   65
Of entrance to a quarrel, but, being in,
Bear 't that th' opposéd may beware of thee.
Give every man thine ear, but few thy voice;
Take each man's censure, but reserve thy judgment.
Costly thy habit as thy purse can buy,   70
But not express'd in fancy; rich, not gaudy;
For the apparel oft proclaims the man,
And they in France of the best rank and station
Are most select and generous, chief in that.
Neither a borrower, nor a lender be;   75
For loan oft loses both itself and friend,
And borrowing dulls the edge of husbandry.
This above all: to thine own self be true,
And it must follow, as the night the day,
Thou canst not then be false to any man.   80
Farewell; my blessing season this in thee!
   Laertes. Most humbly do I take my leave, my lord.
   Polonius. The time invites you; go, your servants tend.
   Laertes. Farewell, Ophelia; and remember well
What I have said to you.
   Ophelia.   'Tis in my memory lock'd,   85

---

59 **character**: inscribe, engrave (Greek χαρακτήρ, a stamp on a seal
or coin).   60 **unproportion'd**: unweighed, unsuitable.
64 **dull thy palm**: i.e. lose your power of discrimination.   69
censure: judgement, opinion (Lat. *censere*, to judge).   73–4 i.e.
the French nobility display their taste and breeding particularly in
their apparel.   77 **husbandry**: thrift.   81 **season**: ripen.
83 **tend**: attend you.

And you yourself shall keep the key of it.

Laertes. Farewell.   [*Exit.*

Polonius. What is 't, Ophelia, he hath said to you?

Ophelia. So please you, something touching the Lord
    Hamlet.

Polonius. Marry, well bethought: 90

'Tis told me, he hath very oft of late

Given private time to you; and you yourself

Have of your audience been most free and bounteous.

If it be so,—as so 'tis put on me,

And that in way of caution,—I must tell you,   95

You do not understand yourself so clearly

As it behoves my daughter and your honour.

What is between you? give me up the truth.

Ophelia. He hath, my lord, of late made many tenders

Of his affection to me.   100

Polonius. Affection! pooh! you speak like a green girl,

Unsifted in such perilous circumstance.

Do you believe his tenders, as you call them?

Ophelia. I do not know, my lord, what I should think.

Polonius. Marry, I'll teach you: think yourself a baby,

That you have ta'en these tenders for true pay,   106

Which are not sterling. Tender yourself more dearly;

Or,—not to crack the wind of the poor phrase,

Running it thus,—you'll tender me a fool.

Ophelia. My lord, he hath importun'd me with love 110

In honourable fashion.

Polonius. Ay, fashion you may call it: go to, go to.

Ophelia. And hath given countenance to his speech, my
    lord,

With almost all the holy vows of heaven.

Pol. Ay, springes to catch woodcocks. I do know,   115

---

99 tenders: offers.   **102 unsifted:** untested.   **107 tender
yourself more dearly:** have a greater regard for yourself.   **108
crack the wind of:** exhaust, overwork.   **115 springes:** snares.

When the blood burns, how prodigal the soul
Lends the tongue vows: these blazes, daughter,
Giving more light than heat, extinct in both,
Even in their promise, as it is a-making,
You must not take for fire. From this time   120
Be somewhat scanter of your maiden presence;
Set your entreatments at a higher rate
Than a command to parley. For Lord Hamlet,
Believe so much in him, that he is young,
And with a larger tether may he walk   125
Than may be given you: in few, Ophelia,
Do not believe his vows, for they are brokers,
Not of that dye which their investments show,
But mere implorators of unholy suits,
Breathing like sanctified and pious bonds,   130
The better to beguile. This is for all:
I would not, in plain terms, from this time forth,
Have you so slander any moment's leisure,
As to give words or talk with the Lord Hamlet.
Look to 't, I charge you; come your ways.   135
    Ophelia. I shall obey, my lord.   [*Exeunt.*

Scene IV. The Platform

Enter HAMLET, HORATIO, *and* MARCELLUS.

Hamlet. The air bites shrewdly; it is very cold.
Horatio. It is a nipping and an eager air.
Hamlet. What hour now?

116 **prodigal:** generously.   117 **blazes:** flashes.   118
extinct in both: their light and heat at once extinguished.   122
entreatments: interviews.   125 **larger tether:** with more
rope, more freely.   127–31 i.e. his vows are not of the colour that
they show; they are go-betweens soliciting an unholy suit, utter-
ing the holy promises of the marriage-service so as to deceive you.
128 **investments:** robes.   131 **this is for all:** to sum up.
133 **slander:** bring shame upon.   2 **eager:** sharp (Fr. *aigre*).

Horatio.   I think it lacks of twelve.
Marcellus. No, it is struck.
Horatio. Indeed? I heard it not: then it draws near the
    season   5
Wherein the spirit held his wont to walk.
    [*A flourish of trumpets, and ordnance shot off, within.*
What does this mean, my lord?
  Ham. The king doth wake to-night and takes his rouse,
Keeps wassail and the swaggering up-spring reels;
And, as he drains his draughts of Rhenish down,   10
The kettle-drum and trumpet thus bray out
The triumph of his pledge.
  Horatio.   Is it a custom?
  Hamlet. Ay, marry, is 't:
But to my mind,—though I am native here
And to the manner born,—it is a custom   15
More honour'd in the breach than the observance.
This heavy-headed revel east and west
Makes us traduc'd and tax'd of other nations;
They clepe us drunkards, and with swinish phrase
Soil our addition; and indeed it takes   20
From our achievements, though perform'd at height,
The pith and marrow of our attribute.
So, oft it chances in particular men,
That for some vicious mole of nature in them,
As, in their birth,—wherein they are not guilty,   25
Since nature cannot choose his origin,—

8 **rouse:** bumper.   9 **swaggering up-spring reels:** blustering new-fangled revels.   11 **bray out:** celebrate.   12 **the triumph
of his pledge:** his triumph as a drinker.   16 **more honour'd
in the breach than the observance:** better disregarded than kept.
18 **traduc'd and tax'd:** defamed and accused.   19 **clepe:** call.
20 **addition:** title, reputation.   **it:** viz. drunkenness.   19–20 i.e.
they dishonour us with the name of drunken swine.   21 **though
perform'd at height:** at their best.   22 **attribute:** reputation,
honour.   24 **vicious mole of nature:** natural blemish.   26 **his:** its.

By the o'ergrowth of some complexion,
Oft breaking down the pales and forts of reason,
Or by some habit that too much o'er-leavens
The form of plausive manners; that these men,   30
Carrying, I say, the stamp of one defect,
Being nature's livery, or fortune's star,
His virtues else, be they as pure as grace,
As infinite as man may undergo,
Shall in the general censure take corruption   35
From that particular fault: the dram of evil
Doth all the noble substance often dout,
To his own scandal.

                    Enter GHOST.

Horatio.   Look, my lord, it comes.
Hamlet. Angels and ministers of grace defend us!
Be thou a spirit of health or goblin damn'd,   40
Bring with thee airs from heaven or blasts from hell,
Be thy intents wicked or charitable,
Thou com'st in such a questionable shape
That I will speak to thee: I'll call thee Hamlet,
King, father; royal Dane, O! answer me: 45
Let me not burst in ignorance; but tell
Why thy canoniz'd bones, hearséd in death,

27–30 **by the o'ergrowth . . . plausive manners:** by the undue development of some natural bent of character which overcomes the restraint imposed by reason, or by some acquired habit which overstrains (or, as it were, ferments) a gracious personality to excess.   32 **nature's livery or fortune's star:** whether the defect be innate or wrought by ill fortune (livery = badge).   34 **undergo:** support, (and so) possess.   35 **general censure:** the estimate of the public.   36–8 **dram of evil . . . scandal:** the taste or dose of ill puts the nobility of the whole man in doubt and brings him to disgrace [*N*].   40 **spirit of health:** *either* beneficent, *or* a spirit that has been saved.   41 **bring:** whether thou bringest.   43 **such a questionable shape:** a form that can be spoken to.   47 **canoniz'd:** consecrated.

Have burst their cerements; why the sepulchre,
Wherein we saw thee quietly inurn'd,
Hath op'd his ponderous and marble jaws,   50
To cast thee up again. What may this mean,
That thou, dead corse, again in complete steel
Revisits thus the glimpses of the moon,
Making night hideous; and we fools of nature
So horridly to shake our disposition   55
With thoughts beyond the reaches of our souls?
Say, why is this? wherefore? what should we do?

                  [*The* Ghost *beckons* HAMLET.

  Horatio. It beckons you to go away with it,
As if it some impartment did desire
To you alone.
  Marcellus. Look, with what courteous action   60
It waves you to a more removéd ground:
But do not go with it.
  Horatio.   No, by no means.
  Hamlet. It will not speak; then, will I follow it.
  Horatio. Do not, my lord.
  Hamlet.   Why, what should be the fear?
I do not set my life at a pin's fee;   65
And for my soul, what can it do to that,
Being a thing immortal as itself?
It waves me forth again; I'll follow it.
  Horatio. What if it tempt you toward the flood, my lord,
Or to the dreadful summit of the cliff   70
That beetles o'er his base into the sea,
And there assume some other horrible form,
Which might deprive your sovereignty of reason
And draw you into madness? think of it;

    49 inurn'd: entombed.   **54 fools of nature**: dupes of nature
(in the face of the supernatural).   **59 impartment**: disclosure.
71 beetles o'er: overhangs.   **73 deprive your sovereignty
of reason**: dethrone your reason.

The very place puts toys of desperation,   **75**
Without more motive, into every brain
That looks so many fathoms to the sea
And hears it roar beneath.

 Hamlet. It waves me still. Go on, I'll follow thee.

 Marcellus. You shall not go, my lord.

 Hamlet.   Hold off your hands! **80**

 Horatio. Be rul'd; you shall not go.

 Hamlet.   My fate cries out,
And makes each petty artery in this body
As hardy as the Nemean lion's nerve. [*Ghost beckons.*
Still am I call'd. Unhand me, gentlemen,

           [*Breaking from them.*
By heaven! I'll make a ghost of him that lets me: **85**
I say, away! Go on, I'll follow thee.

        [*Exeunt* Ghost *and* HAMLET.

 Horatio. He waxes desperate with imagination.

 Marcellus. Let's follow; 'tis not fit thus to obey him.

 Horatio. Have after. To what issue will this come?

 Mar. Something is rotten in the state of Denmark. **90**

 Horatio. Heaven will direct it.

 Marcellus.   Nay, let's follow him.

             [*Exeunt.*

 Scene V. ANOTHER PART OF THE PLATFORM

   Enter Ghost and HAMLET.

 Hamlet. Whither wilt thou lead me? speak; I'll go no
  further.

 Ghost. Mark me.

 Hamlet.   I will.

 Ghost.   My hour is almost come,

---

75 toys of desperation: desperate impulses. **83 hardy:**
bold (Fr. *hardi*). **nerve:** sinew (Lat. *nervus*). **85 lets:** hinders.
91 Heaven will direct it: viz. the issue.

When I to sulphurous and tormenting flames
Must render up myself.
   Hamlet.   Alas! poor ghost.
   Ghost. Pity me not, but lend thy serious hearing   5
To what I shall unfold.
   Hamlet.   Speak; I am bound to hear.
   Ghost. So art thou to revenge, when thou shalt hear.
   Hamlet. What?
   Ghost. I am thy father's spirit;
Doom'd for a certain term to walk the night,   10
And for the day confin'd to fast in fires,
Till the foul crimes done in my days of nature
Are burnt and purg'd away. But that I am forbid
To tell the secrets of my prison-house,
I could a tale unfold whose lightest word   15
Would harrow up thy soul, freeze thy young blood,
Make thy two eyes like stars start from their spheres,
Thy knotted and combinéd locks to part,
And each particular hair to stand an end,
Like quills upon the fretful porpentine: 20
But this eternal blazon must not be
To ears of flesh and blood. List, list, O list!
If thou didst ever thy dear father love—
   Hamlet. O God!
   Ghost. Revenge his foul and most unnatural murder.   25
   Hamlet. Murder!
   Ghost. Murder most foul, as in the best it is;
But this most foul, strange, and unnatural.
   Ham. Haste me to know 't, that I, with wings as swift
As meditation or the thoughts of love,   30
May sweep to my revenge.

---

   6 bound: ready. The Ghost interprets it as 'obliged'.   **17**
spheres: orbits of the stars.   **19 an:** on.   **21 eternal**
blazon: revelation of the secrets of eternity.   **27 in the best:**
at best.

Ghost.   I find thee apt,
And duller shouldst thou be than the fat weed
That rots itself in ease on Lethe wharf,
Wouldst thou not stir in this. Now, Hamlet, hear;
'Tis given out, that sleeping in mine orchard,   35
A serpent stung me; so the whole ear of Denmark
Is by a forgéd process of my death
Rankly abus'd; but know, thou noble youth,
The serpent that did sting thy father's life
Now wears his crown.
Hamlet.   O my prophetic soul!   40
My uncle?
Ghost. Ay, that incestuous, that adulterate beast,
With witchcraft of his wit, with traitorous gifts,—
O wicked wit and gifts, that have the power
So to seduce!—won to his shameful lust   45
The will of my most seeming-virtuous queen.
O Hamlet! what a falling-off was there;
From me, whose love was of that dignity
That it went hand in hand even with the vow
I made to her in marriage; and to decline   50
Upon a wretch whose natural gifts were poor
To those of mine!
But virtue, as it never will be mov'd,
Though lewdness court it in a shape of heaven,
So lust, though to a radiant angel link'd,   55
Will sate itself in a celestial bed,
And prey on garbage.
But, soft! methinks I scent the morning air;
Brief let me be. Sleeping within mine orchard,
My custom always of the afternoon,   60

37 **forgéd process**: false report.   38 **abus'd**: deceived.
40 **O . . . soul!** i.e. this is what I feared.   50–1 **decline upon**:
degrade herself to.   54 **lewdness**: sensuality, viciousness.
56 **sate itself . . . bed**: weary of a heavenly union.

Upon my secure hour thy uncle stole,
With juice of cursed hebona in a vial,
And in the porches of mine ears did pour
The leperous distilment; whose effect
Holds such an enmity with blood of man 65
That swift as quicksilver it courses through
The natural gates and alleys of the body,
And with a sudden vigour it doth posset
And curd, like eager droppings into milk,
The thin and wholesome blood: so did it mine; 70
And a most instant tetter bark'd about,
Most lazar-like, with vile and loathsome crust,
All my smooth body.
Thus was I, sleeping, by a brother's hand,
Of life, of crown, of queen, at once dispatch'd; 75
Cut off even in the blossoms of my sin,
Unhousel'd, disappointed, unanel'd,
No reckoning made, but sent to my account
With all my imperfections on my head:
O, horrible! O, horrible! most horrible! 80
If thou hast nature in thee, bear it not;
Let not the royal bed of Denmark be
A couch for luxury and damned incest.
But, howsoever thou pursu'st this act,
Taint not thy mind, nor let thy soul contrive 85
Against thy mother aught; leave her to heaven,
And to those thorns that in her bosom lodge,
To prick and sting her. Fare thee well at once!

61 **secure**: free from care (Lat. *securus*).   62 **hebona**: yew
[*N*].   68 **posset**: curdle.   69 **eager** cf. l. 2 of sc. iv.
71 **tetter**: scurf, eruption.   **bark'd about**: encrusted, coated.
72 **lazar-like**: like a leper.   75 **dispatch'd**: deprived.
77 **unhousel'd**: without receiving the sacrament. **disappointed**:
ill-equipped, unprepared.   **unanel'd**: unanointed, without Extreme
Unction.   81 **nature**: natural feeling and sense of kinship.
83 **luxury**: lust.

The glow-worm shows the matin to be near,
And 'gins to pale his uneffectual fire;   90
Adieu, adieu! Hamlet, remember me.   [*Exit.*
   Hamlet. O all you host of heaven! O earth! What else?
And shall I couple hell? O fie! Hold, hold, my heart!
And you, my sinews, grow not instant old,
But bear me stiffly up! Remember thee!   95
Ay, thou poor ghost, while memory holds a seat
In this distracted globe. Remember thee!
Yea, from the table of my memory
I'll wipe away all trivial fond records,
All saws of books, all forms, all pressures past   100
That youth and observation copied there;
And thy commandment all alone shall live
Within the book and volume of my brain,
Unmix'd with baser matter: yes, by heaven!
O most pernicious woman!   105
O villain, villain, smiling, damnéd villain!
My tables,—meet it is I set it down,
That one may smile, and smile, and be a villain;
At least I'm sure it may be so in Denmark: [*Writing.*
So, uncle, there you are. Now to my word;   110
It is, 'Adieu, adieu! remember me.'
I have sworn 't.
   Horatio. [*Within.*] My lord, my lord!
   Marcellus. [*Within.*]   Lord Hamlet!
   Horatio. [*Within.*]   Heaven secure him!
   Marcellus. [*Within.*] So be it!
   Horatio. [*Within.*] Hillo, ho, ho, my lord!   115
   Hamlet. Hillo, ho, ho, boy! come, bird, come.

---

   94 **instant**: immediately.   97 **globe**: viz. his skull.   98
table: tablet.   99 **fond**: foolish.   100 i.e. all maxims,
sketches, and past impressions.   107 **my tables**: ivory tablets
for note-taking.   110 **word**: *either* watchword, password *or*
motto, device.

Enter HORATIO *and* MARCELLUS.

Marcellus. How is't, my noble lord?
Horatio.   What news, my lord?
Hamlet. O! wonderful.
Horatio.   Good my lord, tell it.
Hamlet. No; you will reveal it.
Horatio. Not I, my lord, by heaven!
Marcellus.   Nor I, my lord.   120
Hamlet. How say you then, would heart of man once
    think it?
But you'll be secret?
  Horatio. ⎫
  Marcellus.⎭   Ay, by heaven, my lord.
Hamlet. There's ne'er a villain dwelling in all Denmark
But he's an arrant knave.
  Horatio. There needs no ghost, my lord, come from the
    grave,   125
To tell us this.
  Hamlet.   Why, right; you are i' the right;
And so without more circumstance at all,
I hold it fit that we shake hands and part;
You, as your business and desire shall point you,—
For every man hath business and desire,   130
Such as it is,—and, for mine own poor part,
Look you, I'll go pray.
  Hor. These are but wild and whirling words, my lord.
  Hamlet. I am sorry they offend you, heartily;
Yes, faith, heartily.
  Horatio.   There's no offence, my lord.   135
  Hamlet. Yes, by Saint Patrick, but there is, Horatio,
And much offence, too. Touching this vision here,
It is an honest ghost, that let me tell you;
For your desire to know what is between us,

121 **think it:** i.e. believe what I have been told.

O'ermaster 't as you may. And now, good friends,   140
As you are friends, scholars, and soldiers,
Give me one poor request.

  Horatio. What is 't, my lord? we will.

  Hamlet. Never make known what you have seen to-night.

  Horatio. ⎫
  Marcellus.⎭ My lord, we will not.

  Hamlet.   Nay, but swear 't.

  Horatio.   In faith,   145
My lord, not I.

  Marcellus.   Nor I, my lord, in faith.

  Hamlet. Upon my sword.

  Marcellus.   We have sworn, my lord, already.

  Hamlet. Indeed, upon my sword, indeed.

  Ghost. [*Beneath.*] Swear.

  Hamlet. Ha, ha, boy! sayst thou so? art thou there,
    true-penny?   150
Come on,—you hear this fellow in the cellarage,—
Consent to swear.

  Horatio.   Propose the oath, my lord.

  Hamlet. Never to speak of this that you have seen,
Swear by my sword.

  Ghost. [*Beneath.*] Swear.   155

  Hamlet. *Hic et ubique?* then we'll shift our ground.
Come hither, gentlemen,
And lay your hands again upon my sword:
Never to speak of this that you have heard,
Swear by my sword.   160

  Ghost. [*Beneath.*] Swear.

  Ham. Well said, old mole! canst work i' the earth so fast?
A worthy pioner! once more remove, good friends.

  Horatio. O day and night, but this is wondrous strange!

  Hamlet. And therefore as a stranger give it welcome. 165

---

150 **true-penny:** good fellow.   163 **pioner:** digger (cf. the
pioneer corps).

There are more things in heaven and earth, Horatio,
Than are dreamt of in your philosophy.
But come;
Here, as before, never, so help you mercy,
How strange or odd soe'er I bear myself,   170
As I perchance hereafter shall think meet
To put an antic disposition on,
That you, at such times seeing me, never shall,
With arms encumber'd thus, or this head-shake,
Or by pronouncing of some doubtful phrase,   175
As, 'Well, well, we know,' or, 'We could, an if we would;'
Or, 'If we list to speak,' or, 'There be, an if they might;'
Or such ambiguous giving out, to note
That you know aught of me: this not to do,
So grace and mercy at your most need help you,
Swear.   180
  Ghost. [*Beneath.*] Swear.   [*They swear.*
  Hamlet. Rest, rest, perturbéd spirit! So, gentlemen,
With all my love I do commend me to you:
And what so poor a man as Hamlet is
May do, to express his love and friending to you,   185
God willing, shall not lack. Let us go in together;
And still your fingers on your lips, I pray.
The time is out of joint; O curséd spite,
That ever I was born to set it right!
Nay, come, let's go together.   [*Exeunt.*

167 **philosophy:** i.e. natural philosophy or science as then understood.   169 **mercy:** i.e. God's (cf. l. 179).   172 **antic:** odd,
fantastic.   174 **encumber'd:** folded.   177 **there be, an if
they might:** i.e. some could tell a tale if they were permitted.

ACT II

Scene I. A Room in Polonius' House

Enter POLONIUS and REYNALDO.

Pol. Give him this money and these notes, Reynaldo.
Reynaldo. I will, my lord.
Pol. You shall do marvellous wisely, good Reynaldo,
Before you visit him, to make inquiry
Of his behaviour.
    Reynaldo.   My lord, I did intend it.   5
Pol. Marry, well said, very well said. Look you, sir,
Inquire me first what Danskers are in Paris;
And how, and who, what means, and where they keep,
What company, at what expense; and finding
By this encompassment and drift of question   10
That they do know my son, come you more nearer
Than your particular demands will touch it:
Take you, as 'twere, some distant knowledge of him;
As thus, 'I know his father, and his friends,
And, in part, him;' do you mark this, Reynaldo?   15
  Reynaldo. Ay, very well, my lord.
  Pol. 'And, in part, him; but,' you may say, 'not well:
But if 't be he I mean, he's very wild,
Addicted so and so;' and there put on him
What forgeries you please; marry, none so rank   20
As may dishonour him; take heed of that;
But, sir, such wanton, wild, and usual slips

---

1 him: i.e. Laertes. **notes:** letters.   **7 Danskers:**
Danes.   **8 keep:** lodge.   **10 encompassment and
drift of question:** roundabout and indirect inquiry.   **11–12
more nearer . . . touch it:** i.e. find out more about him without asking any direct questions.   **19 put on him:** charge
him with.

As are companions noted and most known
To youth and liberty.
    Reynaldo.   As gaming, my lord?
    Polonius. Ay, or drinking, fencing, swearing, quarrelling,
Drabbing; you may go so far.   26
    Reynaldo. My lord, that would dishonour him.
    Polonius. Faith, no; as you may season it in the charge.
You must not put another scandal on him,
That he is open to incontinency;   30
That's not my meaning; but breathe his faults so quaintly
That they may seem the taints of liberty,
The flash and outbreak of a fiery mind,
A savageness in unreclaiméd blood,
Of general assault.
    Reynaldo.   But, my good lord,—   35
    Polonius. Wherefore should you do this?
    Reynaldo.   Ay, my lord,
I would know that.
    Polonius.   Marry, sir, here's my drift;
And I believe it is a fetch of warrant:
You laying these slight sullies on my son,
As 'twere a thing a little soil'd i' the working,   40
Mark you,
Your party in converse, him you would sound,
Having ever seen in the prenominate crimes
The youth you breathe of guilty, be assur'd,
He closes with you in this consequence;   45
'Good sir,' or so; or 'friend,' or 'gentleman,'
According to the phrase or the addition

26 **drabbing:** frequenting women.   28 **season:** qualify.
30 **incontinency:** debauchery.   31 **quaintly:** artfully.   34
unreclaiméd: untamed.   35 **of general assault:** to which
many are liable.   38 **a fetch of warrant:** a device likely to
succeed.   43 **prenominate:** before-mentioned.   45 i.e.
comes to grips with you as follows.   47 **addition:** title, mode
of address.

Of man and country.

   Reynaldo.   Very good, my lord.

   Polonius. And then, sir, does he this,—he does,—what
was I about to say? By the mass I was about to say something: where did I leave?   51

   Reynaldo. At 'closes in the consequence.'
At 'friend or so,' and 'gentleman.'

   Polonius. At 'closes in the consequence,' ay, marry;
He closes with you thus: 'I know the gentleman;   55
I saw him yesterday, or t' other day,
Or then, or then; with such, or such; and, as you say,
There was a' gaming; there o'ertook in 's rouse;
There falling out at tennis;' or perchance,
'I saw him enter such a house of sale,'   60
Videlicet, a brothel, or so forth.
See you now;
Your bait of falsehood takes this carp of truth;
And thus do we of wisdom and of reach,
With windlasses, and with assays of bias,   65
By indirections find directions out:
So by my former lecture and advice
Shall you my son. You have me, have you not?

   Reynaldo. My lord, I have.

   Polonius.   God be wi' you; fare you well.

   Reynaldo. Good my lord!   70

   Polonius. Observe his inclination in yourself.

   Reynaldo. I shall, my lord.

   Polonius. And let him ply his music.

---

58 **a':** he.   **o'ertook in 's rouse:** the worse for liquor (rouse =
carousal).   64 **of reach:** who are men of range of understanding.   65 **windlasses** (windlaces): roundabout devices
(*lit.* circuits to intercept game).   **assays of bias:** indirect course (a
metaphor from bowls: bias is the weight in the bowl which makes it
run in a curved line).   66 **directions:** i.e. how to proceed.
71 **in yourself:** towards you *or* keep it to yourself.   73 **let him
ply his music:** *perhaps* 'let him go his own way and enjoy himself'.

Reynaldo.   Well, my lord.
Polonius. Farewell!   [*Exit* REYNALDO.

Enter OPHELIA.

          How now, Ophelia! what's the matter?
Ophelia. O! my lord, my lord, I have been so affrighted! 75
Polonius. With what, in the name of God?
Ophelia. My lord, as I was sewing in my closet,
Lord Hamlet, with his doublet all unbrac'd;
No hat upon his head; his stockings foul'd,
Ungarter'd, and down-gyvéd to his ancle;   80
Pale as his shirt; his knees knocking each other;
And with a look so piteous in purport
As if he had been looséd out of hell
To speak of horrors, he comes before me.
  Polonius. Mad for thy love?
  Ophelia.   My lord, I do not know; 85
But truly I do fear it.
  Polonius.   What said he?
  Ophelia. He took me by the wrist and held me hard,
Then goes he to the length of all his arm,
And with his other hand thus o'er his brow,
He falls to such perusal of my face   90
As he would draw it. Long stay'd he so;
At last, a little shaking of mine arm,
And thrice his head thus waving up and down,
He rais'd a sigh so piteous and profound
That it did seem to shatter all his bulk   95
And end his being. That done, he lets me go,
And with his head over his shoulder turn'd,
He seem'd to find his way without his eyes;
For out o' doors he went without their help,
And to the last bended their light on me.   100

    80 **down-gyvéd**: fallen to the ankle—like fetters.

Polonius. Come, go with me; I will go seek the king.
This is the very ecstasy of love,
Whose violent property fordoes itself
And leads the will to desperate undertakings
As oft as any passion under heaven   105
That does afflict our natures. I am sorry.
What! have you given him any hard words of late?
  Ophelia. No, my good lord; but, as you did command,
I did repel his letters and denied
His access to me.
  Polonius.   That hath made him mad.   110
I am sorry that with better heed and judgment
I had not quoted him; I fear'd he did but trifle,
And meant to wrack thee; but, beshrew my jealousy!
By heaven, it is as proper to our age
To cast beyond ourselves in our opinions   115
As it is common for the younger sort
To lack discretion. Come, go we to the king:
This must be known; which, being kept close, might move
More grief to hide than hate to utter love.
Come.   [*Exeunt.*

Scene II. A Room in the Castle

Enter KING, QUEEN, ROSENCRANTZ, GUILDENSTERN,
and Attendants.

  King. Welcome, dear Rosencrantz and Guildenstern!
Moreover that we much did long to see you,
The need we have to use you did provoke
Our hasty sending. Something have you heard

---

102 **ecstasy**: madness.   103 **property**: nature. **fordoes**:
undoes.   112 **quoted**: noted.   113 **wrack**: ruin.   115
cast . . . opinions: overdo suspicion.   118–19 **which . . .
love**: i.e. if we conceal it we may do more harm than the displeasure
which will be caused by informing Claudius of Hamlet's love.   2
moreover: over and above.

Of Hamlet's transformation; so call it,   5
Sith nor the exterior nor the inward man
Resembles that it was. What it should be
More than his father's death, that thus hath put him
So much from the understanding of himself,
I cannot dream of: I entreat you both,   10
That, being of so young days brought up with him,
And sith so neighbour'd to his youth and humour,
That you vouchsafe your rest here in our court
Some little time; so by your companies
To draw him on to pleasures, and to gather,   15
So much as from occasion you may glean,
Whe'r aught to us unknown afflicts him thus,
That open'd lies within our remedy.

   Queen. Good gentlemen, he hath much talk'd of you;
And sure I am two men there are not living   20
To whom he more adheres. If it will please you
To show us so much gentry and good will
As to expend your time with us awhile,
For the supply and profit of our hope,
Your visitation shall receive such thanks   25
As fits a king's remembrance.

   Rosencrantz.   Both your majesties
Might, by the sovereign power you have of us,
Put your dread pleasures more into command
Than to entreaty.

   Guildenstern.   But we both obey,
And here give up ourselves in the full bent,   30
To lay our service freely at your feet,
To be commanded.

   King. Thanks, Rosencrantz and gentle Guildenstern.

   Queen. Thanks, Guildenstern and gentle Rosencrantz;

  6 sith: because.   **7 should:** can.   **11 of so young:** from
such early.   **12 sith:** since then.   **17 whe'r:** whether.
22 gentry: courtesy.   **30 in the full bent:** completely.

And I beseech you instantly to visit 85
My too much changéd son. Go, some of you,
And bring these gentlemen where Hamlet is.

  Guil. Heavens make our presence and our practices
Pleasant and helpful to him!

  Queen.   Ay, amen!

            [*Exeunt* ROSENCRANTZ, GUILDENSTERN, *and some*
                                  Attendants.

            Enter POLONIUS.

  Polonius. The ambassadors from Norway, my good lord,
Are joyfully return'd.   41

  King. Thou still hast been the father of good news.

  Polonius. Have I, my lord? Assure you, my good liege,
I hold my duty, as I hold my soul,
Both to my God and to my gracious king;   45
And I do think—or else this brain of mine
Hunts not the trail of policy so sure
As it hath us'd to do—that I have found
The very cause of Hamlet's lunacy.

  King. O! speak of that; that do I long to hear.   50

  Polonius. Give first admittance to the ambassadors;
My news shall be the fruit to that great feast.

  King. Thyself do grace to them, and bring them in.
                                    [*Exit* POLONIUS.

He tells me, my dear Gertrude, he hath found
The head and source of all your son's distemper.   55

  Queen. I doubt it is no other but the main;
His father's death, and our o'erhasty marriage.

  King. Well, we shall sift him.

     Re-enter POLONIUS, *with* VOLTIMAND *and* CORNELIUS.

                          Welcome, my good friends!
Say, Voltimand, what from our brother Norway?

  38 **practices:** proceedings.   42 **still:** always.   52 **the fruit:**
the dessert.   56 **the main:** the main cause.

Voltimand. Most fair return of greetings and desires. 60
Upon our first, he sent out to suppress
His nephew's levies, which to him appear'd
To be a preparation 'gainst the Polack;
But, better look'd into, he truly found
It was against your highness: whereat griev'd, 65
That so his sickness, age, and impotence
Was falsely borne in hand, sends out arrests
On Fortinbras; which he, in brief, obeys,
Receives rebuke from Norway, and, in fine,
Makes vow before his uncle never more 70
To give the assay of arms against your majesty.
Whereon old Norway, overcome with joy,
Gives him three thousand crowns in annual fee,
And his commission to employ those soldiers,
So levied as before, against the Polack; 75
With an entreaty, herein further shown, [*Giving a paper.*
That it might please you to give quiet pass
Through your dominions for this enterprise,
On such regards of safety and allowance
As therein are set down.
　　King.　　　　　　It likes us well; 80
And at our more consider'd time we'll read,
Answer, and think upon this business:
Meantime we thank you for your well-took labour.
Go to your rest; at night we'll feast together:
Most welcome home. [*Exeunt* VOLTIMAND *and* CORNELIUS.
　　Polonius.　　　　This business is well ended. 85
My liege, and madam, to expostulate
What majesty should be, what duty is,
Why day is day, night night, and time is time,

61 **upon our first:** at our first representation.　　67 **borne in
hand:** deceived.　**arrests:** orders to desist.　　79 **regards . . .
allowance:** with such safeguards and on such conditions.　　86
expostulate: debate.

Were nothing but to waste night, day, and time.
Therefore, since brevity is the soul of wit,   90
And tediousness the limbs and outward flourishes,
I will be brief. Your noble son is mad:
Mad call I it; for, to define true madness,
What is 't but to be nothing else but mad?
But let that go.
    Queen.   More matter, with less art.   95
    Polonius. Madam, I swear I use no art at all.
That he is mad, 'tis true; 'tis true 'tis pity;
And pity 'tis 'tis true: a foolish figure;
But farewell it, for I will use no art.
Mad let us grant him, then; and now remains   100
That we find out the cause of this effect,
Or rather say, the cause of this defect,
For this effect defective comes by cause;
Thus it remains, and the remainder thus.
Perpend.   105
I have a daughter, have while she is mine;
Who, in her duty and obedience, mark,
Hath given me this: now, gather, and surmise.
To the celestial, and my soul's idol, the most beautified
      Ophelia.—
That's an ill phrase, a vile phrase; 'beautified' is a vile
phrase; but you shall hear. Thus: 111
In her excellent white bosom, these, &c.—
    Queen. Came this from Hamlet to her?
    Polonius. Good madam, stay awhile; I will be faithful.
              Doubt thou the stars are fire;   115
                Doubt that the sun doth move;
              Doubt truth to be a liar;
              But never doubt I love.

---

    90 **wit:** wisdom.   103 i.e. for there is some cause for this
madness.   105 **perpend:** consider well.   117 **doubt:** suspect
(in this line).

O dear Ophelia! I am ill at these numbers: I have not art
to reckon my groans; but that I love thee best, O most best!
believe it. Adieu.   121

> *Thine evermore, most dear lady, whilst this*
> *machine is to him,*
>
> *Hamlet.*

This in obedience hath my daughter shown me;   125
And more above, hath his solicitings,
As they fell out by time, by means, and place,
All given to mine ear.
  King.   But how hath she
Receiv'd his love?
  Polonius.   What do you think of me?
  King. As of a man faithful and honourable.   130
  Pol. I would fain prove so. But what might you think,
When I had seen this hot love on the wing,—
As I perceiv'd it (I must tell you that)
Before my daughter told me,—what might you,
Or my dear majesty, your queen here, think,   135
If I had play'd the desk or table-book,
Or given my heart a winking, mute and dumb,
Or look'd upon this love with idle sight;
What might you think? No, I went round to work,
And my young mistress thus I did bespeak: 140
'Lord Hamlet is a prince, out of thy star;
This must not be:' and then I prescripts gave her,
That she should lock herself from his resort,
Admit no messengers, receive no tokens.
Which done, she took the fruits of my advice;   145
And he, repulsèd,—a short tale to make,—
Fell into a sadness, then into a fast,

---

119 **numbers**: verse (Lat. *numeri*).   123 **machine**: body.
126 **more above**: moreover.   136–7 i.e. noted the matter
privately, and kept it secret, or connived at, or ignored it.   139
round: outspokenly, frankly.   142 **prescripts**: commands.

Thence to a watch, thence into a weakness,
Thence to a lightness; and by this declension
Into the madness wherein he raves,   150
And all we mourn for.

King.   Do you think 'tis this?

Queen. It may be, very like.

Pol. Hath there been such a time,—I'd fain know that,—
That I have positively said, ' 'Tis so,'
When it prov'd otherwise?

King.   Not that I know.   155

Polonius. Take this from this, if this be otherwise:
                    [*Pointing to his head and shoulder.*
If circumstances lead me, I will find
Where truth is hid, though it were hid indeed
Within the centre.

King.   How may we try it further?

Pol. You know sometimes he walks four hours together
Here in the lobby.

Queen.   So he does indeed.   161

Pol. At such a time I'll loose my daughter to him;
Be you and I behind an arras then;
Mark the encounter; if he love her not,
And be not from his reason fallen thereon,   165
Let me be no assistant for a state,
But keep a farm, and carters.

King.   We will try it.

Queen. But look, where sadly the poor wretch comes
          reading.

Polonius. Away! I do beseech you, both away.
I'll board him presently.

                    [*Exeunt* KING, QUEEN, *and* Attendants.

---

148 **watch:** sleeplessness.   149 **lightness:** light-headedness.
159 **the centre:** the bowels of the earth.   162 **loose . . . to**
him: i.e. throw them together deliberately.   163 **arras:** tapestry.
170 **board:** accost.   **presently:** at once.

Enter HAMLET, *reading.*

O! give me leave.   170
How does my good Lord Hamlet?
Hamlet. Well, God a-mercy.
Polonius. Do you know me, my lord?
Hamlet. Excellent well; you are a fishmonger.
Polonius. Not I, my lord.   175
Hamlet. Then I would you were so honest a man.
Polonius. Honest, my lord!
Hamlet. Ay, sir; to be honest, as this world goes, is to
be one man picked out of ten thousand.
Polonius. That's very true, my lord.   180
Hamlet. For if the sun breed maggots in a dead dog,
being a good kissing carrion,—Have you a daughter?
Polonius. I have, my lord.
Hamlet. Let her not walk i' the sun: conception is a bless-
ing; but as your daughter may conceive, friend, look to 't.
Polonius. [*Aside.*] How say you by that? Still harp-   186
ing on my daughter: yet he knew me not at first; he
said I was a fishmonger: he is far gone, far gone: and
truly in my youth I suffered much extremity for love;
very near this. I'll speak to him again. What do you   190
read, my lord?
Hamlet. Words, words, words.
Polonius. What is the matter, my lord?
Hamlet. Between who?
Polonius. I mean the matter that you read, my lord.   195
Hamlet. Slanders, sir: for the satirical rogue says
here that old men have grey beards, that their faces
are wrinkled, their eyes purging thick amber and
plum-tree gum, and that they have a plentiful lack of
wit, together with most weak hams: all which, sir,   200

182 **good kissing carrion:** dead flesh good enough to kiss [*N*].
198 **purging:** discharging. **amber:** resin.   200 **hams:**

though I most powerfully and potently believe, yet I
hold it not honesty to have it thus set down; for yourself, sir, shall grow old as I am, if, like a crab, you
could go backward.

Polonius. [*Aside.*]   Though this be madness, yet   205
there is method in 't. Will you walk out of the air, my
lord?

Hamlet. Into my grave?

Polonius. Indeed, that is out o' the air. [*Aside.*] How
pregnant sometimes his replies are! a happiness that   210
often madness hits on, which reason and sanity could
not so prosperously be delivered of. I will leave him,
and suddenly contrive the means of meeting between
him and my daughter. My honourable lord, I will
most humbly take my leave of you.   215

Hamlet. You cannot, sir, take from me any thing that
I will more willingly part withal; except my life, except
my life, except my life.

Polonius. Fare you well, my lord.   [*Going.*

Hamlet. These tedious old fools!   220

Enter ROSENCRANTZ *and* GUILDENSTERN.

Polonius. You go to seek the Lord Hamlet; there he is.

Rosencrantz. [*To* POLONIUS.] God save you, sir!

                                        [*Exit* POLONIUS.

Guildenstern. Mine honoured lord!

Rosencrantz. My most dear lord!   224

Hamlet. My excellent good friends! How dost thou,
Guildenstern? Ah, Rosencrantz! Good lads, how do ye
both?

Rosencrantz. As the indifferent children of the earth.

Guildenstern. Happy in that we are not over-happy;
On Fortune's cap we are not the very button.   230

---

210 **pregnant:** significant.

Hamlet. Nor the soles of her shoe?

Rosencrantz. Neither, my lord.

Hamlet. Then you live about her waist, or in the middle of her favours?

Guildenstern. Faith, her privates we. 235

Hamlet. In the secret parts of Fortune? O! most true; she is a strumpet. What news?

Ros. None, my lord, but that the world's grown honest.

Hamlet. Then is doomsday near; but your news is not true. Let me question more in particular: what have you, my good friends, deserved at the hands of Fortune, that she sends you to prison hither? 242

Guildenstern. Prison, my lord!

Hamlet. Denmark's a prison.

Rosencrantz. Then is the world one. 245

Hamlet. A goodly one; in which there are many confines, wards, and dungeons, Denmark being one o' the worst.

Rosencrantz. We think not so, my lord.

Hamlet. Why, then, 'tis none to you; for there is nothing either good or bad, but thinking makes it so: to me it is a prison. 251

Rosencrantz. Why, then your ambition makes it one; 'tis too narrow for your mind.

Hamlet. O God! I could be bounded in a nutshell, and count myself a king of infinite space, were it not that I have bad dreams. 256

Guildenstern. Which dreams, indeed, are ambition, for the very substance of the ambitious is merely the shadow of a dream.

Hamlet. A dream itself is but a shadow. 260

Rosencrantz. Truly, and I hold ambition of so airy and light a quality that it is but a shadow's shadow.

235 **privates:** intimates.　　246 **confines:** cells.　　258-9 i.e. even the successes of an ambitious man are but the shadows of his desire.

Hamlet. Then are our beggars bodies, and our monarchs
and outstretched heroes the beggars' shadows. Shall we to
the court? for, by my fay, I cannot reason.   265

Rosencrantz. ⎫
Guildenstern. ⎭ We'll wait upon you.

Hamlet. No such matter; I will not sort you with the
rest of my servants, for, to speak to you like an honest
man, I am most dreadfully attended. But, in the beaten
way of friendship, what make you at Elsinore?   270

Rosencrantz. To visit you, my lord; no other occasion.

Hamlet. Beggar that I am, I am even poor in thanks; but
I thank you: and sure, dear friends, my thanks are too
dear a halfpenny. Were you not sent for? Is it your own
inclining? Is it a free visitation? Come, come, deal justly
with me: come, come; nay, speak.   276

Guildenstern. What should we say, my lord?

Hamlet. Why anything, but to the purpose. You were
sent for; and there is a kind of confession in your looks
which your modesties have not craft enough to colour: I
know the good king and queen have sent for you.   281

Rosencrantz. To what end, my lord?

Hamlet. That you must teach me. But let me con-
jure you, by the rights of our fellowship, by the
consonancy of our youth, by the obligation of our   285
ever-preserved love, and by what more dear a better
proposer could charge you withal, be even and direct
with me, whether you were sent for or no!

Rosencrantz. [*Aside to* GUILDENSTERN.] What say you?

263–4 i.e. Kings, the type of ambition, must then be to their anti-
type, beggars, as shadows are to the bodies which cast them (**outstretched** = puffed up, aspiring) [*N*].   267 **sort:** class.   269–70
in the beaten way of friendship: i.e. as tried and trusted friends.
273–4 i.e. the thanks of such a beggar as I am are not worth a halfpenny.   285 **consonancy:** companionship (cf. l. 11).   286–7
what more . . . withal: i.e. by any more moving appeal that a more
eloquent speaker would make to you.

Hamlet. [*Aside.*] Nay, then, I have an eye of you. If you
love me, hold not off.   291

Guildenstern. My lord, we were sent for.

Hamlet. I will tell you why; so shall my anticipation
prevent your discovery, and your secrecy to the king
and queen moult no feather. I have of late,—but 295
wherefore I know not,—lost all my mirth, forgone
all custom of exercises; and indeed it goes so heavily
with my disposition that this goodly frame, the earth,
seems to me a sterile promontory; this most excellent canopy, the air, look you, this brave o'erhanging 300
firmament, this majestical roof fretted with golden
fire, why, it appears no other thing to me but a foul
and pestilent congregation of vapours. What a piece
of work is a man! How noble in reason! how infinite in
faculty! in form, in moving, how express and admir- 305
able! in action how like an angel! in apprehension how
like a god! the beauty of the world! the paragon of
animals! And yet, to me, what is this quintessence of
dust? man delights not me; no, nor woman neither,
though, by your smiling, you seem to say so.   310

Rosencrantz. My lord, there was no such stuff in my
thoughts.

Hamlet. Why did you laugh then, when I said, 'man
delights not me?'   314

Rosencrantz. To think, my lord, if you delight not in man,
what lenten entertainment the players shall receive from
you: we coted them on the way; and hither are they
coming, to offer you service.

Hamlet. He that plays the King shall be welcome;

---

290 **I have . . . you:** I see what you are at.   294 **prevent:**
forestall.   301 **fretted:** embossed, decorated.   305 **express:**
active, purposeful, *or* well-modelled (Lat. *exprimere*, to portray).
307 **paragon:** perfection, flower.   316 **lenten:** meagre.   317
coted: outstripped.

his majesty shall have tribute of me; the adventurous 320
Knight shall use his foil and target; the Lover shall
not sigh gratis; the Humorous Man shall end his part
in peace; the Clown shall make those laugh whose
lungs are tickle o' the sere; and the Lady shall say her
mind freely, or the blank verse shall halt for 't. What 325
players are they?

Rosencrantz. Even those you were wont to take delight
in, the tragedians of the city.

Hamlet. How chances it they travel? their residence,
both in reputation and profit, was better both ways.   330

Rosencrantz. I think their inhibition comes by the means
of the late innovation.

Hamlet. Do they hold the same estimation they did when
I was in the city? Are they so followed?

Rosencrantz. No, indeed they are not.   335

Hamlet. How comes it? Do they grow rusty?

Rosencrantz. Nay, their endeavour keeps in the
wonted pace: but there is, sir, an aery of children,
little eyases, that cry out on the top of question, and
are most tyrannically clapped for 't: these are now the 340
fashion, and so berattle the common stages,—so they
call them,—that many wearing rapiers are afraid of
goose-quills, and dare scarce come thither.

---

321 **foil**: blunted rapier for fencing. **target**: shield.   322
Humorous Man: actor of character parts (humours).   **324 tickle
o' the sere**: easily set off ('sere' is part of a gun).   329 **travel**: are
on tour. **residence**: i.e. in the capital.   331 **inhibition**:
either prohibition *or* loss of favour [N].   332 **innovation**: upheaval.   338 **aery**: nestful.   339 **little eyases**: young hawks.
that cry out on the top of question: i.e. whose shrill voices are
heard above all others in the controversy.   340 **tyrannically**: out-
rageously.   341 **berattle**: abuse.   342-3 **many wearing
rapiers . . . thither**: i.e. the gallants are afraid to visit the public
theatres because of the ridicule of those who write ('goose-quills')
for boy-actors.

Hamlet. What! are they children? who maintains
'em? how are they escoted? Will they pursue the 345
quality no longer than they can sing? will they not say
afterwards, if they should grow themselves to common players,—as it is most like, if their means are not
better,—their writers do them wrong, to make them
exclaim against their own succession?   350

Rosencrantz. Faith, there has been much to-do on both
sides: and the nation holds it no sin to tarre them to controversy: there was, for a while, no money bid for argument,
unless the Poet and the Player went to cuffs in the question.

Hamlet. Is it possible?   355

Guil. O! there has been much throwing about of brains.

Hamlet. Do the boys carry it away?

Rosencrantz. Ay, that they do, my lord; Hercules and
his load too.   359

Hamlet. It is not very strange; for my uncle is King of
Denmark, and those that would make mows at him while
my father lived, give twenty, forty, fifty, a hundred ducats
a-piece for his picture in little. 'Sblood, there is something
in this more than natural, if philosophy could find it out.
                    [*Flourish of trumpets within.*

Guildenstern. There are the players.   365

Hamlet. Gentlemen, you are welcome to Elsinore.
Your hands, come then; the appurtenance of welcome
is fashion and ceremony: let me comply with you in
this garb, lest my extent to the players—which, I tell

---

345 **escoted:** paid for.   346 **quality:** profession.   348 **means:**
resources.   350 **exclaim against their own succession:** decry
their own future employment.   352 **tarre:** incite.   353–4 i.e.
theatre managers would offer nothing for the plot of a play ('argument') unless it dealt with the controversy.   357 **carry it away:**
win the day.   361 **make mows:** grimace (Fr. *moue*).   367
appurtenance: that which belongs to (something).   368–9
let me comply with you in this garb: let me show you ceremony
in a formal handshake.   369 **extent:** condescension.

you, must show fairly outward—should more appear 370
like entertainment than yours. You are welcome; but
my uncle-father and aunt-mother are deceived.

Guildenstern. In what, my dear lord?

Hamlet. I am but mad north-north-west: when the wind
is southerly I know a hawk from a handsaw.   375

Enter POLONIUS.

Polonius. Well be with you, gentlemen!

Hamlet. Hark you, Guildenstern; and you too; at each
ear a hearer: that great baby you see there is not yet out
of his swaddling-clouts.   379

Rosencrantz. Happily he's the second time come to them;
for they say an old man is twice a child.

Hamlet. I will prophesy he comes to tell me of the
players; mark it. You say right, sir; o' Monday morning;
'twas so indeed.

Polonius. My lord, I have news to tell you.   385

Hamlet. My lord, I have news to tell you. When Roscius
was an actor in Rome,—

Polonius. The actors are come hither, my lord.

Hamlet. Buz, buz!

Polonius. Upon my honour,—   390

Hamlet. Then came each actor on his ass,—

Polonius. The best actors in the world, either for
tragedy, comedy, history, pastoral, pastoral-comical,
historical-pastoral, tragical-historical, tragical-comi-
cal-historical-pastoral, scene individable, or poem un- 395
limited: Seneca cannot be too heavy, nor Plautus too
light. For the law of writ and the liberty, these are
the only men.

Hamlet. O Jephthah, judge of Israel, what a treasure
hadst thou!   400

Polonius. What a treasure had he, my lord?

375 **handsaw:** heron [*N*].

Hamlet. Why

> *One fair daughter and no more,*
> *The which he lovéd passing well.*

Polonius. [*Aside.*] Still on my daughter. 405

Hamlet. Am I not i' the right, old Jephthah?

Polonius. If you call me Jephthah, my lord, I have a daughter that I love passing well.

Hamlet. Nay, that follows not.

Polonius. What follows, then, my lord? 410

Hamlet. Why,

> *As by lot, God wot.*

And then, you know,

> *It came to pass, as most like it was.—*

The first row of the pious chanson will show you more; for look where my abridgment comes. 416

Enter four or five Players.

You are welcome, masters; welcome, all. I am glad to see thee well: welcome, good friends. O, my old friend! Why, thy face is valanced since I saw thee last: comest thou to beard me in Denmark? What! my young 420 lady and mistress! By 'r lady, your ladyship is nearer heaven than when I saw you last, by the altitude of a chopine. Pray God, your voice, like a piece of uncurrent gold, be not cracked within the ring. Masters, you are all welcome. We'll e'en to 't like French 425 falconers, fly at anything we see: we'll have a speech straight. Come, give us a taste of your quality; come, a passionate speech.

First Player. What speech, my good lord?

Hamlet. I heard thee speak me a speech once, but it 430

---

415 **first row of the pious chanson:** first verse of the godly ballad. 416 **abridgment:** interruption (*also*, dramatic interlude). 419 **valanced:** fringed. 423 **chopine:** high-heeled shoe. 423–4 **uncurrent gold:** bad gold coin.

was never acted; or, if it was, not above once; for
the play, I remember, pleased not the million; 'twas
caviare to the general: but it was—as I received it,
and others, whose judgments in such matters cried in
the top of mine—an excellent play, well digested in   435
the scenes, set down with as much modesty as cunning. I remember one said there were no sallets in the
lines to make the matter savoury, nor no matter in the
phrase that might indict the author of affectation; but
called it an honest method, as wholesome as sweet,   440
and by very much more handsome than fine. One
speech in it I chiefly loved; 'twas Æneas' tale to Dido;
and thereabout of it especially, where he speaks of
Priam's slaughter. If it live in your memory, begin at
this line: let me see, let me see:—   445
The rugged Pyrrhus, like the Hyrcanian beast,—
'tis not so, it begins with Pyrrhus:—
The rugged Pyrrhus, he, whose sable arm,
Black as his purpose, did the night resemble
When he lay couchéd in the ominous horse,   450
Hath now this dread and black complexion smear'd
With heraldry more dismal; head to foot
Now is he total gules; horridly trick'd
With blood of fathers, mothers, daughters, sons,
Bak'd and impasted with the parching streets,   455
That lend a tyrannous and damnéd light
To their vile murders: roasted in wrath and fire,

---

433 caviare to the general: too great a delicacy for the multitude
(caviare = the roe of the sturgeon).   **434–5 cried in the top of:**
surpassed.   **436 modesty:** restraint.   **437 sallets:** spicy
flavours (*lit.* salads).   **440 honest:** clean.   **441 more
handsome than fine:** more splendid than delicate.   **446 the
Hyrcanian beast:** the tiger.   **451 complexion:** whole appearance.   **453 total gules:** red with blood from head to foot.
trick'd: blazoned (heraldic terms).   **455 impasted:** formed
into a paste.

And thus o'er-sizéd with coagulate gore,
With eyes like carbuncles, the hellish Pyrrhus
Old grandsire Priam seeks.   460
So proceed you.

   Polonius. 'Fore God, my lord, well spoken; with good
accent and good discretion.

   First Player.   *Anon, he finds him*
Striking too short at Greeks; his antique sword,
Rebellious to his arm, lies where it falls,   465
Repugnant to command. Unequal match'd,
Pyrrhus at Priam drives; in rage strikes wide;
But with the whiff and wind of his fell sword
The unnerved father falls. Then senseless Ilium,
Seeming to feel this blow, with flaming top   470
Stoops to his base, and with a hideous crash
Takes prisoner Pyrrhus' ear: for lo! his sword,
Which was declining on the milky head
Of reverend Priam, seem'd i' the air to stick:
So, as a painted tyrant, Pyrrhus stood,   475
And like a neutral to his will and matter,
Did nothing.
But, as we often see, against some storm,
A silence in the heavens, the rack stand still,
The bold winds speechless and the orb below   480
As hush as death, anon the dreadful thunder
Doth rend the region; so, after Pyrrhus' pause,
Aroused vengeance sets him new a-work;
And never did the Cyclops' hammers fall
On Mars's armour, forg'd for proof eterne,   485
With less remorse than Pyrrhus' bleeding sword
Now falls on Priam.

   458 **o'er-sizéd**: painted over. **coagulate**: clotted.   469
Ilium: Troy.   476 **like a neutral to**: as if indifferent to.
matter: purpose.   478 **against**: before.   479 **rack**: cloud
formations.   482 **region**: the space of air.   483 **him**:
himself.   485 **proof eterne**: everlasting durability.

Out, out, thou strumpet, Fortune! All you gods,
In general synod, take away her power;
Break all the spokes and fellies from her wheel,   490
And bowl the round nave down the hill of heaven,
As low as to the fiends!

  Polonius. This is too long.

  Hamlet. It shall to the barber's, with your beard. Prithee,
say on: he's for a jig or a tale of bawdry, or he sleeps. Say
on; come to Hecuba.   496

  First Player.   But who, O! who had seen the mobled queen—

  Hamlet. 'The mobled queen?'—

  Polonius. That's good; 'mobled queen' is good.

  First Player.   Run barefoot up and down, threat'ning the
        flames   500
With bisson rheum; a clout upon that head
Where late the diadem stood; and, for a robe,
About her lank and all o'er-teeméd loins,
A blanket, in the alarm of fear caught up;
Who this had seen, with tongue in venom steep'd,   505
'Gainst Fortune's state would treason have pronounc'd:
But if the gods themselves did see her then,
When she saw Pyrrhus make malicious sport
In mincing with his sword her husband's limbs,
The instant burst of clamour that she made—   510
Unless things mortal move them not at all—
Would have made milch the burning eyes of heaven,
And passion in the gods.

  Polonius. Look! wh'er he has not turned his colour and
has tears in 's eyes. Prithee, no more.   515

  Hamlet. 'Tis well; I'll have thee speak out the rest
soon. Good my lord, will you see the players well

---

489 **synod:** council.   490 **fellies:** sections of the rim.   491
nave: hub.   497 **mobled:** muffled.   501 **bisson rheum:**
blinding tears.   503 **o'er-teeméd:** worn out by child-bearing.
512 **milch:** moist (*lit.* giving milk).

bestowed? Do you hear, let them be well used; for
they are the abstracts and brief chronicles of the time:
after your death you were better have a bad epitaph 520
than their ill report while you live.

Pol. My lord, I will use them according to their desert.

Hamlet. God's bodikins, man, much better; use every
man after his desert, and who shall 'scape whipping? Use
them after your own honour and dignity: the less they
deserve, the more merit is in your bounty. Take them in.

Polonius. Come, sirs.   527

Hamlet. Follow him, friends: we'll hear a play to-morrow.
[*Exit* POLONIUS, *with all the* Players *but the* First.] Dost
thou hear me, old friend; can you play The Murder of
Gonzago?   531

First Player. Ay, my lord.

Hamlet. We'll ha 't to-morrow night. You could, for a
need, study a speech of some dozen or sixteen lines, which
I would set down and insert in 't, could you not?   535

First Player. Ay, my lord.

Hamlet. Very well. Follow that lord; and look you mock
him not. [*Exit* First Player.] [*To* ROSENCRANTZ *and*
GUILDENSTERN.] My good friends, I'll leave you till night;
you are welcome to Elsinore.   540

Rosencrantz. Good my lord!

[*Exeunt* ROSENCRANTZ *and* GUILDENSTERN.

Hamlet. Ay, so, God be wi' ye! Now I am alone.
O! what a rogue and peasant slave am I:
Is it not monstrous that this player here,
But in a fiction, in a dream of passion,   545
Could force his soul so to his own conceit
That from her working all his visage wann'd,

---

518 **bestowed**: provided for.   519 **abstracts and brief
chronicles**: epitomes and histories in little.   534 **study**: get by
heart.   545 **but**: only.   546 **to his own conceit**: to the level
of his imagination.

Tears in his eyes, distraction in 's aspect,
A broken voice, and his whole function suiting
With forms to his conceit? and all for nothing!   550
For Hecuba!
What's Hecuba to him or he to Hecuba
That he should weep for her? What would he do
Had he the motive and the cue for passion
That I have? He would drown the stage with tears,   555
And cleave the general ear with horrid speech,
Make mad the guilty and appal the free,
Confound the ignorant, and amaze indeed
The very faculties of eyes and ears.
Yet I,   560
A dull and muddy-mettled rascal, peak,
Like John-a-dreams, unpregnant of my cause,
And can say nothing; no, not for a king,
Upon whose property and most dear life
A damn'd defeat was made. Am I a coward?   565
Who calls me villain? breaks my pate across?
Plucks off my beard and blows it in my face?
Tweaks me by the nose? gives me the lie i' the throat,
As deep as to the lungs? Who does me this?
Ha!   570
Swounds, I should take it, for it cannot be
But I am pigeon-liver'd, and lack gall
To make oppression bitter, or ere this
I should have fatted all the region kites
With this slave's offal. Bloody, bawdy villain!   575
Remorseless, treacherous, lecherous, kindless villain!
O! vengeance!

549 **function**: bearing, action.   557 **free**: innocent.   560–2
i.e. I am so listless and confused that I waste myself in idle dream-
ing (**peak**: pine).   562 **unpregnant of my cause**: inactive
in my duty.   564 **property**: *either* possessions (i.e. crown and
queen) *or* his very self.   572 **but**: but that.   574 **the region
kites**: the kites of the air.   576 **kindless**: unnatural.

Why, what an ass am I! This is most brave
That I, the son of a dear father murder'd,
Prompted to my revenge by heaven and hell,   580
Must, like a whore, unpack my heart with words,
And fall a-cursing, like a very drab,
A scullion! Fie upon't! foh!
About, my brain; hum, I have heard,
That guilty creatures sitting at a play   585
Have by the very cunning of the scene
Been struck so to the soul that presently
They have proclaim'd their malefactions;
For murder, though it have no tongue, will speak
With most miraculous organ. I'll have these players 590
Play something like the murder of my father
Before mine uncle; I'll observe his looks;
I'll tent him to the quick: if he but blench
I know my course. The spirit that I have seen
May be the devil: and the devil hath power   595
To assume a pleasing shape; yea, and perhaps
Out of my weakness and my melancholy—
As he is very potent with such spirits—
Abuses me to damn me. I'll have grounds
More relative than this: the play's the thing   600
Wherein I'll catch the conscience of the king.   [*Exit.*

584 **about:** to work!   587 **presently:** immediately.   593
tent: probe.   **blench:** flinch.   597 **weakness:** weak-mindedness.
599 **abuses:** misleads, deceives.   600 **relative:** relevant, to the
purpose.

ACT III

Scene I. A Room in the Castle

Enter KING, QUEEN, POLONIUS, OPHELIA, ROSENCRANTZ,
and GUILDENSTERN.

King. And can you, by no drift of conference,
Get from him why he puts on this confusion,
Grating so harshly all his days of quiet
With turbulent and dangerous lunacy?

Rosencrantz. He does confess he feels himself distracted;
But from what cause he will by no means speak.   6

Guildenstern. Nor do we find him forward to be sounded,
But, with a crafty madness, keeps aloof,
When we would bring him on to some confession
Of his true state.

Queen.   Did he receive you well?   10

Rosencrantz. Most like a gentleman.

Guildenstern. But with much forcing of his disposition.

Rosencrantz. Niggard of question, but of our demands
Most free in his reply.

Queen.   Did you assay him
To any pastime?   15

Rosencrantz. Madam, it so fell out that certain players
We o'er-raught on the way; of these we told him,
And there did seem in him a kind of joy
To hear of it: they are here about the court,
And, as I think, they have already order   20
This night to play before him.

Polonius.   'Tis most true;
And he beseech'd me to entreat your majesties

---

1 **drift of conference:** i.e. leading Hamlet on in conversation.
12 **forcing of his disposition:** behaving unnaturally and con-
strainedly.   14 **assay:** challenge, invite.   17 **o'er-raught:**
overtook.

To hear and see the matter.

  King. With all my heart; and it doth much content me
To hear him so inclin'd.   25
Good gentlemen, give him a further edge,
And drive his purpose on to these delights.

  Rosencrantz. We shall, my lord.

               [*Exeunt* ROSENCRANTZ *and* GUILDENSTERN.

  King.   Sweet Gertrude, leave us too;
For we have closely sent for Hamlet hither,
That he, as 'twere by accident, may here   30
Affront Ophelia.
Her father and myself, lawful espials,
Will so bestow ourselves, that, seeing, unseen,
We may of their encounter frankly judge,
And gather by him, as he is behav'd,   35
If 't be the affliction of his love or no
That thus he suffers for.

  Queen.   I shall obey you.
And for your part, Ophelia, I do wish
That your good beauties be the happy cause
Of Hamlet's wildness; so shall I hope your virtues   40
Will bring him to his wonted way again,
To both your honours.

  Ophelia.   Madam, I wish it may.

                   [*Exit* QUEEN.

  Pol. Ophelia, walk you here. Gracious, so please you,
We will bestow ourselves. [*To* OPHELIA.] Read on this
    book;
That show of such an exercise may colour   45
Your loneliness. We are oft to blame in this,
'Tis too much prov'd, that with devotion's visage
And pious action we do sugar o'er

---

  26 give him a further edge: whet him.   **29 closely:** secretly.
31 affront: encounter.   **32 espials:** spies.   **45 exercise:**
i.e. religious exercise. **colour:** give an excuse for.

The devil himself.

   King. [*Aside.*]   O! 'tis too true;

How smart a lash that speech doth give my conscience! 50

The harlot's cheek, beautied with plastering art,

Is not more ugly to the thing that helps it

Than is my deed to my most painted word:

O heavy burden!

   Polonius. I hear him coming; let's withdraw, my lord.

               [*Exeunt* KING *and* POLONIUS.

Enter HAMLET.

   Hamlet. To be, or not to be: that is the question: 56

Whether 'tis nobler in the mind to suffer

The slings and arrows of outrageous fortune,

Or to take arms against a sea of troubles,

And by opposing end them? To die: to sleep; 60

No more; and, by a sleep to say we end

The heart-ache and the thousand natural shocks

That flesh is heir to, 'tis a consummation

Devoutly to be wish'd. To die, to sleep;

To sleep: perchance to dream: ay, there's the rub; 65

For in that sleep of death what dreams may come

When we have shuffled off this mortal coil,

Must give us pause. There's the respect

That makes calamity of so long life;

For who would bear the whips and scorns of time, 70

The oppressor's wrong, the proud man's contumely,

The pangs of dispriz'd love, the law's delay,

---

   52 to: compared to.   **53 painted:** fair-seeming.   **56 to be, or not to be:** i.e. shall I endure my sorrows or shall I take my own life?   **58 slings:** field-guns *or* culverins.   **61 to say:** suppose.   **63 consummation:** fulfilment, crowning conclusion.   **67 this mortal coil:** the turmoil of our mortal life.   **68 respect:** consideration.   **69 of so long life:** so enduring and long-lived.   **71 contumely:** contempt.   **72 dispriz'd:** held of little account.

The insolence of office, and the spurns
That patient merit of the unworthy takes,
When he himself might his quietus make   75
With a bare bodkin? who would fardels bear,
To grunt and sweat under a weary life,
But that the dread of something after death,
The undiscover'd country from whose bourn
No traveller returns, puzzles the will,   80
And makes us rather bear those ills we have
Than fly to others that we know not of?
Thus conscience does make cowards of us all;
And thus the native hue of resolution
Is sicklied o'er with the pale cast of thought,   85
And enterprises of great pitch and moment
With this regard their currents turn awry,
And lose the name of action. Soft you now!
The fair Ophelia! Nymph, in thy orisons
Be all my sins remember'd.

   Ophelia.   Good my lord,   90
How does your honour for this many a day?

   Hamlet. I humbly thank you; well, well, well.

   Ophelia. My lord, I have remembrances of yours,
That I have longéd long to re-deliver;
I pray you, now receive them.

   Hamlet.   No, not I;   95
I never gave you aught.

   Ophelia. My honour'd lord, you know right well you did;
And, with them, words of so sweet breath compos'd
As made the things more rich: their perfume lost,
Take these again; for to the noble mind   100

75 **quietus:** discharge, settlement of an account.   **76 bare
bodkin:** mere dagger. **fardels:** burdens (Fr. *fardeau*).   **79
bourn:** boundary.   **83 conscience:** reflection, consciousness.
85 cast: tinge, hue.   **86 pitch and moment:** height and importance.   **87 with this regard:** on account of this.   **89 orisons:**
prayers (Old Fr. *oraison*).   **93 remembrances:** love-tokens.

Rich gifts wax poor when givers prove unkind.
There, my lord.

Hamlet. Ha, ha! are you honest?

Ophelia. My lord!

Hamlet. Are you fair? 105

Ophelia. What means your lordship?

Hamlet. That if you be honest and fair, your honesty should admit no discourse to your beauty.

Ophelia. Could beauty, my lord, have better commerce than with honesty? 110

Hamlet. Ay, truly; for the power of beauty will sooner transform honesty from what it is to a bawd than the force of honesty can translate beauty into his likeness: this was sometime a paradox, but now the time gives it proof. I did love you once. 115

Ophelia. Indeed, my lord, you made me believe so.

Hamlet. You should not have believed me; for virtue cannot so inoculate our old stock but we shall relish of it: I loved you not.

Ophelia. I was the more deceived. 120

Hamlet. Get thee to a nunnery: why wouldst thou be a breeder of sinners? I am myself indifferent honest; but yet I could accuse me of such things that it were better my mother had not borne me. I am very proud, revengeful, ambitious; with more offences 125 at my beck than I have thoughts to put them in, imagination to give them shape, or time to act them in. What should such fellows as I do crawling between heaven and earth? We are arrant knaves, all; believe none of us. Go thy ways to a nunnery. Where's your 130 father?

---

103 **honest:** chaste.　　108 **no discourse to:** no intercourse with.　　113 **translate:** transform.　　118 **inoculate:** engraft.　**relish of it:** i.e. have a touch or taste of the old evil stock.　　122 **indifferent:** more or less.

Ophelia. At home, my lord.

Hamlet. Let the doors be shut upon him, that he may play the fool nowhere but in 's own house. Farewell.

Ophelia. O! help him, you sweet heavens! 135

Hamlet. If thou dost marry, I'll give thee this plague for thy dowry: be thou as chaste as ice, as pure as snow, thou shalt not escape calumny. Get thee to a nunnery, go; farewell. Or, if thou wilt needs marry, marry a fool; for wise men know well enough what 140 monsters you make of them. To a nunnery, go; and quickly too. Farewell.

Ophelia. O heavenly powers, restore him!

Hamlet. I have heard of your paintings too, well enough; God hath given you one face, and you make 145 yourselves another: you jig, you amble, and you lisp, and nickname God's creatures, and make your wantonness your ignorance. Go to, I'll no more on 't; it hath made me mad. I say, we will have no more marriages; those that are married already, all but one, 150 shall live; the rest shall keep as they are. To a nunnery, go. [*Exit.*

Ophelia. O! what a noble mind is here o'erthrown:
The courtier's, soldier's, scholar's, eye, tongue, sword;
The expectancy and rose of the fair state, 155
The glass of fashion and the mould of form,
The observ'd of all observers, quite, quite down!
And I, of ladies most deject and wretched,
That suck'd the honey of his music vows,
Now see that noble and most sovereign reason, 160
Like sweet bells jangled, out of tune and harsh;
That unmatch'd form and feature of blown youth
Blasted with ecstasy: O! woe is me,

147–8 make your wantonness your ignorance: plead ignorance in excuse of your follies. 155 expectancy: one of whom much is expected. 162 blown: in its prime. 163 ecstasy: madness.

To have seen what I have seen, see what I see!

Re-enter KING *and* POLONIUS.

  King. Love! his affections do not that way tend;   165
Nor what he spake, though it lack'd form a little,
Was not like madness. There's something in his soul
O'er which his melancholy sits on brood;
And, I do doubt, the hatch and the disclose
Will be some danger; which for to prevent,   170
I have in quick determination
Thus set it down: he shall with speed to England,
For the demand of our neglected tribute:
Haply the seas and countries different
With variable objects shall expel   175
This something-settled matter in his heart,
Whereon his brains still beating puts him thus
From fashion of himself. What think you on't?
  Polonius. It shall do well: but yet do I believe
The origin and commencement of his grief   180
Sprung from neglected love. How now, Ophelia!
You need not tell us what Lord Hamlet said;
We heard it all. My lord, do as you please;
But, if you hold it fit, after the play,
Let his queen mother all alone entreat him   185
To show his griefs: let her be round with him;
And I'll be plac'd, so please you, in the ear
Of all their conference. If she find him not,
To England send him, or confine him where
Your wisdom best shall think.
  King.   It shall be so: 190
Madness in great ones must not unwatch'd go.   [*Exeunt.*

---

   165 **affections:** emotions, state of mind.   169 **doubt:** suspect.
175 **variable objects:** change of environment.   176 **something-
settled:** partly established.   186 **griefs:** grievances.
round: stern.

Scene II. A HALL IN THE CASTLE

Enter HAMLET *and certain* Players.

Hamlet. Speak the speech, I pray you, as I pronounced it to you, trippingly on the tongue; but if you
mouth it, as many of your players do, I had as lief the
town-crier spoke my lines. Nor do not saw the air too
much with your hand, thus; but use all gently: for 5
in the very torrent, tempest, and—as I may say—
whirlwind of passion, you must acquire and beget
a temperance, that may give it smoothness. O! it
offends me to the soul to hear a robustious periwig-
pated fellow tear a passion to tatters, to very rags, to 10
split the ears of the groundlings, who for the most part
are capable of nothing but inexplicable dumb-shows
and noise: I would have such a fellow whipped for
o'er-doing Termagant; it out-herods Herod: pray you,
avoid it. 15

First Player. I warrant your honour.

Hamlet. Be not too tame neither, but let your own
discretion be your tutor: suit the action to the word,
the word to the action; with this special observance,
that you o'erstep not the modesty of nature; for any- 20
thing so overdone is from the purpose of playing, whose
end, both at the first and now, was and is, to hold, as
'twere, the mirror up to nature; to show virtue her
own feature, scorn her own image, and the very age and
body of the time his form and pressure. Now, this 25

---

8 **temperance**: control.   9 **robustious**: blustering.
periwig-pated: bewigged (Fr. *perruque*).   11 **groundlings**:
spectators who stood on the ground, i.e. 'the pit'.   12 **capable
of nothing but**: only able to appreciate.   **inexplicable**: unin-
telligible.   14 **out-herods**: i.e. outdoes Herod in rant [*N*].
20 **modesty**: moderation.   21 **from**: away from, contrary to.
24–5 **the very . . . pressure**: i.e. to express the spirit of the age
and of contemporary manners (**pressure** = impression).

overdone, or come tardy off, though it make the unskil-
ful laugh, cannot but make the judicious grieve; the
censure of which one must in your allowance o'erweigh
a whole theatre of others. O! there be players that
I have seen play, and heard others praise, and that 30
highly, not to speak it profanely, that, neither having
the accent of Christians nor the gait of Christian,
pagan, nor man, have so strutted and bellowed that I
have thought some of nature's journeymen had made
men and not made them well, they imitated humanity 35
so abominably.

First Player. I hope we have reformed that indifferently
with us.

Hamlet. O! reform it altogether. And let those that
play your clowns speak no more than is set down for 40
them; for there be of them that will themselves laugh,
to set on some quantity of barren spectators to laugh
too, though in the mean time some necessary question
of the play be then to be considered; that's villanous,
and shows a most pitiful ambition in the fool that uses 45
it. Go, make you ready.   [*Exeunt* Players.

Enter POLONIUS, ROSENCRANTZ, *and* GUILDENSTERN.

How now, my lord! will the king hear this piece of work?
Polonius. And the queen too, and that presently.
Hamlet. Bid the players make haste.   [*Exit* POLONIUS.
Will you two help to hasten them?   50
Rosencrantz. ⎫
Guildenstern. ⎬ We will, my lord.

                    [*Exeunt* ROSENCRANTZ *and* GUILDENSTERN.
Hamlet. What, ho! Horatio!

26 **come tardy off:** inadequately presented.   27–8 **the
censure of which one:** the judgement of a single judicious spectator.
28 **allowance:** estimate.   34 **journeymen:** hired workmen.
37 **indifferently:** more or less.   48 **presently:** immediately.

Enter HORATIO.

Horatio. Here, sweet lord, at your service.

Hamlet. Horatio, thou art e'en as just a man

As e'er my conversation cop'd withal.   55

Horatio. O! my dear lord,—

Hamlet.   Nay, do not think I flatter;

For what advancement may I hope from thee,

That no revenue hast but thy good spirits

To feed and clothe thee? Why should the poor be flat-
    ter'd?

No; let the candied tongue lick absurd pomp,   60

And crook the pregnant hinges of the knee

Where thrift may follow fawning. Dost thou hear?

Since my dear soul was mistress of her choice

And could of men distinguish, her election

Hath seal'd thee for herself; for thou hast been   65

As one, in suffering all, that suffers nothing,

A man that fortune's buffets and rewards

Hast ta'en with equal thanks; and bless'd are those

Whose blood and judgment are so well co-mingled

That they are not a pipe for fortune's finger   70

To sound what stop she please. Give me that man

That is not passion's slave, and I will wear him

In my heart's core, ay, in my heart of heart,

As I do thee. Something too much of this.

There is a play to-night before the king;   75

One scene of it comes near the circumstance

Which I have told thee of my father's death;

I prithee, when thou seest that act afoot,

Even with the very comment of thy soul

Observe mine uncle; if his occulted guilt   80

55 **conversation:** acquaintance, intercourse.   **cop'd:** met.
60 **candied:** fed with sweetmeats, pampered.   **61 pregnant:**
prompt.   62 **thrift:** profit.   69 **blood:** passion.   79 **com-**
ment: observation (mental).   80 **occulted:** hidden.

Do not itself unkennel in one speech,
It is a damnéd ghost that we have seen,
And my imaginations are as foul
As Vulcan's stithy. Give him heedful note;
For I mine eyes will rivet to his face, 85
And after we will both our judgments join
In censure of his seeming.

    Horatio.   Well, my lord:
If he steal aught the whilst this play is playing,
And 'scape detecting, I will pay the theft.

    Hamlet. They are coming to the play; I must be idle:
Get you a place. 91

Danish march. A Flourish. Enter KING, QUEEN, POLONIUS,
    OPHELIA, ROSENCRANTZ, GUILDENSTERN, *and Others.*

    King. How fares our cousin Hamlet?

    Hamlet. Excellent, i' faith; of the chameleon's dish: I eat
the air, promise-crammed; you cannot feed capons so.

    King. I have nothing with this answer, Hamlet; these
words are not mine. 96

    Hamlet. No, nor mine now. [*To* POLONIUS.] My lord,
you played once i' the university, you say?

    Polonius. That did I, my lord, and was accounted a good
actor. 100

    Hamlet. And what did you enact?

    Polonius. I did enact Julius Cæsar: I was killed i' the
Capitol; Brutus killed me.

    Hamlet. It was a brute part of him to kill so capital a calf
there. Be the players ready? 105

    Rosencrantz. Ay, my lord; they stay upon your patience.

    Queen. Come hither, my good Hamlet, sit by me.

---

82 **a damnéd ghost:** a devil.   84 **stithy:** forge (**stith:** anvil).
87 **censure:** judging.   90 **be idle:** play the fool, i.e. assume
my antic disposition.   94 **capons:** young cocks fattened for
killing [*N*].   95 **have nothing with:** can make nothing of.

Hamlet. No, good mother, here's metal more attractive.
Polonius. [*To the* KING.] O ho! do you mark that?
Hamlet. Lady, shall I lie in your lap?   110
                              [*Lying down at* OPHELIA'S *feet.*
Ophelia. No, my lord.
Hamlet. I mean, my head upon your lap?
Ophelia. Ay, my lord.
Hamlet. Do you think I meant country matters?
Ophelia. I think nothing, my lord.   115
Hamlet. That's a fair thought to lie between maids' legs.
Ophelia. What is, my lord?
Hamlet. Nothing.
Ophelia. You are merry, my lord.
Hamlet. Who, I?   120
Ophelia. Ay, my lord.
Hamlet. O God, your only jig-maker. What should a
man do but be merry? for, look you, how cheerfully my
mother looks, and my father died within's two hours.
Ophelia. Nay, 'tis twice two months, my lord.   125
Hamlet. So long? Nay, then, let the devil wear black,
for I'll have a suit of sables. O heavens! die two months
ago, and not forgotten yet? Then there's hope a
great man's memory may outlive his life half a year;
but, by'r lady, he must build churches then, or else   130
shall he suffer not thinking on, with the hobby-horse,
whose epitaph is, 'For, O! for, O! the hobby-horse
is forgot.'

Hautboys play. The dumb-show enters.

Enter a King *and a* Queen, *very lovingly; the* Queen *embracing him, and he her. She kneels, and makes show of protestation unto him. He takes her up, and declines his*

122 **jig-maker:** comedian, i.e. I am a born jester (ironic).   131
not thinking on: being forgotten.   **hautboys:** oboes
(Fr. *hautbois*).

head upon her neck; lays him down upon a bank of
flowers: she, seeing him asleep, leaves him. Anon comes
in a fellow, takes off his crown, kisses it, and pours poison
in the King's *ears, and exit. The* Queen *returns, finds the*
King *dead, and makes passionate action. The* Poisoner,
with some two or three Mutes, *comes in again, seeming to*
lament with her. The dead body is carried away. The
Poisoner *wooes the* Queen *with gifts; she seems loath and*
unwilling awhile, but in the end accepts his love. [*Exeunt.*

Ophelia. What means this, my lord?

Hamlet. Marry, this is miching mallecho; it means mis-
chief.   136

Oph. Belike this show imports the argument of the play.

Enter Prologue.

Hamlet. We shall know by this fellow: the players cannot keep counsel; they'll tell all.

Ophelia. Will he tell us what this show meant?   140

Hamlet. Ay, or any show that you'll show him; be not
you ashamed to show, he'll not shame to tell you what it
means.

Ophelia. You are naught, you are naught. I'll mark the
play.   145

Prologue.   *For us and for our tragedy,*
                Here stooping to your clemency,
                We beg your hearing patiently.

Hamlet. Is this a prologue, or the posy of a ring?

Ophelia. 'Tis brief, my lord.   150

Hamlet. As woman's love.

Enter two Players, King *and* Queen.

P. King. Full thirty times hath Phœbus' cart gone round

---

135 **miching mallecho:** sneaking wickedness (Span. *malhecho*).
137 **argument:** plot.   144 **naught:** naughty, licentious.
149 **posy:** motto (and therefore brief).

Neptune's salt wash and Tellus' orbéd ground,
And thirty dozen moons with borrow'd sheen
About the world have times twelve thirties been,   155
Since love our hearts and Hymen did our hands
Unite commutual in most sacred bands.

  P. Queen. So many journeys may the sun and moon
Make us again count o'er ere love be done!
But, woe is me! you are so sick of late,   160
So far from cheer and from your former state,
That I distrust you. Yet, though I distrust,
Discomfort you, my lord, it nothing must;
For women's fear and love holds quantity,
In neither aught, or in extremity.   165
Now, what my love is, proof hath made you know;
And as my love is siz'd, my fear is so.
Where love is great, the littlest doubts are fear;
Where little fears grow great, great love grows there.

  P. King. Faith, I must leave thee, love, and shortly too;   170
My operant powers their functions leave to do:
And thou shalt live in this fair world behind,
Honour'd, belov'd; and haply one as kind
For husband shalt thou—

  P. Queen.   *O! confound the rest;*
Such love must needs be treason in my breast: 175
In second husband let me be accurst;
None wed the second but who kill'd the first.

  Hamlet. [Aside.] Wormwood, wormwood.

  P. Queen. The instances that second marriage move,
Are base respects of thrift, but none of love;   180
A second time I kill my husband dead,

---

162 **distrust you:** am anxious about you.   164 **holds quantity:** are in equal proportion.   165 i.e. either absent or excessive.
171 **operant:** active. **leave:** cease.   178 **wormwood:** bitterness.   179 **instances:** motives.   180 **respects of thrift:** considerations of gain.

When second husband kisses me in bed.
  P. King. I do believe you think what now you speak;
But what we do determine oft we break.
Purpose is but the slave to memory,   185
Of violent birth, but poor validity;
Which now, like fruit unripe, sticks on the tree,
But fall unshaken when they mellow be.
Most necessary 'tis that we forget
To pay ourselves what to ourselves is debt;   190
What to ourselves in passion we propose,
The passion ending, doth the purpose lose.
The violence of either grief or joy
Their own enactures with themselves destroy;
Where joy most revels grief doth most lament,   195
Grief joys, joy grieves, on slender accident.
This world is not for aye, nor 'tis not strange,
That even our love should with our fortunes change;
For 'tis a question left us yet to prove
Whe'r love lead fortune or else fortune love.   200
The great man down, you mark his favourite flies;
The poor advanc'd makes friends of enemies.
And hitherto doth love on fortune tend,
For who not needs shall never lack a friend;
And who in want a hollow friend doth try   205
Directly seasons him his enemy.
But, orderly to end where I begun,
Our wills and fates do so contrary run
That our devices still are overthrown,
Our thoughts are ours, their ends none of our own: 210
So think thou wilt no second husband wed;
But die thy thoughts when thy first lord is dead.

189–90 i.e. inevitably we forget what is due to ourselves (our previous resolves).   194 **enactures:** accomplishment.   **196 on
slender accident:** with little cause.   **206 seasons him:** prepares for himself.

P. Queen. Nor earth to me give food, nor heaven light!
Sport and repose lock from me day and night!
To desperation turn my trust and hope!   215
An anchor's cheer in prison be my scope!
Each opposite that blanks the face of joy
Meet what I would have well, and it destroy!
Both here and hence pursue me lasting strife,
If, once a widow, ever I be wife!   220

  Hamlet. If she should break it now!

  P. King. 'Tis deeply sworn. Sweet, leave me here awhile;
My spirits grow dull, and fain I would beguile
The tedious day with sleep.   [*Sleeps.*

  P. Queen.   Sleep rock thy brain;
And never come mischance between us twain!   [*Exit.*

  Hamlet. Madam, how like you this play?   226

  Queen. The lady doth protest too much, methinks.

  Hamlet. O! but she'll keep her word.

  King. Have you heard the argument? Is there no offence
in 't?   230

  Hamlet. No, no, they do but jest, poison in jest; no
offence i' the world.

  King. What do you call the play?

  Hamlet. The Mouse-trap. Marry, how? Tropically.
This play is the image of a murder done in Vienna: 235
Gonzago is the duke's name; his wife, Baptista. You
shall see anon; 'tis a knavish piece of work: but what
of that? your majesty and we that have free souls, it
touches us not: let the galled jade wince, our withers
are unwrung.   240

---

214 i.e. may I have no pleasure by day nor rest by night.   216
anchor's cheer: an anchorite's or hermit's existence.   217
blanks: blanches.   234 **tropically:** figuratively (**trope:** a turn
of speech. Gr. τρόπος).   238 **free:** innocent.   239 **galled
jade:** a sore and sorry nag.   **withers:** the ridge between the shoulder-
bones of a horse.

Enter Player *as* Lucianus.

This is one Lucianus, nephew to the king.

Ophelia. You are a good chorus, my lord.

Hamlet. I could interpret between you and your love, if I could see the puppets dallying.

Ophelia. You are keen, my lord, you are keen.   245

Hamlet. It would cost you a groaning to take off my edge.

Ophelia. Still better, and worse.

Hamlet. So you mis-take your husbands. Begin, murderer; pox, leave thy damnable faces, and begin. Come; the croaking raven doth bellow for revenge.   251

Lucianus. *Thoughts black, hands apt, drugs fit, and time*
     agreeing;
Confederate season, else no creature seeing;
Thou mixture rank, of midnight weeds collected,
With Hecate's ban thrice blasted, thrice infected,   255
Thy natural magic and dire property,
On wholesome life usurp immediately.

               [*Pours the poison into the Sleeper's ears.*

Hamlet. He poisons him i' the garden for 's estate. His name's Gonzago; the story is extant, and writ in very choice Italian. You shall see anon how the murderer gets the love of Gonzago's wife.   261

Ophelia. The king rises.

Hamlet. What! frighted with false fire?

Queen. How fares my lord?

Polonius. Give o'er the play.   265

---

243 **your love:** your lover.   243–4 the showman, like the Chorus, 'interprets' as he manipulates the puppets.   253 **confederate season:** time being favourable. **else no creature:** no other creature.   256 i.e. may thy magic, &c. **dire property:** dreadful power.   257 **usurp:** seize.   263 **false fire:** a blank discharge.

King. Give me some light: away!

All. Lights, lights, lights!

> [*Exeunt all except* HAMLET *and* HORATIO.

Hamlet. Why, let the stricken deer go weep,

> The hart ungalled play;   269

> For some must watch, while some must sleep:

> So runs the world away.

Would not this, sir, and a forest of feathers, if the rest of
my fortunes turn Turk with me, with two Provincial
roses on my razed shoes, get me a fellowship in a cry of
players, sir?   275

Horatio. Half a share.

Hamlet. A whole one, I.

> For thou dost know, O Damon dear,

> This realm dismantled was

> Of Jove himself; and now reigns here   280

> A very, very—pajock.

Horatio. You might have rhymed.

Hamlet. O good Horatio! I'll take the ghost's word for
a thousand pound. Didst perceive?

Horatio. Very well, my lord.   285

Hamlet. Upon the talk of the poisoning?

Horatio. I did very well note him.

Re-enter ROSENCRANTZ *and* GUILDENSTERN.

Hamlet. Ah, ha! Come, some music! come, the recorders!

> For if the king like not the comedy,

> Why then, belike he likes it not, perdy.   290

Come, some music!

---

269 **hart** (with a pun on heart).   272 **a forest of feathers: a**
plumed hat.   273 **turn Turk:** go to the bad.   **Provincial
roses:** Provençal rosettes.   274 **razed:** slashed (Fr. *raser*).
a fellowship in a cry of players: a partnership in a theatrical
company.   278 **Damon:** friend (Damon and Pythias).   281
pajock: peacock (instead of 'ass') (supposed to be very lustful).
290 **perdy:** *par Dieu.*

Guil. Good my lord, vouchsafe me a word with you.

Hamlet. Sir, a whole history.

Guildenstern. The king, sir,—

Hamlet. Ay, sir, what of him?   295

Guildenstern. Is in his retirement marvellous distempered.

Hamlet. With drink, sir?

Guildenstern. No, my lord, rather with choler.   298

Hamlet. Your wisdom should show itself more richer to signify this to his doctor; for, for me to put him to his purgation would perhaps plunge him into far more choler.

Guildenstern. Good my lord, put your discourse into some frame, and start not so wildly from my affair.

Hamlet. I am tame, sir; pronounce.

Guildenstern. The queen, your mother, in most great affliction of spirit, hath sent me to you.   306

Hamlet. You are welcome.

Guildenstern. Nay, good my lord, this courtesy is not of the right breed. If it shall please you to make me a wholesome answer, I will do your mother's commandment; if not, your pardon and my return shall be the end of my business.   312

Hamlet. Sir, I cannot.

Guildenstern. What, my lord?

Hamlet. Make you a wholesome answer; my wit's diseased; but, sir, such answer as I can make, you shall command; or, rather, as you say, my mother: therefore no more, but to the matter: my mother, you say,—

Rosencrantz. Then, thus she says: your behaviour hath struck her into amazement and admiration.   320

Hamlet. O wonderful son, that can so astonish a mother! But is there no sequel at the heels of this mother's admiration? Impart.

---

296 **distempered:** disorder, upset (Hamlet takes it literally in a medical sense).   298 **choler:** anger (*lit.* bile).   303 **frame:** order.   320 **admiration:** astonishment.

Rosencrantz. She desires to speak with you in her closet
ere you go to bed.   325

Hamlet. We shall obey, were she ten times our mother.
Have you any further trade with us?

Rosencrantz. My lord, you once did love me.

Hamlet. So I do still, by these pickers and stealers. 329

Rosencrantz. Good my lord, what is your cause of distemper? you do surely bar the door upon your own
liberty, if you deny your griefs to your friend.

Hamlet. Sir, I lack advancement.

Rosencrantz. How can that be when you have the voice
of the king himself for your succession in Denmark?   335

Hamlet. Ay, sir, but 'While the grass grows,'—the proverb is something musty.

Enter Players, *with recorders.*

O! the recorders: let me see one. To withdraw with you:
why do you go about to recover the wind of me, as if you
would drive me into a toil?   340

Guildenstern. O! my lord, if my duty be too bold, my
love is too unmannerly.

Hamlet. I do not well understand that. Will you play
upon this pipe?

Guildenstern. My lord, I cannot.   345

Hamlet. I pray you.

Guildenstern. Believe me, I cannot.

Hamlet. I do beseech you.

Guildenstern. I know no touch of it, my lord.   349

326 i.e. I intend to speak with her whether she is my mother or
not.   327 **trade:** business.   329 **by these pickers and
stealers:** by these hands.   331-2 i.e. you will surely find
yourself in confinement if you refuse to communicate your grievances.
339 **to recover the wind of me:** to get to windward of me [*N*].
340 **toil:** net.   341-2 i.e. if my behaviour seem overbold, impute
it to the eagerness of my affection.   343 **I do not well understand that:** I do not think so.

E

Hamlet. 'Tis as easy as lying; govern these ventages with your finger and thumb, give it breath with your mouth, and it will discourse most eloquent music. Look you, these are the stops.

Guildenstern. But these cannot I command to any utterance of harmony; I have not the skill. 355

Hamlet. Why, look you now, how unworthy a thing you make of me. You would play upon me; you would seem to know my stops; you would pluck out the heart of my mystery; you would sound me from my lowest note to the top of my compass; and there is much 360 music, excellent voice, in this little organ, yet cannot you make it speak. 'Sblood, do you think I am easier to be played on than a pipe? Call me what instrument you will, though you can fret me, you cannot play upon me. 365

Enter POLONIUS.

God bless you, sir!

Polonius. My lord, the queen would speak with you, and presently.

Hamlet. Do you see yonder cloud that's almost in shape of a camel? 370

Polonius. By the mass, and 'tis like a camel, indeed.

Hamlet. Methinks it is like a weasel.

Polonius. It is backed like a weasel.

Hamlet. Or like a whale?

Polonius. Very like a whale. 375

Hamlet. Then I will come to my mother by and by. [*Aside.*] They fool me to the top of my bent. [*Aloud.*] I will come by and by.

Polonius. I will say so. [*Exit.*

---

350 **ventages:** wind-holes, stops.   364 **fret** (a pun or play upon words): (*a*) vex; (*b*) furnish with frets or bars of wood to regulate the fingering.

Hamlet. 'By and by' is easily said. Leave me, friends.

[*Exeunt all but* HAMLET.

'Tis now the very witching time of night, 381
When churchyards yawn and hell itself breathes out
Contagion to this world: now could I drink hot blood,
And do such bitter business as the day
Would quake to look on. Soft! now to my mother. 385
O heart! lose not thy nature; let not ever
The soul of Nero enter this firm bosom;
Let me be cruel, not unnatural;
I will speak daggers to her, but use none;
My tongue and soul in this be hypocrites; 390
How in my words soever she be shent,
To give them seals never, my soul, consent! [*Exit.*

Scene III. A Room in the Castle

Enter KING, ROSENCRANTZ, *and* GUILDENSTERN.

King. I like him not, nor stands it safe with us
To let his madness range. Therefore prepare you;
I your commission will forthwith dispatch,
And he to England shall along with you.
The terms of our estate may not endure 5
Hazard so dangerous as doth hourly grow
Out of his lunacies.

Guildenstern. We will ourselves provide.
Most holy and religious fear it is
To keep those many many bodies safe
That live and feed upon your majesty. 10

Rosencrantz. The single and peculiar life is bound

391 **shent:** reproached, shamed. 392 **to give them seals:**
i.e. to ratify the words by actions. 5 **the terms of our estate:**
our office as king and ruler of the state. 7 **provide:** prepare.
11 **peculiar:** private.

With all the strength and armour of the mind
To keep itself from noyance; but much more
That spirit upon whose weal depend and rest
The lives of many. The cease of majesty   15
Dies not alone, but, like a gulf doth draw
What's near it with it; it is a massy wheel,
Fix'd on the summit of the highest mount,
To whose huge spokes ten thousand lesser things
Are mortis'd and adjoin'd; which, when it falls,   20
Each small annexment, petty consequence,
Attends the boisterous ruin. Never alone
Did the king sigh, but with a general groan.

   King. Arm you, I pray you, to this speedy voyage;
For we will fetters put upon this fear,   25
Which now goes too free-footed.

   Rosencrantz. ⎫
   Guildenstern. ⎭   We will haste us.

       [*Exeunt* ROSENCRANTZ *and* GUILDENSTERN.

Enter POLONIUS.

   Polonius. My lord, he's going to his mother's closet:
Behind the arras I'll convey myself
To hear the process; I'll warrant she'll tax him home;
And, as you said, and wisely was it said,   30
'Tis meet that some more audience than a mother,
Since nature makes them partial, should o'erhear
The speech, of vantage. Fare you well, my liege:
I'll call upon you ere you go to bed
And tell you what I know.

   King.   Thanks, dear my lord.   35

       [*Exit* POLONIUS.

13 **noyance:** hurt.   **15 cease of majesty:** death of a king.
16 **gulf:** whirlpool.   **20 mortis'd:** fixed, dove-tailed.   **23 a**
general groan: the grief of all his people.   **29 process:** proceedings. **home:** effectually (bring it 'home' to him).   **33 of**
vantage: *either* from a favourable point *or* in addition.

O! my offence is rank, it smells to heaven;
It hath the primal eldest curse upon 't;
A brother's murder! Pray can I not,
Though inclination be as sharp as will:
My stronger guilt defeats my strong intent;   40
And like a man to double business bound,
I stand in pause where I shall first begin,
And both neglect. What if this curséd hand
Were thicker than itself with brother's blood,
Is there not rain enough in the sweet heavens   45
To wash it white as snow? Whereto serves mercy
But to confront the visage of offence?
And what's in prayer but this two-fold force,
To be forestalléd, ere we come to fall,
Or pardon'd, being down? Then, I'll look up;   50
My fault is past. But, O! what form of prayer
Can serve my turn? 'Forgive me my foul murder?'
That cannot be since I am still possess'd
Of those effects for which I did the murder,
My crown, mine own ambition, and my queen.   55
May one be pardon'd and retain the offence?
In the corrupted currents of this world
Offence's gilded hand may shove by justice,
And oft 'tis seen the wicked prize itself
Buys out the law; but 'tis not so above;   60
There is no shuffling, there the action lies
In his true nature, and we ourselves compell'd
Even to the teeth and forehead of our faults
To give in evidence. What then? what rests?
Try what repentance can: what can it not?   65

37 **primal**: original (viz. the curse of Cain).   47 **the visage
of offence**: the very presence of sin.   56 **offence**: the prize of
sin.   58 i.e. the criminal may bribe the judge.   59–60 e.g.
kingship or power once seized puts a man above the law.   61
action: in the double sense of an act and an action at law.   64
rests: remains (Lat. *quid restat*).

Yet what can it, when one can not repent?
O wretched state! O bosom black as death!
O liméd soul, that struggling to be free
Art more engaged! Help, angels! make assay;
Bow, stubborn knees; and heart with strings of steel   **70**
Be soft as sinews of the new-born babe.
All may be well.   [*Retires and kneels.*

Enter HAMLET.

Hamlet. Now might I do it pat, now he is praying;
And now I'll do 't: and so he goes to heaven;
And so am I reveng'd. That would be scann'd: **75**
A villain kills my father; and for that,
I, his sole son, do this same villain send
To heaven.
Why, this is hire and salary, not revenge.
He took my father grossly, full of bread,   **80**
With all his crimes broad blown, as flush as May;
And how his audit stands who knows save heaven?
But in our circumstance and course of thought
'Tis heavy with him. And am I then reveng'd,
To take him in the purging of his soul,   **85**
When he is fit and season'd for his passage?
No.
Up, sword, and know thou a more horrid hent;
When he is drunk asleep, or in his rage,
Or in the incestuous pleasure of his bed,   **90**
At gaming, swearing, or about some act
That has no relish of salvation in 't;
Then trip him, that his heels may kick at heaven,

---

68 **liméd**: snared.   69 **engaged**: entangled.   75 **that would
be scann'd**: that calls for scrutiny.   79 **hire and salary**: pay-
ment and reward.   81 **flush**: lusty.   82 **audit**: reckoning,
final account.   83 i.e. according to our evidence and speculation.   85 **to take**: by taking.   88 **hent**: grasp.

And that his soul may be as damn'd and black
As hell, whereto it goes. My mother stays: 95
This physic but prolongs thy sickly days.   [*Exit.*

The KING *rises and advances.*

King. My words fly up, my thoughts remain below:
Words without thoughts never to heaven go.   [*Exit.*

Scene IV. THE QUEEN'S APARTMENT

Enter QUEEN *and* POLONIUS.

Pol. He will come straight. Look you lay home to him;
Tell him his pranks have been too broad to bear with,
And that your Grace hath screen'd and stood between
Much heat and him. I'll silence me e'en here.
Pray you, be round with him.   5
Hamlet. [*Within.*] Mother, mother, mother!
Queen.   I'll warrant you;
Fear me not. Withdraw, I hear him coming.
                        [POLONIUS *hides behind the arras.*

Enter HAMLET.

Hamlet. Now, mother, what's the matter?
Queen. Hamlet, thou hast thy father much offended.
Hamlet. Mother, you have my father much offended. 10
Queen. Come, come, you answer with an idle tongue.
Hamlet. Go, go, you question with a wicked tongue.
Queen. Why, how now, Hamlet!
Hamlet.   What's the matter now?
Queen. Have you forgot me?
Hamlet.   No, by the rood, not so:
You are the queen, your husband's brother's wife;   15

4 **heat**: anger.   5 **round**: plain-spoken.   14 **the rood**:
the Cross.

And,—would it were not so!—you are my mother.

   Queen. Nay then, I'll set those to you that can speak.

   Hamlet. Come, come, and sit you down; you shall not
     budge;

You go not, till I set you up a glass

Where you may see the inmost part of you.   20

   Queen. What wilt thou do? thou wilt not murder me?

Help, help, ho!

   Polonius. [*Behind.*] What, ho! help! help! help!

   Hamlet. [*Draws.*] How now! a rat? Dead, for a ducat,
     dead!   [*Makes a pass through the arras.*

   Polonius. [*Behind.*] O! I am slain.

   Queen. O me! what hast thou done?   25

   Hamlet. Nay, I know not: is it the king?

   Queen. O! what a rash and bloody deed is this!

   Hamlet. A bloody deed! almost as bad, good mother,

As kill a king, and marry with his brother.

   Queen. As kill a king!

   Hamlet.   Ay, lady, 'twas my word.   30

     [*Lifts up the arras and discovers* POLONIUS.

[*To* POLONIUS.] Thou wretched, rash, intruding fool,
     farewell!

I took thee for thy better; take thy fortune;

Thou find'st to be too busy is some danger.

Leave wringing of your hands: peace! sit you down,

And let me wring your heart; for so I shall   35

If it be made of penetrable stuff,

If damnéd custom have not brass'd it so

That it is proof and bulwark against sense.

   Queen. What have I done that thou dar'st wag thy tongue

In noise so rude against me?

   Hamlet.   Such an act   40

That blurs the grace and blush of modesty,

---

   23 for a ducat: I would stake a ducat on it.   **37 damnéd**
custom: habitual vice.   **38 sense:** feeling.

Calls virtue hypocrite, takes off the rose
From the fair forehead of an innocent love
And sets a blister there, makes marriage vows
As false as dicers' oaths; O! such a deed   45
As from the body of contraction plucks
The very soul, and sweet religion makes
A rhapsody of words; heaven's face doth glow,
Yea, this solidity and compound mass,
With tristful visage, as against the doom,   50
Is thought-sick at the act.
   Queen.   Ay me! what act,
That roars so loud and thunders in the index?
   Hamlet. Look here, upon this picture, and on this;
The counterfeit presentment of two brothers.
See, what a grace was seated on this brow;   55
Hyperion's curls, the front of Jove himself,
An eye like Mars to threaten and command,
A station like the herald Mercury
New-lighted on a heaven-kissing hill,
A combination and a form indeed,   60
Where every god did seem to set his seal,
To give the world assurance of a man.
This was your husband: look you now, what follows.
Here is your husband; like a mildew'd ear,
Blasting his wholesome brother. Have you eyes?   65
Could you on this fair mountain leave to feed,
And batten on this moor? Ha! have you eyes?
You cannot call it love, for at your age
The hey-day in the blood is tame, it's humble,

---

46 contraction: the contract and sacrament of marriage.   **48
rhapsody**: medley, a string of words.   **49** i.e. the earth.   **50
tristful**: sorrowing.   **as against the doom**: as before the Day of
Judgement.   **52 index**: prelude [*N*].   **54 counterfeit**:
pictured.   **56 front**: forehead (Lat. *frons*).   **58 station**:
attitude.   **69 hey-day**: wildness of spirits.

And waits upon the judgment; and what judgment   70
Would step from this to this? Sense, sure, you have,
Else could you not have motion; but sure, that sense
Is apoplex'd; for madness would not err,
Nor sense to ecstasy was ne'er so thrall'd
But it reserv'd some quantity of choice,   75
To serve in such a difference. What devil was 't
That thus hath cozen'd you at hoodman-blind?
Eyes without feeling, feeling without sight,
Ears without hands or eyes, smelling sans all,
Or but a sickly part of one true sense   80
Could not so mope.
O shame! where is thy blush? Rebellious hell,
If thou canst mutine in a matron's bones,
To flaming youth let virtue be as wax,
And melt in her own fire: proclaim no shame   85
When the compulsive ardour gives the charge,
Since frost itself as actively doth burn,
And reason panders will.

Queen.   O Hamlet! speak no more;
Thou turn'st mine eyes into my very soul;
And there I see such black and grainéd spots   90
As will not leave their tinct.

Hamlet.   Nay, but to live
In the rank sweat of an enseaméd bed,
Stew'd in corruption, honeying and making love
Over the nasty sty,—

---

71 **sense**: feeling.   72 **motion**: impulses.   73 **apoplex'd**:
paralysed.   74 **ecstasy**: madness.   74–6 i.e. feeling was
never so enslaved by madness as to be quite unable to choose and
discriminate in so extreme a case.   77 **cozen'd**: cheated.
hoodman-blind: blind-man's-buff.   83 **mutine**: rebel.   86
compulsive ardour: the compelling passions of youth.   87
frost: i.e. middle age.   88 **panders**: serves. **will**: desire.
90 **grainéd**: deep-dyed.   91 **leave**: give up. **tinct**: stain.
92 **enseaméd**: greasy.

Queen.   O! speak to me no more;
These words like daggers enter in mine ears;   95
No more, sweet Hamlet!
   Hamlet.   A murderer, and a villain;
A slave that is not twentieth part the tithe
Of your precedent lord; a vice of kings;
A cut-purse of the empire and the rule,
That from a shelf the precious diadem stole,   100
And put it in his pocket!
   Queen.   No more!
   Hamlet. A king of shreds and patches,—

        Enter Ghost.

Save me and hover o'er me with your wings,
You heavenly guards! What would your gracious figure?
   Queen. Alas! he's mad!   105
   Hamlet. Do you not come your tardy son to chide,
That, laps'd in time and passion, lets go by
The important acting of your dread command?
O! say.
   Ghost. Do not forget: this visitation
Is but to whet thy almost blunted purpose.   110
But, look! amazement on thy mother sits;
O! step between her and her fighting soul;
Conceit in weakest bodies strongest works;
Speak to her, Hamlet.
   Hamlet.   How is it with you, lady?
   Queen. Alas! how is't with you,   115
That you do bend your eye on vacancy
And with the incorporal air do hold discourse?

  97 tithe: tenth part.   **98 precedent:** previous. **vice:** clown,
caricature.   **99 cut-purse:** pickpocket, petty thief.   102
king of shreds and patches: i.e. a king in motley, a clown king.
107 laps'd in time and passion: 'having suffered time to slip and
passion to cool' (Johnson).   **108 important:** urgent.   113
conceit: imagination.

Forth at your eyes your spirits wildly peep;
And, as the sleeping soldiers in the alarm,
Your bedded hair, like life in excrements,   120
Starts up and stands an end. O gentle son!
Upon the heat and flame of thy distemper
Sprinkle cool patience. Whereon do you look?
    Hamlet. On him, on him! Look you, how pale he glares!
His form and cause conjoin'd, preaching to stones,   125
Would make them capable. Do not look upon me;
Lest with this piteous action you convert
My stern effects: then what I have to do
Will want true colour; tears perchance for blood.
    Queen. To whom do you speak this?
    Hamlet.   Do you see nothing there?
    Queen. Nothing at all; yet all that is I see.   131
    Hamlet. Nor did you nothing hear?
    Queen.   No, nothing but ourselves.
    Hamlet. Why, look you there! look, how it steals away;
My father, in his habit as he liv'd;
Look! where he goes, even now, out at the portal.   135
                                        [*Exit* Ghost.
    Queen. This is the very coinage of your brain:
This bodiless creation ecstasy
Is very cunning in.
    Hamlet. Ecstasy!
My pulse, as yours, doth temperately keep time,   140
And makes as healthful music. It is not madness
That I have utter'd: bring me to the test,
And I the matter will re-word, which madness

---

120 **bedded**: supine, flat. **excrements**: outgrowths (e.g. nails).
126 **capable**: impressionable, capable of feeling.   128 **stern
effects**: *either* stern intentions *or* outward signs of my stern feelings.
129 **colour**: excuse. **tears . . . for blood**: i.e. I may shed tears
instead of exacting blood.   134 **habit**: clothing.   137-8 i.e.
madness is skilful in creating shapes and phantoms.

Would gambol from. Mother, for love of grace,
Lay not that flattering unction to your soul,   145
That not your trespass but my madness speaks;
It will but skin and film the ulcerous place,
Whiles rank corruption, mining all within,
Infects unseen. Confess yourself to heaven;
Repent what's past; avoid what is to come;   150
And do not spread the compost on the weeds
To make them ranker. Forgive me this my virtue;
For in the fatness of these pursy times
Virtue itself of vice must pardon beg,
Yea, curb and woo for leave to do him good.   155
  Queen. O Hamlet! thou hast cleft my heart in twain.
  Hamlet. O! throw away the worser part of it,
And live the purer with the other half.
Good night; but go not to mine uncle's bed;
Assume a virtue, if you have it not.   160
That monster, custom, who all sense doth eat,
Of habits devil, is angel yet in this,
That to the use of actions fair and good
He likewise gives a frock or livery,
That aptly is put on. Refrain to-night;   165
And that shall lend a kind of easiness
To the next abstinence: the next more easy;
For use almost can change the stamp of nature,
And exorcise the devil or throw him out
With wondrous potency. Once more, good-night: 170
And when you are desirous to be bless'd,

145 **flattering unction**: salve of self-deception.   151 **compost**: manure.   153 **pursy**: short-winded, out of condition.
155 **curb**: bend (Fr. *courber*).   161–5 that monster, custom, who destroys all sensibility, being the evil genius of our habits, is yet a good angel in that he makes us more prompt in our good actions.
168 **stamp of nature**: innate qualities.   171 **desirous to be bless'd**: (*viz.* by heaven) penitent.

I'll blessing beg of you.   For this same lord,
> [*Pointing to* POLONIUS.

I do repent: but heaven hath pleas'd it so,
To punish me with this, and this with me,
That I must be their scourge and minister.   175
I will bestow him, and will answer well
The death I gave him. So, again, good-night.
I must be cruel only to be kind:
Thus bad begins and worse remains behind.
One word more, good lady.
 Queen.   What shall I do?   180
 Hamlet. Not this, by no means, that I bid you do:
Let the bloat king tempt you again to bed;
Pinch wanton on your cheek; call you his mouse;
And let him, for a pair of reechy kisses,
Or paddling in your neck with his damn'd fingers,   185
Make you to ravel all this matter out,
That I essentially am not in madness,
But mad in craft. 'Twere good you let him know;
For who that's but a queen, fair, sober, wise,
Would from a paddock, from a bat, a gib,   190
Such dear concernings hide? who would do so?
No, in despite of sense and secrecy,
Unpeg the basket on the house's top,
Let the birds fly, and, like the famous ape,
To try conclusions, in the basket creep,   195
And break your own neck down.
 Queen. Be thou assur'd, if words be made of breath,
And breath of life, I have no life to breathe
What thou hast said to me.

181-96 The speech is bitter and sarcastic. Hamlet wishes to en-
sure secrecy by again taunting her with her lustful life.   184
reechy: filthy (*lit.* smoky).   188 **in craft:** by design.   **'twere**
good, &c.: (sarcastic).   190 **paddock:** toad.   **gib:** tom-cat.
191 **such dear concernings:** matters of such near concern.   195
to try conclusions: to see what will happen.

Hamlet. I must to England; you know that?

Queen.   Alack! 200
I had forgot: 'tis so concluded on.

Hamlet. There's letters seal'd; and my two schoolfellows,
Whom I will trust as I will adders fang'd,
They bear the mandate; they must sweep my way,
And marshal me to knavery. Let it work;   205
For 'tis the sport to have the enginer
Hoist with his own petar: and 't shall go hard
But I will delve one yard below their mines,
And blow them at the moon. O! 'tis most sweet,
When in one line two crafts directly meet.   210
This man shall set me packing;
I'll lug the guts into the neighbour room.
Mother, good-night. Indeed this counsellor
Is now most still, most secret, and most grave,
Who was in life a foolish prating knave.   215
Come, sir, to draw toward an end with you.
Good-night, mother.

        [*Exeunt severally;* HAMLET *tugging in* POLONIUS.

207 **hoist with his own petar:** blown up by his own bomb.
211 **packing:** *both* plotting *and* hastening on my journey.   216
to draw toward an end: to close my conversation.

ACT IV

Scene I. A ROOM IN THE CASTLE

Enter KING, QUEEN, ROSENCRANTZ, *and* GUILDENSTERN.

King. There's matter in these sighs, these profound
　　heaves:
You must translate; 'tis fit we understand them.
Where is your son?
　Queen. [*To* ROSENCRANTZ *and* GUILDENSTERN.] Bestow
　　this place on us a little while.
　　　　　　　　[*Exeunt* ROSENCRANTZ *and* GUILDENSTERN.
Ah! my good lord, what have I seen to-night.　　　　　　5
　King. What, Gertrude? How does Hamlet?
　Queen. Mad as the sea and wind, when both contend
Which is the mightier. In his lawless fit,
Behind the arras hearing something stir,
Whips out his rapier, cries, 'A rat! a rat!'　　　　　　10
And, in his brainish apprehension, kills
The unseen good old man.
　King.　　　　　　　　O heavy deed!
It had been so with us had we been there.
His liberty is full of threats to all;
To you yourself, to us, to every one.　　　　　　　　15
Alas! how shall this bloody deed be answer'd?
It will be laid to us, whose providence
Should have kept short, restrain'd, and out of haunt,
This mad young man: but so much was our love,
We would not understand what was most fit,　　　　　20
But, like the owner of a foul disease,
To keep it from divulging, let it feed

---

11 **brainish apprehension:** headstrong fancy.　　17 **providence:** foresight.　　18 **out of haunt:** private.　　22 **divulging:**
becoming public.

Even on the pith of life. Where is he gone?

  Queen. To draw apart the body he hath kill'd;

O'er whom his very madness, like some ore   25

Among a mineral of metals base,

Shows itself pure: he weeps for what is done.

  King. O Gertrude! come away.

The sun no sooner shall the mountains touch

But we will ship him hence; and this vile deed   30

We must, with all our majesty and skill,

Both countenance and excuse. Ho! Guildenstern!

     Re-enter ROSENCRANTZ *and* GUILDENSTERN.

Friends both, go join you with some further aid:

Hamlet in madness hath Polonius slain,

And from his mother's closet hath he dragg'd him: 35

Go seek him out; speak fair, and bring the body

Into the chapel. I pray you, haste in this.

       [*Exeunt* ROSENCRANTZ *and* GUILDENSTERN.

Come, Gertrude, we'll call up our wisest friends;

And let them know both what we mean to do,

And what's untimely done: so, haply, slander,   40

Whose whisper o'er the world's diameter,

As level as the cannon to his blank

Transports his poison'd shot, may miss our name,

And hit the woundless air. O! come away;   44

My soul is full of discord and dismay.   [*Exeunt.*

   Scene II. ANOTHER ROOM IN THE SAME

      Enter HAMLET.

  Hamlet. Safely stowed.

  Rosencrantz. ⎫
  Guildenstern. ⎭ [*Within.*] Hamlet! Lord Hamlet!

---

   25 ore: gold (as heraldic *or*).   **26 mineral**: mine.   42
level: straight to the mark. **blank**: centre of the target.

Hamlet. What noise? who calls on Hamlet?
O! here they come.

Enter ROSENCRANTZ *and* GUILDENSTERN.

Rosencrantz. What have you done, my lord, with the
     dead body?   5

Hamlet. Compounded it with dust, whereto 'tis kin.

Rosencrantz. Tell us where 'tis, that we may take it thence
And bear it to the chapel.

Hamlet. Do not believe it.

Rosencrantz. Believe what?   10

Hamlet. That I can keep your counsel and not mine
own. Besides, to be demanded of a sponge! what replication should be made by the son of a king?

Rosencrantz. Take you me for a sponge, my lord?

Hamlet. Ay, sir, that soaks up the king's countenance, 15
his rewards, his authorities. But such officers do the
king best service in the end: he keeps them, like an
ape, in the corner of his jaw; first mouthed, to be last
swallowed: when he needs what you have gleaned,
it is but squeezing you, and, sponge, you shall be dry 20
again.

Rosencrantz. I understand you not, my lord.

Hamlet. I am glad of it: a knavish speech sleeps in a
foolish ear.

Rosencrantz. My lord, you must tell us where the body is,
and go with us to the king.   26

Hamlet. The body is with the king, but the king is not
with the body. The king is a thing—

Guildenstern. A thing, my lord!

Hamlet. Of nothing: bring me to him. Hide fox, and all
after.   [*Exeunt.*

---

   11 counsel: i.e. secrets.   **12 replication:** rejoinder.   **17–18
like an ape:** as an ape 'keeps nuts' [*Q* 1].

Scene III. ANOTHER ROOM IN THE SAME

Enter KING, *attended.*

King. I have sent to seek him, and to find the body.
How dangerous is it that this man goes loose!
Yet must not we put the strong law on him:
He's lov'd of the distracted multitude,
Who like not in their judgment, but their eyes;   5
And where 'tis so, the offender's scourge is weigh'd,
But never the offence. To bear all smooth and even,
This sudden sending him away must seem
Deliberate pause: diseases desperate grown
By desperate appliance are reliev'd,   10
Or not at all.

Enter ROSENCRANTZ.

         How now! what hath befall'n?
Rosencrantz. Where the dead body is bestow'd, my lord,
We cannot get from him.
King.   But where is he?
Rosencrantz. Without, my lord; guarded, to know your
    pleasure.
King. Bring him before us.   15
Rosencrantz. Ho, Guildenstern! bring in my lord.

Enter HAMLET *and* GUILDENSTERN.

King. Now, Hamlet, where's Polonius?
Hamlet. At supper.
King. At supper! Where?
Hamlet. Not where he eats, but where he is eaten: a   20
certain convocation of politic worms are e'en at him.
Your worm is your only emperor for diet: we fat all

4 **distracted:** unstable.   6 **scourge:** punishment.   **7 bear
all smooth:** pass everything off smoothly.   9 **deliberate
pause:** a politic or considered delay (in calling Hamlet to account).
21 **convocation:** parliament [*N*].

creatures else to fat us, and we fat ourselves for maggots: your fat king and your lean beggar is but variable
service; two dishes, but to one table: that's the end.   25

King. Alas, alas!

Hamlet. A man may fish with the worm that hath eat
of a king, and eat of the fish that hath fed of that worm.

King. What dost thou mean by this?

Hamlet. Nothing, but to show you how a king may go
a progress through the guts of a beggar.   31

King. Where is Polonius?

Hamlet. In heaven; send thither to see: if your messenger
find him not there, seek him i' the other place yourself.
But, indeed, if you find him not within this month, you
shall nose him as you go up the stairs into the lobby.   36

King. [*To some* Attendants.] Go seek him there.

Hamlet. He will stay till you come.

                                        [*Exeunt* Attendants.

King. Hamlet, this deed, for thine especial safety,
Which we do tender, as we dearly grieve   40
For that which thou hast done, must send thee hence
With fiery quickness: therefore prepare thyself;
The bark is ready, and the wind at help,
The associates tend, and every thing is bent
For England.

Hamlet.   For England!

King.   Ay, Hamlet.

Hamlet.   Good.   45

King. So is it, if thou knew'st our purposes.

Hamlet. I see a cherub that sees them. But, come; for
England! Farewell, dear mother.

King. Thy loving father, Hamlet.   49

Hamlet. My mother: father and mother is man and wife.

24–5 **variable service**: different courses.   31 **a progress**: a
state-journey.   40 **tender**: have regard for.   44 **the
associates tend**: your companions await you.

man and wife is one flesh, and so, my mother. Come, for
England! [*Exit.*

King. Follow him at foot; tempt him with speed aboard:
Delay it not, I'll have him hence to-night.
Away! for every thing is seal'd and done 55
That else leans on the affair: pray you, make haste.
[*Exeunt* ROSENCRANTZ *and* GUILDENSTERN.
And, England, if my love thou hold'st at aught,—
As my great power thereof may give thee sense,
Since yet thy cicatrice looks raw and red
After the Danish sword, and thy free awe 60
Pays homage to us,—thou mayst not coldly set
Our sovereign process, which imports at full,
By letters congruing to that effect,
The present death of Hamlet. Do it, England;
For like the hectic in my blood he rages, 65
And thou must cure me. Till I know 'tis done,
Howe'er my haps, my joys were ne'er begun. [*Exit.*

Scene IV. A Plain in Denmark

Enter FORTINBRAS, *a* Captain, *and* Soldiers, *marching.*

Fortinbras. Go, captain, from me greet the Danish king;
Tell him that, by his licence, Fortinbras
Claims the conveyance of a promis'd march
Over his kingdom. You know the rendezvous.
If that his majesty would aught with us, 5
We shall express our duty in his eye,
And let him know so.

53 **at foot:** at his heels. 57 **England:** the King of England.
58 i.e. as my power makes my good will valuable to you. 59 **cicatrice:** scar. 61 **coldly set:** underrate. 62 **sovereign process:** royal mandate. 63 **congruing:** agreeing. 64 **present:**
immediate. 65 **hectic:** fever. 67 **howe'er my haps:** whatever befall me. 3 **conveyance:** convoy, conduct. 6 **in his
eye:** in his presence.

Captain.   I will do 't, my lord.
Fortinbras. Go softly on.
                              [*Exeunt* FORTINBRAS *and* Soldiers.

        Enter HAMLET, ROSENCRANTZ, GUILDENSTERN, *&c.*

Hamlet. Good sir, whose powers are these?
Captain. They are of Norway, sir.   10
Hamlet. How purpos'd, sir, I pray you?
Captain. Against some part of Poland.
Hamlet. Who commands them, sir?
Captain. The nephew to old Norway, Fortinbras.
Hamlet. Goes it against the main of Poland, sir,   15
Or for some frontier?
Captain. Truly to speak, and with no addition,
We go to gain a little patch of ground
That hath in it no profit but the name.
To pay five ducats, five, I would not farm it;   20
Nor will it yield to Norway or the Pole
A ranker rate, should it be sold in fee.
Hamlet. Why, then the Polack never will defend it.
Captain. Yes, 'tis already garrison'd.
Hamlet. Two thousand souls and twenty thousand ducats
Will not debate the question of this straw: 26
This is the imposthume of much wealth and peace,
That inward breaks, and shows no cause without
Why the man dies. I humbly thank you, sir.
Captain. God be wi' you, sir.   [*Exit.*
Rosencrantz.   Will 't please you go, my lord? 30
Hamlet. I'll be with you straight. Go a little before.
                              [*Exeunt all except* HAMLET.
How all occasions do inform against me,
And spur my dull revenge! What is a man,

----

8 **softly:** slowly.   15 **main:** mainland.   20 **to pay:** at a
rent of.   22 **ranker rate:** higher value. **fee:** fee-simple, free-
hold.   27 **imposthume:** abscess.

If his chief good and market of his time
Be but to sleep and feed? a beast, no more.   35
Sure he that made us with such large discourse,
Looking before and after, gave us not
That capability and god-like reason
To fust in us unus'd. Now, whe'r it be
Bestial oblivion, or some craven scruple   40
Of thinking too precisely on the event,
A thought, which, quarter'd, hath but one part wisdom,
And ever three parts coward, I do not know
Why yet I live to say 'This thing 's to do;'
Sith I have cause and will and strength and means   45
To do 't. Examples gross as earth exhort me:
Witness this army of such mass and charge
Led by a delicate and tender prince,
Whose spirit with divine ambition puff'd
Makes mouths at the invisible event,   50
Exposing what is mortal and unsure
To all that fortune, death and danger dare,
Even for an egg-shell. Rightly to be great
Is not to stir without great argument,
But greatly to find quarrel in a straw   55
When honour 's at the stake. How stand I then,
That have a father kill'd, a mother stain'd,
Excitements of my reason and my blood,
And let all sleep, while, to my shame, I see
The imminent death of twenty thousand men,   60
That, for a fantasy and trick of fame,
Go to their graves like beds, fight for a plot

34 **market:** traffic, employment.   36 **discourse:** power of
reasoning.   39 **fust:** moulder.   41 **event:** issue, consequence
(Lat. *eventus*).   45 **sith:** since.   48 **tender:** youthful.
50 **makes mouths ... event:** scorns the uncertainty of the out-
come.   52 **dare:** can inflict upon him.   54 **argument:** cause.
58 **blood:** passion.   61 **fantasy and trick of fame:** merest
idea of glory.

Whereon the numbers cannot try the cause,
Which is not tomb enough and continent
To hide the slain? O! from this time forth,   65
My thoughts be bloody, or be nothing worth!   [*Exit.*

Scene V. ELSINORE. A ROOM IN THE CASTLE

Enter QUEEN, HORATIO, *and a* Gentleman.

Queen. I will not speak with her.
Gentleman. She is importunate, indeed distract:
Her mood will needs be pitied.
Queen.   What would she have?
Gentleman. She speaks much of her father; says she hears
There's tricks i' the world; and hems, and beats her
      heart;   5
Spurns enviously at straws; speaks things in doubt,
That carry but half sense: her speech is nothing,
Yet the unshapéd use of it doth move
The hearers to collection; they aim at it,
And botch the words up fit to their own thoughts;   10
Which, as her winks, and nods, and gestures yield them,
Indeed would make one think there might be thought,
Though nothing sure, yet much unhappily.
Horatio. 'Twere good she were spoken with, for she may
      strew
Dangerous conjectures in ill-breeding minds.   15
Queen. Let her come in.   [*Exit* Gentleman.
To my sick soul, as sin's true nature is,

---

   63 **whereon the numbers . . . cause:** which has not enough
space for an army to settle the dispute.   64 **continent:** cover,
receptacle.   2 **importunate:** insistent.   6 **spurns enviously
at straws:** is vexed and angry for little or no reason.   8 **unshapéd:** incoherent.   9 **collection:** inference. **aim:** guess.
10 **botch up:** piece together clumsily.   12 **thought:** suspected.

Each toy seems prologue to some great amiss;
So full of artless jealousy is guilt,
It spills itself in fearing to be spilt.   20

       Re-enter Gentleman, *with* OPHELIA.

Ophelia. Where is the beauteous majesty of Denmark?
Queen. How now, Ophelia!
Ophelia.

      How should I your true love know
        From another one?
      By his cockle hat and staff,   25
        And his sandal shoon.

Queen. Alas! sweet lady, what imports this song?
Ophelia. Say you? nay, pray you, mark.

      He is dead and gone, lady,
        He is dead and gone;   30
      At his head a grass-green turf;
        At his heels a stone.

O, ho!
Queen. Nay, but Ophelia,—
Ophelia. Pray you, mark.   35

      White his shroud as the mountain snow,—

        Enter KING.

Queen. Alas! look here, my lord.
Ophelia.

      Larded all with sweet flowers;
      Which bewept to the grave did not go
        With true-love showers.   40

King. How do you, pretty lady?

---

18 i.e. every trifle seems to herald a disaster. **19 artless jealousy:** uncontrollable suspicion. 20 i.e. by anticipating discovery guilt betrays itself. 25 **cockle hat and staff:** i.e. pilgrim's dress. 26 **shoon:** shoes. 38 **larded:** decked.

Ophelia. Well, God 'ild you! They say the owl was a baker's daughter. Lord! we know what we are, but know not what we may be. God be at your table!

King. Conceit upon her father.　　　　　　　　45

Ophelia. Pray you, let's have no words of this; but when they ask you what it means, say you this:

> To-morrow is Saint Valentine's day,
> 　　All in the morning betime,
> And I a maid at your window,　　　　　　50
> 　　To be your Valentine:
> Then up he rose, and donn'd his clothes,
> 　　And dupp'd the chamber door;
> Let in the maid, that out a maid
> 　　Never departed more.　　　　　　55

King. Pretty Ophelia!

Oph. Indeed, la! without an oath, I'll make an end on 't:

> By Gis and by Saint Charity,
> 　　Alack, and fie for shame!
> Young men will do 't, if they come to 't;　　60
> 　　By Cock they are to blame.
> Quoth she, before you tumbled me,
> 　　You promis'd me to wed:

(He answers.)

> So would I ha' done, by yonder sun,　　65
> 　　An thou hadst not come to my bed.

King. How long hath she been thus?

Ophelia. I hope all will be well. We must be patient: but I cannot choose but weep, to think they should lay him i' the cold ground. My brother shall know of it: 70 and so I thank you for your good counsel. Come, my coach! Good-night, ladies; good-night, sweet ladies; good-night, good-night.　　　　　　　　　[*Exit.*

---

42 **'ild:** yield, i.e. reward.　　45 **conceit upon:** she thinks of.
53 **dupp'd:** opened.　　58 **Gis:** Jesus.　　61 **Cock:** God.

King. Follow her close; give her good watch, I pray
    you.   [*Exit* HORATIO.
O! this is the poison of deep grief; it springs   75
All from her father's death. O Gertrude, Gertrude!
When sorrows come, they come not single spies,
But in battalions. First, her father slain;
Next, your son gone; but he most violent author
Of his own just remove: the people muddied,   80
Thick and unwholesome in their thoughts and whispers,
For good Polonius' death; and we have done but greenly,
In hugger-mugger to inter him: poor Ophelia
Divided from herself and her fair judgment,
Without the which we are pictures, or mere beasts: 85
Last, and as much containing as all these,
Her brother is in secret come from France,
Feeds on his wonder, keeps himself in clouds,
And wants not buzzers to infect his ear
With pestilent speeches of his father's death;   90
Wherein necessity, of matter beggar'd,
Will nothing stick our person to arraign
In ear and ear. O my dear Gertrude! this,
Like to a murdering-piece, in many places
Gives me superfluous death.   [*A noise within.*
  Queen.   Alack! what noise is this? 95

Enter a Gentleman.

  King. Where are my Switzers? Let them guard the door.
What is the matter?
  Gentleman.   Save yourself, my lord;
The ocean, overpeering of his list,
Eats not the flats with more impetuous haste

---

80 **muddied**: turbulent, confused.   83 **hugger-mugger**:
secrecy.   88 i.e. nurses his amazement and keeps himself aloof.
89 **buzzers**: tale-bearers, whisperers.   91-2 i.e. for lack of
matter they are obliged to accuse us.   98 **overpeering of his
list**: towering above his bounds.

Than young Laertes, in a riotous head,   100
O'erbears your officers. The rabble call him lord;
And, as the world were now but to begin,
Antiquity forgot, custom not known,
The ratifiers and props of every word,
They cry, 'Choose we; Laertes shall be king!'   105
Caps, hands, and tongues, applaud it to the clouds,
'Laertes shall be king, Laertes king!'
   Queen. How cheerfully on the false trail they cry!
O! this is counter, you false Danish dogs!   109
   King. The doors are broke.   [*Noise within.*

      Enter LAERTES, *armed;* Danes *following.*

   Laertes. Where is the king? Sirs, stand you all without.
   Danes. No, let's come in.
   Laertes.   I pray you, give me leave.
   Danes. We will, we will.   [*They retire without the door.*
   Laertes. I thank you: keep the door. O thou vile king!
Give me my father.
   Queen.   Calmly, good Laertes.   115
   Laertes. That drop of blood that's calm proclaims me
     bastard,
Cries cuckold to my father, brands the harlot
Even here, between the chaste unsmirchéd brows
Of my true mother.
   King.   What is the cause, Laertes,
That thy rebellion looks so giant-like?   120
Let him go, Gertrude; do not fear our person:
There's such divinity doth hedge a king,

---

100 **head:** force, body.   102 **as:** as if.   103–4
i.e. prerogative and tradition which sanction and support every
pledge being ignored.   109 **counter:** in the opposite direction (a hunting term), i.e. rebellion.   116–19 i.e. my
mother was false to my father and I am no true son of his if I show
myself calm.

That treason can but peep to what it would,
Acts little of his will. Tell me, Laertes,
Why thou art thus incens'd. Let him go, Gertrude.   125
Speak, man.
   Laertes.   Where is my father?
   King.   Dead.
   Queen.   But not by him.
   King. Let him demand his fill.
   Laertes. How came he dead? I'll not be juggled with.
To hell, allegiance! vows, to the blackest devil!
Conscience and grace, to the profoundest pit!   130
I dare damnation. To this point I stand,
That both the worlds I give to negligence,
Let come what comes; only I'll be reveng'd
Most throughly for my father.
   King.   Who shall stay you?
   Laertes. My will, not all the world: 135
And for my means, I'll husband them so well,
They shall go far with little.
   King.   Good Laertes,
If you desire to know the certainty
Of your dear father's death, is 't writ in your revenge,
That, swoopstake, you will draw both friend and foe,   140
Winner and loser?
   Laertes. None but his enemies.
   King.   Will you know them then?
   Laertes. To his good friends thus wide I'll ope my arms;
And like the kind life-rendering pelican,
Repast them with my blood.
   King.   Why, now you speak   145
Like a good child and a true gentleman.

---

   123 **peep to:** take a hasty glance at.   124 **his:** its.   132 i.e.
I care nothing for this life or the next.   136 **husband:** manage
with economy.   140 **swoopstake:** in a clean sweep.   145
repast: feed (as the pelican her young).

That I am guiltless of your father's death,
And am most sensibly in grief for it,
It shall as level to your judgment pierce
As day does to your eye.
    Danes.   [*Within.*] Let her come in.   150
    Laertes. How now! what noise is that?

Re-enter OPHELIA.

O heat, dry up my brains! tears seven times salt,
Burn out the sense and virtue of mine eye!
By heaven, thy madness shall be paid by weight,
Till our scale turn the beam. O rose of May!   155
Dear maid, kind sister, sweet Ophelia!
O heavens! is 't possible a young maid's wits
Should be as mortal as an old man's life?
Nature is fine in love, and where 'tis fine
It sends some precious instance of itself   160
After the thing it loves.
    Ophelia.

           They bore him barefac'd on the bier;
           Hey non nonny, nonny, hey nonny;
           And in his grave rain'd many a tear;—

Fare you well, my dove!   165
    Laertes. Hadst thou thy wits, and didst persuade revenge,
It could not move thus.
    Ophelia.

           You must sing, a-down a-down,
           And you call him a-down-a.

O how the wheel becomes it! It is the false steward that
stole his master's daughter.   171
    Laertes. This nothing's more than matter.
    Ophelia. There's rosemary, that's for remembrance;

---

148 **sensibly**: feelingly.   160 **instance**: token [*N*].   170
the wheel [*N*].   172 i.e. this nonsense is more than sense.

pray, love, remember: and there is pansies, that's for
thoughts.   175

Laertes. A document in madness, thoughts and remembrance fitted.

Ophelia. There's fennel for you, and columbines;
there's rue for you; and here's some for me; we may
call it herb of grace o' Sundays. O! you must wear 180
your rue with a difference. There's a daisy; I would
give you some violets, but they withered all when my
father died. They say he made a good end,—

       For bonny sweet Robin is all my joy.

Laertes. Thought and affliction, passion, hell itself, 185
She turns to favour and to prettiness.

Ophelia.

      And will a' not come again?
       And will a' not come again?
        No, no, he is dead;
        Go to thy death-bed,   190
      He never will come again.
      His beard was as white as snow
      All flaxen was his poll,
        He is gone, he is gone,
        And we cast away moan: 195
      God ha' mercy on his soul!

And of all Christian souls I pray God. God be wi' ye!

                                       [*Exit.*

Laertes. Do you see this, O God?

King. Laertes, I must commune with your grief,
Or you deny me right. Go but apart,   200
Make choice of whom your wisest friends you will,
And they shall hear and judge 'twixt you and me.

---

176 document: lesson.   **180 herb of grace o' Sundays:** i.e.
by its second, more religious name.   **181 with a difference:**
for a different reason.   **185 thought:** melancholy. **passion:**
suffering. **hell:** spiritual torment.   **186 favour:** beauty.

If by direct or by collateral hand
They find us touch'd, we will our kingdom give,
Our crown, our life, and all that we call ours,   205
To you in satisfaction; but if not,
Be you content to lend your patience to us,
And we shall jointly labour with your soul
To give it due content.
 Laertes.   Let this be so:
His means of death, his obscure burial,   210
No trophy, sword, nor hatchment o'er his bones,
No noble rite nor formal ostentation,
Cry to be heard, as 'twere from heaven to earth,
That I must call 't in question.
 King.   So you shall;
And where the offence is let the great axe fall.   215
I pray you go with me.   [*Exeunt.*

Scene VI. ANOTHER ROOM IN THE SAME

Enter HORATIO *and a* Servant.

Horatio. What are they that would speak with me?
Servant. Sailors, sir: they say, they have letters for you.
Horatio. Let them come in. [*Exit* Servant.
I do not know from what part of the world
I should be greeted, if not from Lord Hamlet.   5

Enter Sailors.

First Sailor. God bless you, sir.
Horatio. Let him bless thee too.
Second Sailor. He shall, sir, an 't please him. There's a
letter for you, sir;—it comes from the ambassador that

 203 **collateral:** indirect. 204 **touch'd:** guilty. 211 **hatchment:** escutcheon. 212 **ostentation:** ceremony. 214 **that:**
so that.

was bound for England;—if your name be Horatio, as I
am let to know it is.   11

Horatio. Horatio, when thou shalt have overlooked this,
give these fellows some means to the king: they have letters
for him. Ere we were two days old at sea, a pirate of very
war-like appointment gave us chase. Finding ourselves too 15
slow of sail, we put on a compelled valour; in the grapple
I boarded them: on the instant they got clear of our ship,
so I alone became their prisoner. They have dealt with
me like thieves of mercy, but they knew what they did;
I am to do a good turn for them. Let the king have the 20
letters I have sent; and repair thou to me with as much haste
as thou wouldst fly death. I have words to speak in thine
ear will make thee dumb, yet are they much too light for the
bore of the matter. These good fellows will bring thee
where I am. Rosencrantz and Guildenstern hold their 25
course for England: of them I have much to tell thee.
Farewell.

> *He that thou knowest thine,*
>   *Hamlet.*

Come, I will give you way for these your letters;   30
And do 't the speedier, that you may direct me
To him from whom you brought them.   [*Exeunt.*

Scene VII. ANOTHER ROOM IN THE SAME

Enter KING *and* LAERTES.

King. Now must your conscience my acquittance seal,
And you must put me in your heart for friend,
Sith you have heard, and with a knowing ear,
That he which hath your noble father slain
Pursu'd my life.

---

13 **means:** means of access.   15 **appointment:** equipment.
19 **thieves of mercy:** merciful thieves.   24 **bore:** calibre.

Laertes.   It well appears: but tell me   5
Why you proceeded not against these feats,
So crimeful and so capital in nature,
As by your safety, wisdom, all things else,
You mainly were stirr'd up.
  King.   O! for two special reasons;
Which may to you, perhaps, seem much unsinew'd,   10
But yet to me they are strong. The queen his mother
Lives almost by his looks, and for myself,—
My virtue or my plague, be it either which,—
She's so conjunctive to my life and soul,
That, as the star moves not but in his sphere,   15
I could not but by her. The other motive,
Why to a public count I might not go,
Is the great love the general gender bear him;
Who, dipping all his faults in their affection,
Would, like the spring that turneth wood to stone,   20
Convert his gyves to graces; so that my arrows,
Too slightly timber'd for so loud a wind,
Would have reverted to my bow again,
And not where I had aim'd them.
  Laertes. And so have I a noble father lost;   25
A sister driven into desperate terms,
Whose worth, if praises may go back again,
Stood challenger on mount of all the age
For her perfections. But my revenge will come.
  King. Break not your sleeps for that; you must not think

6 **feats**: actions.   9 **mainly**: strongly.   10 **unsinew'd**:
feeble.   13 i.e. I know not whether to call my dependence
upon her a blessing or a curse.   14 **conjunctive**: closely united.
15 **sphere**: orbit.   17 **count**: account, trial.   18 **the general
gender**: the common sort.   21 **convert his gyves to graces**:
regard his fetters as an honour, not as a disgrace, i.e. make a martyr
of him.   22 **too slightly timber'd**: too light-weight.   27-9
i.e. should I praise her as she once was, her worth would challenge
the whole age.   28 **on mount**: conspicuously, for all to see.

That we are made of stuff so flat and dull   31
That we can let our beard be shook with danger
And think it pastime. You shortly shall hear more;
I lov'd your father, and we love ourself,
And that, I hope, will teach you to imagine.—   35

Enter a Messenger.

How now! what news?
  Messenger.   Letters, my lord, from Hamlet:
This to your majesty; this to the queen.
  King. From Hamlet! who brought them?
  Messenger. Sailors, my lord, they say; I saw them not:
They were given me by Claudio, he receiv'd them   40
Of him that brought them.
  King.   Laertes, you shall hear them.
Leave us.   [*Exit* Messenger.
  High and mighty, you shall know I am set naked on your
kingdom. To-morrow shall I beg leave to see your kingly
eyes; when I shall, first asking your pardon thereunto, recount
the occasions of my sudden and more strange return.   46
                        Hamlet.
What should this mean? Are all the rest come back?
Or is it some abuse and no such thing?
  Laertes. Know you the hand?
  King.   'Tis Hamlet's character. 'Naked,'   50
And in a postscript here, he says, 'alone.'
Can you advise me?
  Laertes. I'm lost in it, my lord. But let him come!
It warms the very sickness in my heart,
That I shall live and tell him to his teeth,   55
'Thus diddest thou.'
  King.   If it be so, Laertes,
As how should it be so? how otherwise?

---

    43 naked: destitute.   **49 abuse:** imposture, plot.   **57 it:**
Hamlet's return.

Will you be rul'd by me?

Laertes.   Ay, my lord;
So you will not o'er-rule me to a peace.

King. To thine own peace. If he be now return'd,   60
As checking at his voyage, and that he means
No more to undertake it, I will work him
To an exploit, now ripe in my device,
Under the which he shall not choose but fall;
And for his death no wind of blame shall breathe,   65
But even his mother shall uncharge the practice
And call it accident.

Laertes.   My lord, I will be rul'd;
The rather, if you could devise it so
That I might be the organ.

King.   It falls right.
You have been talk'd of since your travel much,   70
And that in Hamlet's hearing, for a quality
Wherein, they say, you shine; your sum of parts
Did not together pluck such envy from him
As did that one, and that, in my regard,
Of the unworthiest siege.

Laertes.   What part is that, my lord?   75

King. A very riband in the cap of youth,
Yet needful too; for youth no less becomes
The light and careless livery that it wears
Than settled age his sables and his weeds,
Importing health and graveness. Two months since   80
Here was a gentleman of Normandy:
I've seen myself, and serv'd against, the French,
And they can well on horseback; but this gallant

---

61 **checking at:** swerving from.   66 **uncharge the practice:**
acquit us of plotting.   75 **siege:** class (*lit.* seat, Fr. *siège*).
79 **sables:** furred gowns. **weeds:** distinctive garments.   80
importing health: denoting well-being.   83 **can well:** are
expert.

Had witchcraft in 't, he grew unto his seat,
And to such wondrous doing brought his horse,   85
As he had been incorps'd and demi-natur'd
With the brave beast; so far he topp'd my thought,
That I, in forgery of shapes and tricks,
Come short of what he did.

   Laertes.   A Norman was 't?

   King. A Norman.   90

   Laertes. Upon my life, Lamord.

   King.   The very same.

   Laertes. I know him well; he is the brooch indeed
And gem of all the nation.

   King. He made confession of you,
And gave you such a masterly report   95
For art and exercise in your defence,
And for your rapier most especially,
That he cried out, 'twould be a sight indeed
If one could match you; the scrimers of their nation,
He swore, had neither motion, guard, nor eye,   100
If you oppos'd them. Sir, this report of his
Did Hamlet so envenom with his envy
That he could nothing do but wish and beg
Your sudden coming o'er, to play with him.
Now, out of this,—

   Laertes.   What out of this, my lord?   105

   King. Laertes, was your father dear to you?
Or are you like the painting of a sorrow,
A face without a heart?

   Laertes.   Why ask you this?

   King. Not that I think you did not love your father,

---

86 i.e. like a Centaur, half-man, half-beast (**incorps'd**: made into one body with).   87–9 i.e. he outdid all I could have imagined in his feats and dexterity.   92 **brooch**: as we say, 'jewel'. 94 **confession**: unwilling acknowledgement.   99 **scrimers**: fencers (Fr. *escrimeur*).   100 **motion**: attack.

But that I know love is begun by time,   110
And that I see, in passages of proof,
Time qualifies the spark and fire of it.
There lives within the very flame of love
A kind of wick or snuff that will abate it,
And nothing is at a like goodness still,   115
For goodness, growing to a plurisy,
Dies in his own too-much. That we would do,
We should do when we would, for this 'would' changes,
And hath abatements and delays as many
As there are tongues, are hands, are accidents;   120
And then this 'should' is like a spendthrift sigh,
That hurts by easing. But, to the quick o' the ulcer;
Hamlet comes back; what would you undertake
To show yourself your father's son in deed
More than in words?
   Laertes.   To cut his throat i' the church.   125
  King. No place indeed should murder sanctuarize;
Revenge should have no bounds. But, good Laertes,
Will you do this, keep close within your chamber.
Hamlet return'd shall know you are come home;
We'll put on those shall praise your excellence,   130
And set a double varnish on the fame
The Frenchman gave you, bring you, in fine, together,
And wager on your heads: he, being remiss,
Most generous and free from all contriving,
Will not peruse the foils; so that, with ease   135
Or with a little shuffling, you may choose

---

110 **begun by time:** created by circumstances.   111 **pas-**
sages of proof: proved examples.   112 **qualifies:** moderates.
116 **plurisy:** excess, plethora.   117–22 i.e. we ought to put our
intentions into action at once. Otherwise we make excuses and
procrastinate and our duty is left undone, perhaps to our relief but
also to our peril.   121 **spendthrift:** wasteful [*N*].   126
murder sanctuarize: protect a murderer from vengeance.   133
remiss: careless.

A sword unbated, and, in a pass of practice
Requite him for your father.
   Laertes.   I will do 't;
And, for that purpose, I'll anoint my sword.
I bought an unction of a mountebank,   140
So mortal that, but dip a knife in it,
Where it draws blood no cataplasm so rare,
Collected from all simples that have virtue
Under the moon, can save the thing from death
That is but scratch'd withal; I'll touch my point   145
With this contagion, that, if I gall him slightly,
It may be death.
   King.   Let's further think of this;
Weigh what convenience both of time and means
May fit us to our shape. If this should fail,
And that our drift look through our bad performance 150
'Twere better not assay'd; therefore this project
Should have a back or second, that might hold,
If this should blast in proof. Soft! let me see;
We'll make a solemn wager on your cunnings:
I ha 't: 155
When in your motion you are hot and dry,—
As make your bouts more violent to that end,—
And that he calls for drink, I'll have prepar'd him
A chalice for the nonce, whereon but sipping,
If he by chance escape your venom'd stuck,   160
Our purpose may hold there. But stay! what noise?

Enter QUEEN.

How now, sweet queen!

137 **unbated:** unblunted.   **a pass of practice:** *both* a bout of exercise *and* a treacherous thrust.   140 **unction:** ointment.   **mounte-**
bank: quack.   142 **cataplasm:** plaster.   143 **simples:** herbs.
148-9 i.e. consider what occasion and means will best secure our purpose.   150 **drift:** plan.   153 **blast in proof:** miscarry in action.
159 **for the nonce:** for the occasion.   160 **stuck:** thrust.

Queen. One woe doth tread upon another's heel,
So fast they follow: your sister's drown'd, Laertes.
   Laertes. Drown'd! O, where?   165
   Queen. There is a willow grows aslant a brook,
That shows his hoar leaves in the glassy stream;
There with fantastic garlands did she come,
Of crow-flowers, nettles, daisies, and long purples,
That liberal shepherds give a grosser name,   170
But our cold maids do dead men's fingers call them:
There, on the pendent boughs her coronet weeds
Clambering to hang, an envious sliver broke,
When down her weedy trophies and herself
Fell in the weeping brook. Her clothes spread wide,   175
And, mermaid-like, awhile they bore her up;
Which time she chanted snatches of old lauds,
As one incapable of her own distress,
Or like a creature native and indu'd
Unto that element; but long it could not be   180
Till that her garments, heavy with their drink,
Pull'd the poor wretch from her melodious lay
To muddy death.
   Laertes.   Alas! then, she is drown'd?
   Queen. Drown'd, drown'd.
   Laertes. Too much of water hast thou, poor Ophelia,
And therefore I forbid my tears; but yet   186
It is our trick, nature her custom holds,
Let shame say what it will; when these are gone
The woman will be out. Adieu, my lord!
I have a speech of fire, that fain would blaze,   190

---

167 **hoar**: greyish-white.   169 **crow-flowers**: buttercups.
long purples: orchids.   170 **liberal**: free-spoken.   172
coronet weeds: garlands of flowers.   173 **sliver**: branch.
177 **lauds**: hymns of praise (to God) [*N*].   178 **incapable of**:
insensitive to.   179–80 **indu'd unto**: belonging to.   187 **trick**:
habit.   188–9 i.e. when these tears are shed I shall be rid of
womanish tenderness [*N*].

But that this folly douts it.   [*Exit.*
   King.   Let's follow, Gertrude.
How much I had to do to calm his rage!
Now fear I this will give it start again;
Therefore let's follow.   [*Exeunt.*

     191 **douts:** quenches (*lit.* do out).

ACT V

Scene I. A Churchyard

Enter two Clowns, *with spades and mattock.*

First Clown. Is she to be buried in Christian burial that
wilfully seeks her own salvation?

Second Clown. I tell thee she is: and therefore make her
grave straight: the crowner hath sat on her, and finds it
Christian burial.   5

First Clown. How can that be, unless she drowned herself in her own defence?

Second Clown. Why, 'tis found so.   8

First Clown. It must be *se offendendo;* it cannot be else.
For here lies the point: if I drown myself wittingly it
argues an act; and an act hath three branches; it is, to act,
to do, and to perform: argal, she drowned herself wittingly.

Second Clown. Nay, but hear you, goodman delver,—

First Clown. Give me leave. Here lies the water;
good: here stands the man; good: if the man go to this   15
water, and drown himself, it is, will he, nill he, he
goes; mark you that? but if the water come to him,
and drown him, he drowns not himself: argal, he that
is not guilty of his own death shortens not his own life.

Second Clown. But is this law?   20

First Clown. Ay, marry, is 't; crowner's quest law.

Second Clown. Will you ha' the truth on 't? If this had
not been a gentlewoman she should have been buried out
o' Christian burial.

First Clown. Why, there thou sayest; and the more   25
pity that great folk should have countenance in this

1–2 i.e. Is she to be laid in sanctified ground although she brought
about her own death? **4 straight:** straightway. **crowner:**
coroner. **finds:** brings a verdict of. **12 argal:** therefore
(Lat. *ergo*). **21 quest:** inquest. **25 there thou sayest:**
you say true.

world to drown or hang themselves more than their
even Christian. Come, my spade. There is no ancient
gentlemen but gardeners, ditchers, and grave-makers;
they hold up Adam's profession.   30

Second Clown. Was he a gentleman?

First Clown. A' was the first that ever bore arms.

Second Clown. Why, he had none.

First Clown. What! art a heathen? How dost thou
understand the Scripture? The Scripture says, Adam
digged; could he dig without arms? I'll put another
question to thee; if thou answerest me not to the purpose,
confess thyself—   38

Second Clown. Go to.

First Clown. What is he that builds stronger than either
the mason, the shipwright, or the carpenter?

Second Clown. The gallows-maker; for that frame out-
lives a thousand tenants.   43

First Clown. I like thy wit well, in good faith; the gallows does well, but how does it well? it does well to those
that do ill; now thou dost ill to say the gallows is built
stronger than the church: argal, the gallows may do well
to thee. To 't again; come.

Second Clown. Who builds stronger than a mason, a
shipwright, or a carpenter?   50

First Clown. Ay, tell me that, and unyoke.

Second Clown. Marry, now I can tell.

First Clown. To 't.

Second Clown. Mass, I cannot tell.   54

Enter HAMLET *and* HORATIO *at a distance.*

First Clown. Cudgel thy brains no more about it, for your
dull ass will not mend his pace with beating; and, when
you are asked this question next, say, 'a grave-maker:'

28 **even Christian:** fellow Christian.   51 **unyoke:** be done
with it; dismiss!   52 **now I can tell:** I know the answer.

the houses that he makes last till doomsday. Go, get thee
to Yaughan; fetch me a stoup of liquor.

> [*Exit Second* Clown.
> *First* Clown *digs, and sings.*

>> In youth, when I did love, did love,　　　60
>>> Methought it was very sweet,
>> To contract o' the time, for-a my behove,
>>> O! methought there was nothing meet.

Hamlet. Has this fellow no feeling of his business, that
he sings at grave-making?　　　65
Horatio. Custom hath made it in him a property of
easiness.
Hamlet. 'Tis e'en so; the hand of little employment hath
the daintier sense.
First Clown.

>> But age, with his stealing steps,　　　70
>>> Hath claw'd me in his clutch,
>> And hath shipped me intil the land,
>>> As if I had never been such.

> [*Throws up a skull.*

Hamlet. That skull had a tongue in it, and could sing
once; how the knave jowls it to the ground, as if it were
Cain's jaw-bone, that did the first murder! This might
be the pate of a politician, which this ass now o'er-reaches,
one that would circumvent God, might it not?　　　78
Horatio. It might, my lord.
Hamlet. Or of a courtier, which could say, 'Good morrow,
sweet lord! How dost thou, good lord?' This might be
my Lord Such-a-one, that praised my Lord Such-a-one's
horse, when he meant to beg it, might it not?
Horatio. Ay, my lord.　　　84

---

59 **stoup**: flagon.　　62 **contract**: marry [*N*].　　66–7 **a property of easiness**: naturally easy *or* a characteristic of indifference.
72 **intil**: into.　　75 **jowls**: dashes.　　77 **politician**: plotter.
o'er-reaches: gets the better of.

Hamlet. Why, e'en so, and now my Lady Worm's; chapless, and knocked about the mazzard with a sexton's spade. Here's fine revolution, an we had the trick to see't. Did these bones cost no more the breeding but to play at loggats with 'em? mine ache to think on 't.

First Clown.

<blockquote>
A pick-axe, and a spade, a spade,   90
  For and a shrouding sheet;
O! a pit of clay for to be made
  For such a guest is meet.
</blockquote>

                             [Throws up another skull.

Hamlet. There's another; why may not that be the skull of a lawyer? Where be his quiddities now, his 95 quillets, his cases, his tenures, and his tricks? why does he suffer this rude knave now to knock him about the sconce with a dirty shovel, and will not tell him of his action of battery? Hum! This fellow might be in's time a great buyer of land, with his statutes, 100 his recognizances, his fines, his double vouchers, his recoveries; is this the fine of his fines, and the recovery of his recoveries, to have his fine pate full of fine dirt? will his vouchers vouch him no more of his purchases, and double ones too, than the length and breadth of 105 a pair of indentures? The very conveyance of his lands will hardly lie in this box, and must the inheritor himself have no more, ha?

Horatio. Not a jot more, my lord.

Hamlet. Is not parchment made of sheep-skins? 110

---

85 **chapless:** jawless.　　86 **mazzard:** skull.　　87 **revolution:** turn of Fortune's wheel.　　89 **loggats:** skittles.　　95 **quiddities:** sophistries.　　96 **quillets:** subtleties.　　98 **sconce:** head.　　100–101 **statutes . . . recognizances:** terms in deeds of purchase.　　101 **vouchers:** witnesses.　　102 **recoveries:** processes of transfer. **fine of his fines:** end of his petitions.　　106 **pair of indentures:** contracts in duplicate.　　107 **inheritor:** possessor.

Horatio. Ay, my lord, and of calf-skins too.

Hamlet. They are sheep and calves which seek out assurance in that. I will speak to this fellow. Whose grave's this, sir?

First Clown. Mine, sir,   115

> O! a pit of clay for to be made
> For such a guest is meet.

Hamlet. I think it be thine, indeed; for thou liest in 't.

First Clown. You lie out on 't, sir, and therefore it is not yours; for my part, I do not lie in 't, and yet it is mine.   120

Hamlet. Thou dost lie in 't, to be in 't and say it is thine: 'tis for the dead, not for the quick; therefore thou liest.

First Clown. 'Tis a quick lie, sir; 'twill away again, from me to you.

Hamlet. What man dost thou dig it for?   125

First Clown. For no man, sir.

Hamlet. What woman, then?

First Clown. For none, neither.

Hamlet. Who is to be buried in 't?

First Clown. One that was a woman, sir; but, rest her soul, she's dead.   131

Hamlet. How absolute the knave is! we must speak by the card, or equivocation will undo us. By the Lord, Horatio, these three years I have taken note of it; the age is grown so picked that the toe of the   135 peasant comes so near the heel of the courtier, he galls his kibe. How long hast thou been a grave-maker?

First Clown. Of all the days i' the year, I came to 't that day that our last King Hamlet overcame Fortinbras.

Hamlet. How long is that since?   140

First Clown. Cannot you tell that? every fool can tell

---

113 **assurance:** security   **that:** i.e. parchment·   132 **absolute:** positive.   133 **by the card:** precisely (**card:** the mariner's compass-card).   **equivocation:** quibbling.   135 **picked:** fastidious, spruce.   137 **kibe:** chilblain.

that; it was the very day that young Hamlet was born;
he that is mad, and sent into England.

Hamlet. Ay, marry; why was he sent into England? 144

First Clown. Why, because he was mad: he shall recover
his wits there; or, if he do not, 'tis no great matter there.

Hamlet. Why?

First Clown. 'Twill not be seen in him there; there the
men are as mad as he.

Hamlet. How came he mad? 150

First Clown. Very strangely, they say.

Hamlet. How strangely?

First Clown. Faith, e'en with losing his wits.

Hamlet. Upon what ground?

First Clown. Why, here in Denmark; I have been sexton
here, man and boy, thirty years. 156

Hamlet. How long will a man lie i' the earth ere he rot?

First Clown. Faith, if he be not rotten before he die,—
as we have many pocky corses now-a-days, that will
scarce hold the laying in,—he will last you some eight year
or nine year; a tanner will last you nine year. 161

Hamlet. Why he more than another?

First Clown. Why, sir, his hide is so tanned with his trade
that he will keep out water a great while, and your water
is a sore decayer of your whoreson dead body. Here's a
skull now; this skull hath lain you i' the earth three-and-
twenty years. 167

Hamlet. Whose was it?

First Clown. A whoreson mad fellow's it was: whose do
you think it was? 170

Hamlet. Nay, I know not.

First Clown. A pestilence on him for a mad rogue! a'
poured a flagon of Rhenish on my head once. This same
skull, sir, was, sir, Yorick's skull, the king's jester.

Hamlet. This! 175

159 **pocky:** pock-marked.   165 **whoreson:** scurvy (*lit.* bastard).

First Clown. E'en that.

Hamlet. Let me see.—[*Takes the skull*.]—Alas! poor
Yorick. I knew him, Horatio; a fellow of infinite jest,
of most excellent fancy; he hath borne me on his back
a thousand times; and now, how abhorred in my 180
imagination it is! my gorge rises at it. Here hung
those lips that I have kissed I know not how oft.
Where be your gibes now? your gambols? your songs?
your flashes of merriment, that were wont to set the
table on a roar? Not one now, to mock your own grin- 185
ning? quite chapfallen? Now get you to my lady's
chamber, and tell her, let her paint an inch thick, to
this favour she must come; make her laugh at that.
Prithee, Horatio, tell me one thing.

Horatio. What's that, my lord? 190

Hamlet. Dost thou think Alexander looked o' this fashion
i' the earth?

Horatio. E'en so.

Hamlet. And smelt so? pah!   [*Puts down the skull.*

Horatio. E'en so, my lord. 195

Hamlet. To what base uses we may return, Horatio! Why
may not imagination trace the noble dust of Alexander,
till he find it stopping a bung-hole?

Horatio. 'Twere to consider too curiously, to consider so.

Hamlet. No, faith, not a jot; but to follow him thither 200
with modesty enough, and likelihood to lead it; as
thus: Alexander died, Alexander was buried, Alexander returneth into dust; the dust is earth; of earth
we make loam, and why of that loam, whereto he was
converted, might they not stop a beer-barrel? 205
  Imperious Cæsar, dead and turn'd to clay,

---

181 **gorge:** stomach (*lit.* throat). 186 **chapfallen:** (a) jaw-less,
(b) downcast.   188 **favour:** face, complexion. 199 **curiously:**
precisely.   201 i.e. without exaggeration and in all probability.
206 **imperious:** imperial.

Might stop a hole to keep the wind away:
O! that that earth, which kept the world in awe,
Should patch a wall to expel the winter's flaw.
But soft! but soft! aside: here comes the king.   210

Enter KING, QUEEN, LAERTES, *and a coffin with* Lords
attendant *and* Priest.

The queen, the courtiers: who is that they follow?
And with such maiméd rites? This doth betoken
The corse they follow did with desperate hand
Fordo its own life; 'twas of some estate.   214
Couch we awhile, and mark.   [*Retiring with* HORATIO.
  Laertes. What ceremony else?
  Hamlet.   That is Laertes,
A very noble youth: mark.
  Laertes. What ceremony else?
  First Priest. Her obsequies have been as far enlarg'd
As we have warrantise: her death was doubtful,   220
And, but that great command o'ersways the order,
She should in ground unsanctified have lodg'd
Till the last trumpet; for charitable prayers,
Shards, flints, and pebbles should be thrown on her;
Yet here she is allow'd her virgin crants,   225
Her maiden strewments, and the bringing home
Of bell and burial.
  Laertes. Must there no more be done?
  First Priest.   No more be done:
We should profane the service of the dead,
To sing sage requiem, and such rest to her   230
As to peace-parted souls.
  Laertes.   Lay her i' th'earth;
And from her fair and unpolluted flesh

209 **flaw**: gust.   220 **warrantise**: authority.   224 **shards**:
broken pots.   225 **crants**: wreaths (Germ. *Kranz*).
226 **maiden strewments**: flowers strewn on a girl's grave.
230 **sage**: solemn.   231 **peace-parted**: departed in peace.

May violets spring! I tell thee, churlish priest,
A ministering angel shall my sister be,
When thou liest howling.

    Hamlet.   What! the fair Ophelia?   235
    Queen. Sweets to the sweet: farewell! *[Scattering flowers.*
I hop'd thou shouldst have been my Hamlet's wife;
I thought thy bride-bed to have deck'd, sweet maid,
And not have strew'd thy grave.

    Laertes.   O! treble woe
Fall ten times treble on that cursèd head   240
Whose wicked deed thy most ingenious sense
Depriv'd thee of. Hold off the earth awhile,
Till I have caught her once more in mine arms.

                          [Leaps into the grave.
Now pile your dust upon the quick and dead,
Till of this flat a mountain you have made,   245
To o'ertop old Pelion or the skyish head
Of blue Olympus.

    Hamlet. [*Advancing.*] What is he whose grief
Bears such an emphasis? whose phrase of sorrow
Conjures the wandering stars, and makes them stand
Like wonder-wounded hearers? this is I,   250
Hamlet the Dane.   *[Leaps into the grave.*
    Laertes.   The devil take thy soul!

                          [Grapples with him.
    Hamlet. Thou pray'st not well.
I prithee, take thy fingers from my throat;
For though I am not splenetive and rash
Yet have I in me something dangerous,   255
Which let thy wisdom fear. Away thy hand!
    King. Pluck them asunder.
    Queen.   Hamlet! Hamlet!

---

    241 **most ingenious sense**: wits, understanding.   249 **the
wandering stars**: the planets.   254 **splenetive**: passionate,
easily angered.

All. Gentlemen,—
Horatio.   Good my lord, be quiet.
                    [*The* Attendants *part them, and they come out
                                             of the grave.*

Hamlet. Why, I will fight with him upon this theme
Until my eyelids will no longer wag.   260
   Queen. O my son! what theme?
   Hamlet. I lov'd Ophelia: forty thousand brothers
Could not, with all their quantity of love,
Make up my sum. What wilt thou do for her?
   King. O! he is mad, Laertes.   265
   Queen. For love of God, forbear him.
   Hamlet. 'Swounds, show me what thou'lt do:
Woo't weep? woo't fight? woo't fast? woo't tear thyself?
Woo't drink up eisel? eat a crocodile?
I'll do't. Dost thou come here to whine?   270
To outface me with leaping in her grave?
Be buried quick with her, and so will I:
And, if thou prate of mountains, let them throw
Millions of acres on us, till our ground,
Singeing his pate against the burning zone,   275
Make Ossa like a wart! Nay, an thou'lt mouth,
I'll rant as well as thou.
   Queen.   This is mere madness:
And thus a while the fit will work on him;
Anon as patient as the female dove,
When that her golden couplets are disclos'd,   280
His silence will sit drooping.
   Hamlet.   Hear you, sir;
What is the reason that you use me thus?
I lov'd you ever: but it is no matter;
Let Hercules himself do what he may,

268 woo't: wouldst thou.   **269 eisel:** vinegar.   **275 the
burning zone:** the sun.   **280** i.e. when her pair of yellow chicks
are hatched out.

The cat will mew and dog will have his day.   [*Exit.*

  King. I pray you, good Horatio, wait upon him.   286

[*Exit* HORATIO.

[*To* LAERTES.] Strengthen your patience in our last night's
    speech;

We'll put the matter to the present push.

Good Gertrude, set some watch over your son.

This grave shall have a living monument: 290

An hour of quiet shortly shall we see;

Till then, in patience our proceeding be.   [*Exeunt.*

Scene II. A HALL IN THE CASTLE

Enter HAMLET *and* HORATIO.

  Hamlet. So much for this, sir: now shall you see the
    other;

You do remember all the circumstance?

  Horatio. Remember it, my lord?

  Hamlet. Sir, in my heart there was a kind of fighting

That would not let me sleep; methought I lay   5

Worse than the mutines in the bilboes. Rashly,—

And prais'd be rashness for it, let us know,

Our indiscretion sometimes serves us well

When our deep plots do pall; and that should teach us

There's a divinity that shapes our ends,   10

Rough-hew them how we will.

  Horatio.   That is most certain.

  Hamlet. Up from my cabin,

My sea-gown scarf'd about me, in the dark

Groped I to find out them, had my desire,

Finger'd their packet, and in fine withdrew   15

288 **present push:** immediate trial.   290 **a living monument:** an enduring memorial.   6 **mutines in the bilboes:**
mutineers in shackles.   8 **indiscretion:** lack of judgement.
9 **pall:** fail.   15 **finger'd:** pilfered.

To mine own room again; making so bold—
My fears forgetting manners—to unseal
Their grand commission; where I found, Horatio,
O royal knavery! an exact command,
Larded with many several sorts of reasons   20
Importing Denmark's health, and England's too,
With, ho! such bugs and goblins in my life,
That, on the supervise, no leisure bated,
No, not to stay the grinding of the axe,
My head should be struck off.

   Horatio.   Is 't possible?   25

   Hamlet. Here's the commission: read it at more leisure.
But wilt thou hear me how I did proceed?

   Horatio. I beseech you.

   Hamlet. Being thus be-netted round with villanies,—
Ere I could make a prologue to my brains   30
They had begun the play,—I sat me down,
Devis'd a new commission, wrote it fair;
I once did hold it, as our statists do,
A baseness to write fair, and labour'd much
How to forget that learning; but, sir, now   85
It did me yeoman's service. Wilt thou know
The effect of what I wrote?

   Horatio.   Ay, good my lord.

   Hamlet. An earnest conjuration from the king,
As England was his faithful tributary,
As love between them like the palm should flourish,   40
As peace should still her wheaten garland wear,
And stand a comma 'tween their amities,
And many such-like 'As'es of great charge,

---

22 **bugs:** bogies.   23 **supervise:** first reading. **no leisure
bated:** no respite allowed.   30 **make a prologue to:** expound
the plot to.   31 **they:** my brains.   33 **statists:** statesmen.
42 **comma:** *either* link *or* a brief pause in their (so-called) friendly
relations.

That, on the view and knowing of these contents,
Without debatement further, more or less,   45
He should the bearers put to sudden death,
Not shriving-time allow'd.

  Horatio.   How was this seal'd?

  Hamlet. Why, even in that was heaven ordinant.
I had my father's signet in my purse,
Which was the model of that Danish seal;   50
Folded the writ up in form of the other,
Subscrib'd it, gave 't th' impression, plac'd it safely,
The changeling never known. Now, the next day
Was our sea-fight, and what to this was sequent
Thou know'st already.   55

  Horatio. So Guildenstern and Rosencrantz go to 't.

  Hamlet. Why, man, they did make love to this employ-
    ment;
They are not near my conscience; their defeat
Does by their own insinuation grow.
'Tis dangerous when the baser nature comes   60
Between the pass and fell-incenséd points
Of mighty opposites.

  Horatio.   Why, what a king is this!

  Hamlet. Does it not, thinks 't thee, stand me now upon—
He that hath kill'd my king and whor'd my mother,
Popp'd in between the election and my hopes,   65
Thrown out his angle for my proper life,
And with such cozenage—is 't not perfect conscience
To quit him with this arm? and is 't not to be damn'd
To let this canker of our nature come
In further evil?   70

48 **ordinant**: arranging matters (cf. l. 10).   50 **model**: copy.
52 **subscrib'd it, gave 't th' impression**: signed and sealed it.
57 **make love to**: ask for it, *as we say.*   59 **insinuation**:
currying of favour, intervention.   61 **pass**: thrust (of weapon).
62 **opposites**: adversaries.   63 i.e. is it not now my duty ...?
66 **my proper life**: even for my very life.

Horatio. It must be shortly known to him from England
What is the issue of the business there.

Hamlet. It will be short: the interim is mine;
And a man's life's no more than to say 'One.'
But I am very sorry, good Horatio,   75
That to Laertes I forgot myself;
For, by the image of my cause, I see
The portraiture of his: I'll court his favours:
But, sure, the bravery of his grief did put me
Into a towering passion.

Horatio.   Peace! who comes here?   80

Enter OSRIC.

Osric. Your lordship is right welcome back to Denmark.

Hamlet. I humbly thank you, sir. [*Aside to* HORATIO.]
Dost know this water-fly?

Horatio. [*Aside to* HAMLET.] No, my good lord.   84

Hamlet. [*Aside to* HORATIO.] Thy state is the more
gracious; for 'tis a vice to know him. He hath much land,
and fertile: let a beast be lord of beasts, and his crib shall
stand at the king's mess: 'tis a chough; but, as I say,
spacious in the possession of dirt.

Osric. Sweet lord, if your lordship were at leisure, I
should impart a thing to you from his majesty.   91

Hamlet. I will receive it, sir, with all diligence of spirit.
Put your bonnet to his right use; 'tis for the head.

Osric. I thank your lordship, 'tis very hot.

Ham. No, believe me, 'tis very cold; the wind is northerly.

Osric. It is indifferent cold, my lord, indeed.   96

Hamlet. But yet methinks it is very sultry and hot for
my complexion.

---

79 **bravery:** bravado.   83 **water-fly:** gnat.   87 **lord of
beasts:** i.e. any ass who owns enough cattle gets the entry at court.
88 **chough:** jackdaw (i.e. chatterer).   89 **spacious in the possession of dirt:** a landlord of many acres.

Osric. Exceedingly, my lord; it is very sultry, as 'twere, I cannot tell how. But, my lord, his majesty bade me signify to you that he has laid a great wager on your head. Sir, this is the matter,—   102

Hamlet. I beseech you, remember—

[HAMLET *moves him to put on his hat.*

Osric. Nay, good my lord; for mine ease, in good faith. Sir, here is newly come to court Laertes; believe 105 me, an absolute gentleman, full of most excellent differences, of very soft society and great showing; indeed, to speak feelingly of him, he is the card or calendar of gentry, for you shall find in him the continent of what part a gentleman would see.   110

Hamlet. Sir, his definement suffers no perdition in you; though, I know, to divide him inventorially would dizzy the arithmetic of memory, and yet but yaw neither, in respect of his quick sail. But, in the verity of extolment, I take him to be a soul of great 115 article; and his infusion of such dearth and rareness, as, to make true diction of him, his semblable is his mirror; and who else would trace him, his umbrage, nothing more.

Osric. Your lordship speaks most infallibly of him. 120

Hamlet. The concernancy, sir? why do we wrap the gentleman in our more rawer breath?

---

107 differences: marks of distinction.   **soft:** polite.   **108-9**
card or calendar of gentry: map or register of good breeding.
110 continent: container.   **part:** qualities.   **111-19** i.e. his
graces, sir, lose nothing in your specification of them.   To make a detailed inventory of them would puzzle a man's mental arithmetic and
yet lag behind his speedy progress.   To praise Laertes truly, I think
of him as a soul of great worth.   His essential quality is so valuable
and so rare that I can indeed compare him with nothing except his
own looking-glass: any other representation of him would be a mere
shadow, nothing more.   **121 the concernancy, sir?** i.e. but
what is all this about?   **122 rawer:** less refined.

Osric. Sir?

Horatio. Is 't not possible to understand in another tongue? You will do 't, sir, really.   125

Hamlet. What imports the nomination of this gentleman?

Osric. Of Laertes?

Horatio. His purse is empty already; all's golden words are spent.   130

Hamlet. Of him, sir.

Osric. I know you are not ignorant—

Hamlet. I would you did, sir; in faith, if you did, it would not much approve me. Well, sir.   134

Osr. You are not ignorant of what excellence Laertes is—

Hamlet. I dare not confess that, lest I should compare with him in excellence; but, to know a man well, were to know himself.

Osric. I mean, sir, for his weapon; but in the imputation laid on him by them in his meed, he's unfellowed.   140

Hamlet. What's his weapon?

Osric. Rapier and dagger.

Hamlet. That's two of his weapons; but, well.

Osric. The king, sir, hath wagered with him six Barbary horses; against the which he has imponed, 145 as I take it, six French rapiers and poniards, with their assigns, as girdle, hangers, and so: three of the carriages, in faith, are very dear to fancy, very responsive to the hilts, most delicate carriages, and of very liberal conceit.   150

124–5 **in another tongue:** in more direct language.   125 **you will do 't, sir, really:** you can tackle it, if you try.   133–4 **it would not much approve me:** your opinion would be no testimonial.   139 **imputation:** repute.   140 **by them in his meed:** those in his retinue (**meed:** pay).   145 **imponed:** staked.   147 **assigns:** appurtenances. **hangers:** straps attaching the rapier to the girdle.   148 **carriages:** hangers (154).   149–50 **of very liberal conceit:** of fanciful design.

Hamlet. What call you the carriages?

Horatio. I knew you must be edified by the margent, ere you had done.

Osric. The carriages, sir, are the hangers.

Hamlet. The phrase would be more germane to the 155
matter, if we could carry cannon by our sides; I would
it might be hangers till then. But, on; six Barbary
horses against six French swords, their assigns, and
three liberal-conceited carriages; that's the French
bet against the Danish. Why is this 'imponed,' as you 160
call it?

Osric. The king, sir, hath laid, sir, that in a dozen passes
between yourself and him, he shall not exceed you three
hits; he hath laid on twelve for nine, and it would come
to immediate trial, if your lordship would vouchsafe the
answer. 166

Hamlet. How if I answer no?

Osric. I mean, my lord, the opposition of your person in
trial. 169

Hamlet. Sir, I will walk here in the hall; if it please his
majesty, 'tis the breathing time of day with me; let the
foils be brought, the gentleman willing, and the king hold
his purpose, I will win for him an I can; if not, I will gain
nothing but my shame and the odd hits.

Osric. Shall I re-deliver you e'en so? 175

Hamlet. To this effect, sir; after what flourish your
nature will.

Osric. I commend my duty to your lordship.

Hamlet. Yours, yours. [*Exit* osric.] He does well to
commend it himself; there are no tongues else for 's turn.

152 **edified:** enlightened. **margent:** margin (i.e. explanatory
note).   155 **germane:** appropriate.   164 **he:** Laertes [*N*].
165–6 **vouchsafe the answer:** accept the challenge.   171
breathing time: time of exercise.   174 **the odd hits:** any
successful hits I may chance to make.   179 **yours, yours:**
i.e. at your service.

Horatio. This lapwing runs away with the shell on his head.

Hamlet. He did comply with his dug before he sucked   182
it. Thus has he—and many more of the same bevy,
that I know the drossy age dotes on—only got the
tune of the time and outward habit of encounter, a   185
kind of yesty collection which carries them through and
through the most fond and winnowed opinions; and
do but blow them to their trial, the bubbles are out.

Enter a Lord.

Lord. My lord, his majesty commended him to you by
young Osric, who brings back to him, that you attend him
in the hall; he sends to know if your pleasure hold to play
with Laertes, or that you will take longer time.   192

Hamlet. I am constant to my purposes; they follow the
king's pleasure: if his fitness speaks, mine is ready; now,
or whensoever, provided I be so able as now.

Lord. The king, and queen, and all are coming down.

Hamlet. In happy time.   197

Lord. The queen desires you to use some gentle entertainment to Laertes before you fall to play.

Hamlet. She well instructs me.   [*Exit* Lord.

Horatio. You will lose this wager, my lord.   201

Hamlet. I do not think so; since he went into France,
I have been in continual practice; I shall win at the odds.
But thou wouldst not think how ill all's here about my
heart; but it is no matter.   205

Horatio. Nay, good my lord,—

Hamlet. It is but foolery; but it is such a kind of gain-
giving as would perhaps trouble a woman.

182 **comply with:** observe the formalities of ceremony.   183
bevy: covey.   184 **drossy:** frivolous.   185 **tune of the**
time: fashionable jargon. **encounter:** address, compliment.   186
yesty: frothy.   187 **winnowed:** sifted [*N*].   203 **at the**
odds: with the advantage given me (*see* ll. 162–4 [*N*]).   207
gain-giving: misgiving (cf. gainsay).

Horatio. If your mind dislike any thing, obey it; I will
forestal their repair hither, and say you are not fit.   210

Hamlet. Not a whit, we defy augury; there's a special
providence in the fall of a sparrow. If it be now, 'tis not
to come; if it be not to come, it will be now; if it be not
now, yet it will come: the readiness is all. Since no man
has aught of what he leaves, what is 't to leave betimes?
Let be.   216

Enter KING, QUEEN, LAERTES, Lords, OSRIC, *and*
Attendants *with foils, &c.*

King. Come, Hamlet, come, and take this hand from me.
[*The* KING *puts the hand of* LAERTES *into*
that of HAMLET.

Hamlet. Give me your pardon, sir; I've done you wrong;
But pardon 't, as you are a gentleman.
This presence knows, and you must needs have heard,   220
How I am punish'd with a sore distraction.
What I have done
That might your nature, honour and exception
Roughly awake, I here proclaim was madness.
Was 't Hamlet wrong'd Laertes? Never Hamlet;   225
If Hamlet from himself be ta'en away,
And when he's not himself does wrong Laertes,
Then Hamlet does it not; Hamlet denies it.
Who does it then? His madness. If 't be so,
Hamlet is of the faction that is wrong'd;   230
His madness is poor Hamlet's enemy.
Sir, in this audience,
Let my disclaiming from a purpos'd evil
Free me so far in your most generous thoughts,
That I have shot mine arrow o'er the house,   235

211 **augury:** foreboding.   215 **leave betimes:** die young.
223 **exception:** distaste.   235 **that:** as if, *or* in that.

And hurt my brother.

Laertes.   I am satisfied in nature,
Whose motive, in this case, should stir me most
To my revenge; but in my terms of honour
I stand aloof, and will no reconcilement,
Till by some elder masters, of known honour,   240
I have a voice and precedent of peace,
To keep my name ungor'd. But till that time,
I do receive your offer'd love like love,
And will not wrong it.

Hamlet.   I embrace it freely;
And will this brother's wager frankly play.   245
Give us the foils. Come on.

Laertes.   Come, one for me.

Hamlet. I'll be your foil, Laertes; in mine ignorance
Your skill shall, like a star i' the darkest night,
Stick fiery off indeed.

Laertes.   You mock me, sir.

Hamlet. No, by this hand.   250

King. Give them the foils, young Osric. Cousin Hamlet,
You know the wager?

Hamlet.   Very well, my lord;
Your Grace hath laid the odds o' the weaker side.

King. I do not fear it; I have seen you both;
But since he is better'd, we have therefore odds.   255

Laertes. This is too heavy; let me see another.

Hamlet. This likes me well. These foils have all a length?

Osric. Ay, my good lord.   [*They prepare to play.*

King. Set me the stoups of wine upon that table.
If Hamlet give the first or second hit,   260

236 **nature**: natural affection.   240–2 i.e. until I receive an
authoritative decision justified by precedent to preserve my honour.
245 **frankly**: i.e. without ill feeling.   247 **foil**: i.e. a foil to your
skill as a fencer.   249 **stick fiery off**: stand out brightly.
253 **laid the odds**: backed, betted on (cf. 255, *for which see* l. 203).
255 **better'd**: improved by training.

Or quit in answer of the third exchange,
Let all the battlements their ordnance fire;
The king shall drink to Hamlet's better breath;
And in the cup an union shall he throw,
Richer than that which four successive kings   265
In Denmark's crown have worn. Give me the cups;
And let the kettle to the trumpet speak,
The trumpet to the cannoneer without,
The cannons to the heavens, the heavens to earth,
'Now the king drinks to Hamlet!' Come, begin;   270
And you, the judges, bear a wary eye.

Hamlet. Come on, sir.

Laertes.   Come, my lord.   *[They play.*

Hamlet.   One.

Laertes.   No.

Hamlet.   Judgment.

Osric. A hit, a very palpable hit.

Laertes.   Well; again.

King. Stay; give me drink. Hamlet, this pearl is thine;
Here's to thy health. Give him the cup.   275
       [Trumpets sound; and cannon shot off within.

Hamlet. I'll play this bout first; set it by awhile.
Come.—*[They play.]* Another hit; what say you?

Laertes. A touch, a touch, I do confess.

King. Our son shall win.

Queen.   He's fat, and scant of breath.
Here, Hamlet, take my napkin, rub thy brows;   280
The queen carouses to thy fortune, Hamlet

Hamlet. Good madam!

King.   Gertrude, do not drink.

Queen. I will, my lord; I pray you, pardon me.

King. *[Aside.]* It is the poison'd cup! it is too late.

---

  261 **quit in answer:** score a return hit.   264 **an union:** a
large pearl.   267 **kettle:** kettle-drum.   279 **fat:** puffed, out
of condition, *or* sweaty. ·   280 **napkin:** handkerchief.

Hamlet. I dare not drink yet, madam; by and by.   285
Queen. Come, let me wipe thy face.
Laertes. My lord, I'll hit him now.
King.   I do not think 't.
Laertes. [*Aside.*] And yet 'tis almost 'gainst my con-
science.
Hamlet. Come, for the third, Laertes. You but dally;
I pray you, pass with your best violence.   290
I am afeard you make a wanton of me.
Laertes. Say you so? come on.   [*They play.*
Osric. Nothing, neither way.
Laertes. Have at you now.
            [LAERTES *wounds* HAMLET; *then, in scuffling, they*
                change rapiers, and HAMLET *wounds* LAERTES.
King.   Part them! they are incens'd.
Hamlet. Nay, come, again.   [*The* QUEEN *falls.*
Osric.   Look to the queen there, ho!   295
Horatio. They bleed on both sides. How is it, my lord?
Osric. How is it, Laertes?
Laertes. Why, as a woodcock to mine own springe, Osric;
I am justly kill'd with mine own treachery.
Hamlet. How does the queen?
King.   She swounds to see them bleed.   300
Queen. No, no, the drink, the drink,—O my dear Hamlet!
The drink, the drink; I am poison'd.   [*Dies.*
Hamlet. O villany! Ho! let the door be lock'd:
Treachery! seek it out.   [LAERTES *falls.*
Laertes. It is here, Hamlet. Hamlet, thou art slain;   305
No medicine in the world can do thee good;
In thee there is not half an hour of life;
The treacherous instrument is in thy hand,
Unbated and envenom'd. The foul practice
Hath turn'd itself on me; lo! here I lie,   810

---

290 **pass:** thrust.   291 **make a wanton:** trifle with.   298
springe: snare.   309 **practice:** plot, treachery.

Never to rise again. Thy mother's poison'd.
I can no more. The king, the king's to blame.
   Hamlet. The point envenom'd too!—
Then, venom, to thy work.   [*Stabs the* KING.
   All. Treason! treason!   315
   King. O! yet defend me, friends; I am but hurt.
   Hamlet. Here, thou incestuous, murderous, damnéd Dane,
Drink off this potion;—is thy union here?
Follow my mother.   [KING *dies.*
   Laertes.   He is justly serv'd;
It is a poison temper'd by himself.   320
Exchange forgiveness with me, noble Hamlet:
Mine and my father's death come not upon thee,
Nor thine on me!   [*Dies.*
   Hamlet. Heaven make thee free of it! I follow thee.
I am dead, Horatio. Wretched queen, adieu!   325
You that look pale and tremble at this chance,
That are but mutes or audience to this act,
Had I but time,—as this fell sergeant, death,
Is strict in his arrest,—O! I could tell you—
But let it be. Horatio, I am dead;   330
Thou liv'st; report me and my cause aright
To the unsatisfied.
   Horatio.   Never believe it;
I am more an antique Roman than a Dane:
Here's yet some liquor left.
   Hamlet.   As thou'rt a man,
Give me the cup: let go; by heaven, I'll have 't.   335
O God! Horatio, what a wounded name,
Things standing thus unknown, shall live behind me.
If thou didst ever hold me in thy heart,

---

   324 **make thee free:** acquit thee.   327 **mutes or audience:**
silent spectators.   328 **sergeant:** sheriff's officer.   333 **an
antique Roman:** (and therefore ready to commit suicide).   336
wounded name: tarnished reputation.

Absent thee from felicity awhile,
And in this harsh world draw thy breath in pain,   340
To tell my story.   [*March afar off, and shot within.*
              What war-like noise is this?
  Osr. Young Fortinbras, with conquest come from Poland,
To the ambassadors of England gives
This war-like volley.
  Hamlet.   O! I die, Horatio;
The potent poison quite o'er-crows my spirit: 345
I cannot live to hear the news from England,
But I do prophesy the election lights
On Fortinbras: he has my dying voice;
So tell him, with the occurrents, more and less,
Which have solicited—The rest is silence.   [*Dies.*
  Horatio. Now cracks a noble heart. Good-night, sweet
      prince,   351
And flights of angels sing thee to thy rest!
Why does the drum come hither?   [*March within.*

Enter FORTINBRAS, *the English* Ambassadors, *and Others.*

  Fortinbras. Where is this sight?
  Horatio.   What is it ye would see?
If aught of woe or wonder, cease your search.   355
  Fortinbras. This quarry cries on havoc. O proud death!
What feast is toward in thine eternal cell,
That thou so many princes at a shot
So bloodily hast struck?
  First Ambassador.   The sight is dismal;
And our affairs from England come too late: 360
The ears are senseless that should give us hearing,

345 **o'er-crows**: triumphs over.   349 **the occurrents, more
and less**: the incidents, great and small.   350 **solicited**:
incited me to.   356 **quarry**: heap of slain.   **cries on**: cries
aloud, proclaims.   **havoc**: indiscriminate slaughter.   357
toward: imminent.   **eternal cell**: the grave.

To tell him his commandment is fulfill'd,
That Rosencrantz and Guildenstern are dead.
Where should we have our thanks?
 Horatio.   Not from his mouth,
Had it the ability of life to thank you: 865
He never gave commandment for their death.
But since, so jump upon this bloody question,
You from the Polack wars, and you from England,
Are here arriv'd, give order that these bodies
High on a stage be placéd to the view;   870
And let me speak to the yet unknowing world
How these things came about: so shall you hear
Of carnal, bloody, and unnatural acts,
Of accidental judgments, casual slaughters;
Of deaths put on by cunning and forc'd cause, 875
And, in this upshot, purposes mistook
Fall'n on the inventors' heads; all this can I
Truly deliver.
 Fortinbras. Let us haste to hear it,
And call the noblest to the audience.
For me, with sorrow I embrace my fortune; 880
I have some rights of memory in this kingdom,
Which now to claim my vantage doth invite me.
 Horatio. Of that I shall have also cause to speak,
And from his mouth whose voice will draw on more:
But let this same be presently perform'd, 885
Even while men's minds are wild, lest more mischance
On plots and errors happen.
 Fortinbras.   Let four captains

---

367 **jump upon:** at the very moment of. 373 **carnal:** lustful (Claudius and Gertrude). 374 **accidental judgments:** mistakes of judgement (i.e. Ophelia's madness). **casual:** chance (Polonius's death). 375 **put on:** instigated. 376 **in this upshot:** this final result. 381 **of memory:** not unforgotten. 384 **voice:** *see* l. 348. **more:** i.e. to your advantage. 387 **on:** on top of.

Bear Hamlet, like a soldier, to the stage;
For he was likely, had he been put on,
To have prov'd most royally: and, for his passage,   390
The soldiers' music and the rites of war
Speak loudly for him.
Take up the bodies: such a sight as this
Becomes the field, but here shows much amiss.
Go, bid the soldiers shoot.   395

      [A dead march. Exeunt, bearing off the bodies;
         after which a peal of ordnance is shot off.

389 **put on**: set to the work of a king.   390 **passage**: passing.

NOTES

Q 1 = the first Quarto, published in 1603 and known as the 'Bad' Quarto.

Q 2 = the second Quarto of 1604, known as the 'Good' Quarto.

F = the first Folio of 1623, the first collected edition of the plays. References to other plays are made to the Oxford Shakespeare in one volume.

ACT I, SCENE I

The first Act consists of five scenes (but scenes iv and v are really one) and it serves to lay the foundations of the whole action of the play. It is a first movement, a prologue, an act of exposition. It sets before us (besides Hamlet himself) three things out of which the play is made. First, the Ghost; secondly, Claudius; thirdly, the Polonius family. The Ghost, like the Witches in *Macbeth*, supplies the encompassing *atmosphere*, at once religious and supernatural. Claudius, the usurper of the throne and the seducer of the Queen, is Hamlet's opposite and adversary; this is the play's *theme* of revenge. The Polonius family supply the detail of the *plot*, that is to say, the situations and intrigues, the mechanism by which the *theme* is kept in motion. For Polonius and Laertes and Ophelia are all instruments or tools in the hand of Claudius, and Hamlet's love of Ophelia and trust in Laertes are two weak points in his armour of which Claudius makes the most.

The other play in which Shakespeare devotes a whole act to exposition or preparation for the action is *Othello*.

The atmosphere evoked by the first scene is very powerful: the bitter cold, the sense of anxiety and expectation and mystery, the talk of war-like preparation, of Norway and of young Fortinbras with his band of lawless resolutes, the reference to portents and prodigies in the high and palmy state of Rome before the murder of Caesar, the re-appearance of the Ghost, its silence and majesty—all these combine to prepare the audience for tragedy on the grand scale. And then with the crowing of the cock the dawn breaks in the east and the soldiers dismiss to impart what they have seen to the young prince.

Note the indications of different types even among these minor figures. Francisco is sick at heart. Bernardo is on edge; he gives the challenge instead of Francisco, the sentinel on guard, and he is anxious not to be left alone. Horatio's mood is different. He is sceptical and humorous (l. 19). Marcellus strikes us as a more gentle soldier in his reverence for the apparition. To him also are given the beautiful lines (157–64) about the holy and gracious season of Christmas when no spirits stir abroad.

3. Long live the king! Dramatic irony.

19. A piece of him. Horatio perhaps feels pinched by the cold and hugs himself as he gives this jesting reply.

21. What! has this thing. F and Q 1 give this to Marcellus, but it is more suited to the disbelieving Horatio to whom it is assigned by Q 2. Marcellus's next speech then follows more naturally.

23. Horatio is a student and a scholar. His attitude to ghosts is that of Reginald Scot's 'Discourse upon Divels and Spirits' in *The Discoverie of Witchcraft*, 1584.

33. two nights. 'The play opens on the eve of the coronation and marriage of Claudius; and the Ghost begins to walk three days before the ceremony' (Dover Wilson).

36. westward from the pole: a planet west of the Polar star.

42. a scholar: i.e. Horatio can speak Latin and thus exorcise any evil spirit. Cf. Beaumont and Fletcher, *The Night Walker*, II. i:

> Let's call the butler up, for he speaks Latin,
> And that would daunt the devil.

47. In earlier plays the traditional Ghost wore a sheet or a leather jacket. Hamlet's father appears 'in arms', which makes his son suspect foul play. In III. iv he appears in the Queen's bedchamber 'in his habit as he lived', according to Q 1 his night-gown or dressing-gown.

93. co-mart. F reads Cou'nant (covenant). Co-mart (Q 2) only occurs here.

108–25. These lines are omitted in F and were presumably a 'cut'.

117. As stars, &c. Either we must assume that a line has been lost or some re-arrangement is necessary. Dover Wilson follows Q 2 and reverses the order of the two passages 117–21 and 122–5. A solar eclipse and two total eclipses of the moon were to be seen in 1598.

120. **almost to doomsday.** 'At the second coming of Christ "the moon shall not give her light" (Matthew xxiv. 29)' (Herford).

127. **I'll cross it.** To cross the path of a demon might cause death. Q 2 gives the stage direction 'It spreads his arms'. Dover Wilson thinks that 'it' is a mis-reading for 'he' and refers to Horatio barring the Ghost's way, but it may describe a gesture of the Ghost.

153. **Whether in sea or fire.** 'According to the pneumatology of that time, every element was inhabited by its peculiar order of spirits. The meaning therefore is, that all *spirits extravagant*, wandering out of their element, return to their proper limits, in which they are confined' (Dr. Johnson).

ACT I, SCENE II

Claudius, with the aid of his Prime Minister, Polonius, has won over the Lords of the Council to accept his usurpation of the throne as the Consort of Gertrude, his 'imperial jointress'. Dover Wilson, following the stage direction of Q 2, has revealed that this is a meeting of the Privy Council, the first since the double event of the royal marriage and coronation, to transact matters of foreign policy, to dispatch ambassadors, and to announce Hamlet as next in succession to the throne. We see Claudius as a skilful and smooth diplomatist, gracious to Laertes, the son of the Minister to whom he owes much, and with a sharp eye on his nephew who enters last in the procession and stands apart, a black blot and reproach to this easy-going, self-loving court.

The scene is a striking contrast of warmth and light and colour after the frosty air, the starry sky, the lonely sentinel, the ringing pass-word, the anxious questionings, and the ghostly knight-at-arms of the preceding scene.

As soon as the Queen has won an obedient word from her son Claudius breaks up the Council in triumph and Hamlet is left alone. He bursts out into the first of the soliloquies which brings home to us that it is not his father's death only but his mother's inconstancy and 'incestuous' re-marriage which have broken his heart and sickened him with all the uses of the world, most of all with the falsity of womankind.

65. **A little more than kin.** The Prince's first words are enigmatic, a quibble revealing a mood of bitter irony. He is more than a cousin and less than a son. 'Kind' is the contemporary word for

'nature'; e.g. in *All's Well* 'Your cuckoo sings by kind'. Goneril and Regan are unkind, or unnatural, daughters. Hamlet has no feeling of *kindness* to his uncle, who has, by marrying Gertrude, become his *unnatural* father.

67. too much i' the sun. Q 2 reads 'in the sonne' and it seems that the Prince is punning once more. He objects to being called son by Claudius under cover of the phrase 'i' the sun', which may either be interpreted literally as 'too much in the sunshine of court favour' or according to a proverb of the time ('Out of God's blessing into the warm sun') as meaning homeless, fallen from high estate.

76–84. Are not these lines a reproach levelled at his mother for her *seeming* grief at his father's funeral? Cf. 'The funeral baked meats did coldly furnish forth the marriage tables'.

113. school in Wittenberg: i.e. the university of Wittenberg, in Saxony, founded 1502, 'Luther's university, indicating that Hamlet was of Protestant upbringing' (Dover Wilson).

129. O! that this too too solid flesh. This is the reading of F which editors have always followed. But Q 1 reads 'too much griev'd and sallied'; Q 2 'too too sallied'. In II. i. 39 'sallies' is misprinted for 'sullies' (i.e. 'stains', 'defilement'). The metaphor of stained and besmirched snow would be more in keeping with the line that follows ('thaw') and with the whole soliloquy.

140. Hyperion: one of the Titans and father of Helios, the sun, but identified with Helios as the sun-god from Homer's time.

149. Niobe. Like Rachel mourning for her children, she is a symbol of maternal grief. Her seven sons and seven daughters were slain by Apollo and Artemis because she boasted of them, and Zeus in answer to her prayers transformed her into a weeping stone.

157. incestuous. Because Gertrude had married the brother of her dead husband. Such a marriage was incestuous in the eyes of both the Catholic and Protestant Churches and it is one of the chief causes of the Prince's horror and sick disgust.

169. A truant disposition. Horatio uses the same cheerful, jesting tone as on his first appearance in scene i.

224, 236. Indeed, indeed, sirs ... very like, very like. These repetitions are characteristic of the Prince. With this rapid interchange of dialogue the scene gathers speed and moves forward to the climax of the Prince's resolve: 'I will watch tonight.'

243. **If it assume.** Hamlet realizes that the Ghost may be a devil sent to tempt him.

ACT I, Scene III

Yet another contrast. From ghostly battlements at dead of night and affairs of state in the royal palace we pass to a domestic scene, intimate and private, 'a conversation piece' which serves to under-line even more the loneliness of the Prince's position and his loss of home affections. And now Ophelia, whom he loves, is warned both by her brother and her father to withdraw her sympathy, not to believe his vows, not to give words or talk with him. And she obeys. 'Frailty, thy name is woman.'

The family of Polonius have their own tragic story in the play. In a way they reflect and reinforce the main theme just as the Gloucester story reflects and reinforces that of Lear. Laertes is an illuminating contrast to Hamlet; he is 'a very noble youth'; he loves Ophelia, whose happiness he thinks the Prince may destroy, just as Hamlet loved Gertrude; he has to avenge the murder of his father by his sister's lover; Hamlet avenges the murder of his father by his mother's second husband.

Again the scene is important as establishing for us the person of Laertes and his family affections. He is now to leave the stage until the fifth scene of the fourth Act, when he will return to play an essential part as the tool of Claudius and the adversary of the Prince. Polonius by his spying and intrigue is to keep the play in motion until his death, which is the turning-point in the action. Finally this scene sketches in the delicate outline of Ophelia, who is to show us another side of Hamlet and who shares with Gertrude the second theme of the play, the nature of women.

21. **safety.** F reads 'sanctity'; Q 2 'safty'. Dover Wilson (follow-ing Theobald) reads 'sanity', meaning welfare, soundness.

58. **these few precepts.** Such precepts were common in Elizabethan literature and life, for instance Lyly's *Euphues* and the precepts left by Burleigh and Sir Henry Sidney for their sons. 'Every pre-cept is hedged with caution and pointed with self-interest' (Dover Wilson).

74. **Are.** Or (Q 2). F and Q 1 read 'Are'. The three texts all read, 'of a most select and generous, chief in that.' The text is corrupt. A possible emendation is 'choice' for 'chief' (Collier).

130. **bonds.** It is not necessary to adopt Theobald's emendation 'bawds'.

ACT I, Scene IV

'The scene is begun (as was the first scene) by a brisk, picturesque exchange, which sets us again (this time more easily) in the midnight darkness and cold. Then Shakespeare unexpectedly changes the subject. We have in Q 2

A florish of trumpets and 2 peeces goes of

and, for explanation, the verbal picture of the oblivious King, keeping wassail, drinking deep, reeling the 'swaggering up-spring' in comfortable warmth and light; a contrast heightening the effect of the cloaked, close-standing, nervously expectant three' (Granville Barker).

8–38. These lines are not in F; they may have been omitted for fear of offending Anne of Denmark, Queen to James I, but the passage is one which can be spared in an acting version. Its chief interest lies in the thoughts which rise to Hamlet's mind. When he speaks of a virtuous man whose good qualities may be marred by 'the o'ergrowth of some complexion' and vitiated by a defect of nature or by ill luck, he is surely thinking of himself and his own character. Dover Wilson suggests that the 'judicious' in the audience would have applied the lines in 1601 to the ill-fated Earl of Essex.

36. **evil.** Q 2 reads 'eale'. Shakespeare probably wrote 'eule', i.e. 'evil'. Elsewhere 'deule' and 'deale' are misprints for 'devil'.

37. **often dout.** Q 2 reads 'of a doubt'. The best emendation of this famous textual difficulty is 'often dout'; 'dout' means 'quench'. Cf. 'But that this folly douts it' (iv. vii. 192).

38. The entry of the Ghost comes with the same dramatic surprise as in scene i, when it interrupts Horatio's narrative. Suspense and surprise are the secret of effective drama and are powerfully and continually employed by Shakespeare in his mature plays.

83. **the Nemean lion.** The killing of it was the first of the labours of Hercules.

ACT I, Scene V

There should be no division or break between this and the preceding scene. The Folio text of *Hamlet* has some scene division, but this is the invention of the eighteenth-century editor. Our modern editions, with such directions as 'Another part of the platform', are misleading. The

Elizabethan stage was unlocalized, and scene dissolved into scene
with the fluid continuity to which we are accustomed in the cinema.
We can suppose that the Ghost disappeared by one of the side doors,
followed by Hamlet, and after a brief interchange to keep up the
tension Horatio and Marcellus disappear into the darkness and the
Ghost and Hamlet return, perhaps on the inner stage. The 'business'
of the beckoning enables the dramatist to clear the stage so that
father and son can re-enter alone.

In this last scene of the first movement we come to the first great
climax, elaborately prepared for, when Claudius's crime is revealed
and the dread command is laid upon the young Prince. The foundations of the play are sealed by the couplet:

> The time is out of joint. O curséd spite,
> That ever I was born to set it right!

Hamlet at once realizes both his duty and his incapacity.

11. fast in fires: the punishment inflicted in Dante's *Purgatorio* on
those guilty of the sin of gluttony.

33. Lethe wharf. The bank of Lethe, the river of forgetfulness in
the hell of classical mythology.

45–57. This almost certainly informs Hamlet of his mother's infidelity
while his father still lived.

62. hebona. (Q 1, 2.) F reads 'Hebenon'. Shakespeare may mean
henbane, or ebony, or yew. Cf. 'The juice of hebon and Cocytus'
breath' (Marlowe, *Jew of Malta*, iii. 271).

84–8. Hamlet's task is made far harder by the injunction that his
mother is not to suffer. His mother's 'o'er-hasty marriage' and (as
the Ghost now suggests) her adultery (42–52) are more terrible and
agonizing to Hamlet even than his father's murder.

107–8. Hamlet the student takes out his ivory tablets to note down
that a man may smile and be a villain. Cf. the description of Sinon
in *The Rape of Lucrece*, stanzas ccxvi–ccxxi, and the 'honesty' of
Iago. For the remainder of the scene he is on the verge of hysteria,
concealing his agony of mind in rapid broken phrases and apparent
jesting. A similar effect on a larger scale is to be found in *King
Lear* in the hovel scene when the King has lost his wits and Edgar
affects madness and the Fool intersperses snatches of song.

111. Hamlet perhaps kisses the hilt of his sword before the words
'I have sworn 't'.

116. Hillo, ho, ho, boy! Hamlet mockingly echoes Marcellus with a falconer's call.

136. St. Patrick. It was given out that a serpent stung Hamlet's father, the serpent who now wears his crown. St. Patrick banished serpents from Ireland and is therefore invoked (Dowden). St. Patrick also is the Keeper of Purgatory.

136–42. Dover Wilson points out that the first lines are an aside to Horatio who will learn the truth later. Hamlet then turns to the others and swears them to silence.

147. Upon my sword. The handle and blade form a cross on which the name 'Jesus' was sometimes inscribed. Hence this form of administering an oath.

150. Ha, ha, boy...true-penny. Hamlet's cries to the Ghost suggest the way in which the 'Vice' or Clown in the old Morality plays provokes the Devil. The effect is grotesque and medieval. It serves to bewilder Marcellus, to relieve the Prince's pent-up, hysterical emotion, to prepare for the 'antic disposition', and to keep alive the possibility that the Ghost may be diabolic.

156. *Hic et ubique?* 'The repetition of the oath, the shifting of the ground, and the Latin phrase are taken from the ceremonies of conjurors' (Tschischwitz).

167. your philosophy: either meaning philosophy in general or referring particularly to the philosophical and sceptical scholar, Horatio.

188. The time is out of joint. This has been prepared for by certain moments in earlier scenes. In scene i Horatio says: 'This bodes some strange eruption in our state.' In scene ii, 'My father's spirit in arms! all is not well. I doubt some foul play'; and Marcellus closes scene iv with, 'Something is rotten in the state of Denmark.' Now at last the command is laid upon the Prince himself to cure 'the fatness of these pursy times' (III. iv. 153), to avenge his father's murder, and to restore the sanity and health of the whole state.

ACT II

The second movement is on the grand scale and is almost equal to the first and third movements put together. It runs through to the end of Act IV, scene iv, when the Prince watches Fortinbras pass at the head of his army and leaves Denmark with his two school-fellows in banishment for England. After a slow start it brings us to four major developments in the action: the rejection of Ophelia; the disclosure of the King's undoubted guilt in the Play scene; his escape when Hamlet finds him at his prayers, which is closely linked with the murder of Polonius in his stead; and lastly Hamlet's indictment of Gertrude which completes the secondary theme of the play. The re-appearance of the Ghost, Hamlet's banishment, and his resolve

> From this time forth
> My thoughts be bloody, or be nothing worth!

lead us on to the final movement.

ACT II, SCENE I

The first scene of Act II is a relief, an interlude, a lull, after the excitement and climax of Act I. Again we turn from matters of public import to private life and domestic detail. It serves to keep Laertes in our minds; it illuminates the character and methods of Polonius; it re-introduces the Hamlet–Ophelia situation. Its purpose in the action is the conviction which comes to Polonius that Hamlet is mad with the ecstasy of love.

Further, we get the impression that time is slipping by, and a new phase of manœuvring and plotting and eavesdropping, before 'the mighty opposites' come to grips, is introduced.

1. **Give him this money.** 'Reynaldo is just off on his journey. These last minute injunctions, heaped hastily on one another, give the scene an impetus, which will compensate somewhat for its slackness of fibre' (Granville-Barker).

78–80. Rosalind gives us the signs of a lover: 'Then, your hose should be ungartered, your bonnet unbanded, your sleeve unbuttoned, your shoe untied, and everything about you demonstrating a careless desolation' (*As You Like It*, III. ii).

ACT II, SCENE II

This is a long and leisurely scene, full of interest and variety, very valuable as establishing Hamlet's many-sided nature. But it slows up the action dangerously, although less noticeably so on the stage than in the study. Later the Ghost is to speak of Hamlet's 'almost blunted purpose'. Hamlet's schoolfellows are set on to observe him. The Ambassadors return from Norway. Polonius acquaints their Majesties with the cause of the Prince's madness as he sees it and plans to put it to the proof. The arrival of the strolling Players stirs the listless Hamlet, and the Act closes with the soliloquy in which he proposes on his side to put his uncle to the proof by presenting *The Murder of Gonzago* to the assembled court; at the same time he can thus test for himself the 'honesty' of the Ghost.

60–85. 'This is the third reference to Fortinbras and his affairs. Next we shall see him, but Hamlet and he will pass each other by. At last they will meet, the one living and the other dead' (Granville-Barker). The reception of the Ambassadors and the dilatory verbosity of Polonius, which tries even the Queen's patience, combine to create a sense of delay and to anticipate the apathy of the Prince when he enters sadly reading a book.

86. Polonius employs the regular figures and formalities of sixteenth-century rhetoric, an art much studied by would-be courtiers. Shakespeare had learned the tropes and figures at Stratford Grammar School. He parodies them here.

109. To the celestial. 'Some suppose the whole letter ironical. I see no grounds for this; it is just the love-letter of a young man, beginning à *la mode*, containing a rather forced jingle for which he apologises, and ending on a note of genuine passion. The student comes out in the word "machine" ' (Dover Wilson).

137. winking. Q 2 reads 'working', a word often used of the heart and soul to mean any mental operation.

156. Take this from this. Polonius either touches his head and shoulder (as Theobald's stage direction has it) or he refers to his staff or chain of office.

168. But look, where sadly. Dover Wilson is insistent that Hamlet's entry should come some ten lines earlier on the inner stage, so that he may overhear the trap to be laid for him by Polonius with Ophelia as a decoy, and that the entry in the text signifies his coming forward from the inner stage. Any producer who follows this innovation will find, of course, that it affects the subsequent dialogue between the Prince and Polonius and, which is more important, the playing of the Nunnery scene. Hamlet will be obliged to give a bitter tone to the words, 'Nymph, in thy orisons be all my sins remembered.' It is more effective to play the scene tenderly up to the abrupt suspicion, 'Where's your father?'

174. fishmonger. The word had a hidden meaning for Elizabethan ears. A fishmonger's daughter was a cant term for a prostitute.

181. **For if the sun breed maggots.** 'Honesty may well be rare in
a world where the sun himself breeds maggots in a dog which is
flesh, good enough for kissing when alive.' Warburton emended
'good' to 'god' since elsewhere the sun is called 'common-kissing
Titan' and in *1 Henry IV*, ii. iv we find: 'Didst thou never see
Titan kiss a dish of butter?' Johnson called this a noble emendation, but the text makes sense as it stands.

184. **Let her not walk i' the sun: conception is a blessing.**
Another allusion to the proverb 'Out of God's blessing into the
warm sun', meaning 'Out of grace into ill fortune'. Hamlet, knowing what is in Polonius's mind, warns him that he, Hamlet, is no
husband to breed children by Ophelia as the sun breeds maggots
in a dog.

196. **satirical rogue.** Perhaps Hamlet was reading the tenth satire
of Juvenal.

206. **out of the air.** Fresh air was thought to be bad for the sick.

244. **Denmark's a prison.** In the next few moments of dialogue
Hamlet appears as a man suffering from the Elizabethan malady
of Melancholy, a psychological condition which was much studied.
We note also that Rosencrantz and Guildenstern suspect that
Hamlet's state of mind arises from thwarted ambition in that
Claudius has usurped the succession: a suspicion which receives
some support from the Prince's 'Beggar that I am, I am even poor
in thanks'.

263. **Then are our beggars bodies.** Hamlet explodes their quibbles
in a paradox. If ambition is a shadow's shadow, then heroes are
shadows cast by beggars who are the only reality.

303–4. **What a piece of work is a man!** This is the punctuation of
F, but Dover Wilson prefers that of Q 2 which runs thus: 'What
a piece of work is a man, how noble in reason, how infinite in
faculties, in form and moving, how express and admirable in action,
how like an angel in apprehension, how like a god: the beauty of
the world; the paragon of animals;'. The advantage of this is that
it brings together 'angel' and 'apprehension'. Apprehension is the
faculty peculiar to angels, who dispense with sense perception and
have immediate intuition and understanding.

319. **He that plays the King.** With an ironical reference to Claudius.

325. **the blank verse shall halt.** 'The lady, of course, will have

indecent words to utter; if she omits them, the halting blank verse will betray her delicacy' (Dowden).

328. the tragedians of the city. Probably refers to the Lord Admiral's men, who performed Marlowe's tragedies with Edward Alleyn in the title parts.

331. I think their inhibition. This is obscure. Inhibition suggests a prohibition of playing by the authorities but may mean simply loss of favour. 'Innovation' elsewhere in Shakespeare means a political upheaval. Dover Wilson connects it here with Essex's rebellion in 1601; but Shakespeare's own company were not themselves inhibited on account of the rising.

336–59. How comes it? &c. This passage is omitted in Q 2 possibly because when it was printed Queen Anne of Denmark had taken the Children of the Chapel under her protection. The little eyases were these Children, and the passage refers to the *Poetomachia* or War of the Theatres begun by Jonson's *Cynthia's Revels*, acted by the Children late in 1600, and Jonson's *Poetaster* of the spring of 1601, to which Dekker and Marston replied in the *Satiromastix*, acted by Shakespeare's company in the summer of the same year. The Children played at the Blackfriars, a private playhouse, and their success made 'the common stages' (l. 341) unfashionable (Dover Wilson).

358. Hercules and his load too. The Globe Theatre with its sign of Hercules carrying the globe was opened late in 1599.

374–5. i.e. 'My wits are only a few degrees astray. I can still tell chalk from cheese.'

375. a hawk from a handsaw: usually interpreted to mean a hawk from a hernshaw or heron. But a hawk was also the name of a workman's tool, though not found as early as this. Dowden suggested reading 'hack', the Elizabethan word for several tools.

386. Roscius. The famous Roman actor with whom Alleyn was often compared, but who was in fact a great *comic* actor.

389. Buz, buz! A colloquial interjection meaning 'stale news'.

392. The best actors in the world. Shakespeare is perhaps satirizing the play-bills of the Admiral's company, but the speech is typical of Polonius and officialdom.

395. **scene individable, or poem unlimited**: i.e. classical drama which preserves the unity of place or romantic drama in which none of the unities are preserved.

396. **Seneca.** The Latin tragedian of the Silver Age who was translated and imitated by Shakespeare's predecessors; e.g. *Gorboduc* by Sackville and Norton.

    Plautus. Shakespeare's *The Comedy of Errors* is based on the *Menaechmi* of Plautus, which was translated into English in 1595.

397. **the law of writ and the liberty**: i.e. plays written according to the classical rules or extemporized. Dover Wilson explains the words as 'terms defining the jurisdiction of the Sheriffs in and about the city of London quibblingly applied to types of drama'.

399. **Jephthah, judge of Israel.** Dover Wilson notes that the Admiral's men had a play called *Jephthah* by Dekker and Munday in their repertory. The play is lost, but the ballad from which Hamlet quotes survives in Percy's *Reliques of Ancient English Poetry*.

420. **my young lady**: i.e. a boy-actor whose voice may have cracked since the last visit of the players. Female parts on the Elizabethan stage were taken by trained boy-actors.

442. **'twas Aeneas' tale to Dido.** Shakespeare in the player's speech tries his hand at the outmoded style of Marlowe and his school. It seems more likely to be an imitation than a quotation. *Dido, Queen of Carthage*, ascribed on the title-page to Marlowe and Nashe, has a Pyrrhus speech, but except for two lines it is different from Shakespeare's. A lost *Dido and Aeneas* was acted by the Admiral's men in 1598.

468. *But with the whiff and wind.* Cf. *Dido, Queen of Carthage*:

    Which he disdaining, whisked his sword about,
    And with the wind therof the king fell down.

495. **he's for a jig.** Kempe, the famous Clown who left Shakespeare's company in 1599, excelled in jigs, which consisted of a comic song and dance.

524. **who shall 'scape whipping.** Stage players without a licence were classed as rogues and vagrants and therefore liable by the Act of 1572 to the punishment of whipping.

572. pigeon-liver'd. The pigeon was supposed to secrete no gall, the physical cause of spite and bitterness.

584. I have heard: a commonplace of the age. Heywood gives examples in his *Apology for Actors*. *A Warning for Fair Women*, 1599 tells how a woman at King's Lynn who had murdered her husband thus betrayed herself.

ACT III, Scene I

This Act, packed with crowded action, hurries us on with rising excitement until the moment when Hamlet leaves his mother's chamber tugging in the body of Polonius; but the whole movement is not completed until some way through the following Act. The heart of the play is in this Act, and we see Hamlet alone with Ophelia, alone with Claudius, alone with his mother: three situations of great intensity. And as a dramatic contrast there is 'the Play within the Play', with King and Prince watching each other, cat and mouse, and the whole assembled court intent upon the mimic action which caricatures the play's main theme of murder and revenge.

Scene i presents Rosencrantz and Guildenstern making the best of their unsatisfactory attempt to probe the Prince and the eavesdropping plot which proves that it is not love which is the cause of his 'turbulent and dangerous lunacy', as Claudius overstates it; the action advances with the King's 'quick determination' at the close to dispatch him to England; but the real importance of the scene is that it is the one love scene, that in it Ophelia fails Hamlet, and that he forgets the girl he loves in a general indictment of the frailty and falseness of women. He speaks to her, but he is thinking only of his mother. The dialogue between them is preluded by the most famous of all the speeches Shakespeare ever penned and it exists independently of the play like a poem, a sonnet; like Macbeth's 'Tomorrow and tomorrow and tomorrow' or Portia's 'The quality of mercy is not strained'. When Hamlet leaves her, Ophelia utters what is indeed the Prince's epitaph.

24-7. With all my heart: dramatic irony.

48. we do sugar o'er the devil himself. This may be linked with I. v. 108:

> That one may smile, and smile, and be a villain!

49. O! 'tis too true. This stirring of the King's guilty conscience prepares us for the prayer scene.

58. Hamlet knows that vengeance upon his uncle may bring about his own death, but life means little to him.

59. take arms against a sea. 'To take up arms and rush upon the waves of the sea was a custom attributed by several classical writers to the Celts. Shakespeare probably read of it in Fleming's translation of Aelian's *Histories* (1576), bk. xii, where it is said that "they throw themselves into the fomey floudes with their swordes drawn in their handes, and shaking their javelines as though they were of force and violence to withstand the rough waves"' (Herford).

60. To die: to sleep. In Florio's translation of Montaigne (published 1603) (bk. iii, ch. 12) there is a parallel from the summary of the Apology of Socrates: 'If it (death) be a consummation of ones being, it is also an amendment and entrance into a long and quiet life. Wee finde nothing so sweete in life, as a quiet rest and gentle sleepe, and without dreames' (Brandes).

79. from whose bourn no traveller returns. Has Shakespeare forgotten the play for the sake of the poem? It is more likely that this indicates that Hamlet no longer believes in the honesty of the Ghost. His soul-sickness has bred indifference and despair.

91. How does your honour? 'The meeting for its first few moments, passes as any such meeting may between two sensitive creatures sundered by no quarrel of their own; in reserve, in reproachful sorrow that they have let themselves be sundered, and a provoking of more misunderstanding by which to justify reproach' (Granville-Barker).

130. Where's your father? The sudden abrupt question suggests that he has seen a movement behind the arras or caught a glimpse of peeping Polonius or the King. Ophelia answers with a clumsy, pitiful lie which confirms Hamlet's suspicions. Desdemona answers Othello with just such another frightened lie when he questions her about the handkerchief: 'I have not lost it.'

144. I have heard of your paintings. Note the change from *thou* to *you*. Hamlet is condemning all womankind. Ophelia seems to him with her rejection of him, her return of his gifts, her uncertain answers, to be no better than his mother.

172. he shall with speed to England: a strong contrast to the Prince's 'words, words, words' and incurable delay.

187. **And I'll be plac'd.** The old key-hole diplomat plans another
piece of eavesdropping and little knows that it will result in his own
death.

ACT III, Scene II

Another strong contrast to complicate and heighten our impression
of the Prince. A moment since we have seen him in mournful, listless
meditation, then violent and passionate in his denunciation of himself and of women. Now he is concentrated upon the success of his
plot with all the suppressed excitement of an amateur producer on a
first night. He can speak with sanity and understanding upon the
art of acting and is the first and one of the wisest of English dramatic
critics. With the entry of Polonius and his dispatch by Hamlet as if
he were an errand boy, with Rosencrantz and Guildenstern at his
heels, we feel the familiar bustle before the curtain rises. Then
Horatio enters, and Shakespeare points a contrast of which he is
fond between the sensitive and artistic temperament and 'the strong,
silent man' of action: a contrast also between the professional courtier
who bows and scrapes and the true gentleman. Finally he insists
that the Play will be the test of truth between the Ghost and
the King.

10. **tear a passion to tatters.** Is this a glance at Edward Alleyn
of the Admiral's company, famous performer of Tamburlaine and
such full-bodied roles? Bottom in the *Midsummer Night's Dream*
says: 'yet my chief humour is for a tyrant: I could play Ercles
rarely, or a part to tear a cat in, to make all split.'

12. **inexplicable dumb-shows.** Yet these Players provide a dumb
show.

14. **Termagant:** a Saracen deity who appears in the old Miracles
and Moralities.
    it out-herods Herod: the typical tyrant of the Miracle plays.
John Absalon in the *Miller's Tale* of Chaucer 'playeth Herodes on
a scaffold hye'. The scaffold was the old platform stage.

39. **those that play your clowns.** Perhaps a reference to William
Kempe who had joined a rival company. (See *N* on II. ii. 495.)

90. 'Before our eyes Hamlet puts on, as he might a mask, his "antic
disposition"; it disguises his excitement, is an ambush from which
to shoot his mockeries—arrows, plucked from his own flesh,

poisoned by his own misery, which is assuaged when he can see
them rankling elsewhere' (Granville Barker).

92. **fares.** Hamlet interprets the word as 'feeds'.

93. **of the chameleon's dish.** The chameleon, a kind of lizard, was
supposed to feed on air. Hamlet possibly quibbles on *air* and *heir*
and refers to his thwarted ambition. 'In "capons" Hamlet hints
that the King is plying him with empty promises in preparation
for having him quietly removed from his path, since the word means
young cocks stuffed for killing' (Dover Wilson).

103. **Brutus killed me.** Did Shakespeare know the lost University
play *Caesar Interfectus*, and was it from this play that he culled
the famous *Et tu, Brute?*

127. **suit of sables.** Hamlet speaks ironically and quibbles on the
two meanings of sables: (*a*) mourning, (*b*) the furred gown of
middle age. 'So long? Then I must be getting an old man.'

132. **For, O! for, O! the hobby-horse. . . .** A line from a popular
ballad. The hobby-horse was a character in the old May games and
Morris Dances which the Puritans sought to suppress.

134. The dumb show was part of the old Moralities, but it survived
in the early court dramas. As a rule, for instance in *Gorboduc*, it
anticipates the subsequent action. Claudius does not see the dumb
show which is introduced to show the audience in brief what they
are to expect. Dover Wilson believes that Hamlet is vexed at the
actors inserting a dumb show against his orders and afraid that
the Prologue will give away the plot.

151. **As woman's love.** He reproaches Ophelia, but he has learned
this truth from his mother.

236. **Gonzago.** 'In 1538 the Duke of Urbino, married to a Gonzaga,
was murdered by Luigi Gonzaga, who dropped poison into his ear.
Shakespeare, it is suggested, might have found this writ in choice
Italian, might have transferred the name Gonzaga to the murdered
man, and formed "Lucianus" from Luigi' (Dowden). The story
has not been found in any of the Italian collections of *novelle*. But
there were numerous translations sold in the sixteenth century.

241. **nephew to the king.** Is Hamlet provoking the King to pay
special attention to Lucianus, he himself being Claudius's nephew?
Or is he throwing dust in the eyes of the court so that they think
the Prince contemplates the assassination of the usurper?

249. **mis-take.** The reading of F and Q 2. Q 1 reads 'must take', which is less effective. Hamlet refers to the marriage service, 'take for better, for worse', but suggests that women are not true to their vows.

251. **the croaking raven.** Hamlet parodies the old type of revenge play and in particular a passage in *The True Tragedy of Richard III*:

> The screeking raven sits croking for revenge,
> Whole heards of beasts comes bellowing for revenge.

252. ***Thoughts black, hands apt.*** This, it would seem, is the speech which the Prince himself composed and gave to the First Player to study. The 'some dozen or sixteen lines' are cut short.

268. **Why, let the stricken deer.** As the procession hastens out in confusion Hamlet leaps on to the players' stage and himself utters an epilogue.

288. **Ah, ha! Come, some music!** Hamlet sees his schoolfellow spies enter and breaks off his confidence with Horatio. The couplet which follows is directed at them.

305. **The queen, your mother.** Thus at a critical moment he is distracted from his purpose.

336. **'While the grass grows.'** Cf. Whetstone's *Promos and Cassandra*, 1578:

> Whylst grass doth growe, oft sterves the seely steed.

339. **why do you go about.** The metaphor is drawn from hunting. The stag is approached from the side whence the wind blows and the game, startled by the scent, moves off into the net.

387. **the soul of Nero.** The emperor Nero caused the murder of his mother Agrippina.

ACT III, Scene III

The soliloquy which closes the previous scene reveals that Hamlet is aware of a change in himself. The task laid upon him, the horror of all that he has learned about those about him, his isolation, and his self-distrust have combined to develop in him (partly in disgust, partly in self-defence, partly to meet the necessities of circumstance) a certain callousness and ruthlessness which he fears. That hardness, already finding expression in the dismissal of Ophelia, comes out in

extremest form now when he spares Claudius at his prayers lest,
killing him so, his enemy should escape the everlasting torments
of hell.

The first twenty lines of the scene show that Hamlet's 'lunacy'
can now be considered a State matter. Clearly the king is threatened,
'upon whose weal depend and rest the lives of many'. Claudius is
justified in hastening Hamlet's virtual banishment under the sur-
veillance of the two courtiers. After the busy-body Polonius has
reported that the Prince is going to his mother and that he will take
note of all that occurs, Claudius is left alone. We see him for the first
time as a private man and he wins our sympathy, with the result
that Hamlet's speech as he observes him at his prayers strikes us
with deeper horror. The dramatic dilemma which Shakespeare has
achieved is acute. For a single moment he makes us feel that Claudius
is nearer salvation than the hero, and that feeling helps to keep the
balance of our sympathies even.

30. **as you said.** 'Polonius astutely (or obliviously) attributes his
own suggestion to the king' (Herford).

79. **hire and salary.** F 1 'hyre and Sallery'; Q 2 'base and silly'.
Dover Wilson suggests 'bait' (food, refreshment).

88. **Up, sword.** 'This speech in which Hamlet, represented as a
virtuous character, is not content with taking blood for blood, but
contrives damnation for the man that he would punish, is too
horrible to be read or to be uttered' (Samuel Johnson). But
Claudius had contrived the same damnation for Hamlet's father
and the Prince allows 'not shriving time' for Rosencrantz and
Guildenstern (v. ii. 47).

ACT III, SCENE IV

It has already been suggested that there are two themes in the play.
One is a theme of revenge; a theme which is the motive force of the
plot of the play, of its form and design and sequence of situations;
and this theme is only resolved *in action* when Laertes and Hamlet
'fight it out' in a duel to the death and Hamlet stabs the King and
forces the last drop of poison down his throat. That theme is
advanced here by the murder of Polonius, which is to raise up
Laertes as an avenger, a sword in the hand of Claudius:

> And so have I a noble father lost;
> A sister driven into desperate terms,
> ... But my revenge will come.

But the secondary theme of the play is general rather than particular,
more emotional than dramatic: namely, 'Frailty, thy name is woman.'
It is in this scene that the secondary theme finds final expression.
This scene, in which Hamlet wrings his mother's heart, is the climax
of the second movement just as the duel is the climax of the third
movement and of the play as a whole. This secondary theme begins
with Hamlet's first soliloquy; it is intensified by the Ghost's revelations; it finds utterance in Hamlet's scene with Ophelia; 'you jig,
you amble, and you lisp, ... and make your wantonness your ignorance
... we will have no more marriages'; and now at last all the repressed
emotion and poisoned thoughts are set free in a rush of violent
imagery, in relentless condemnation and piteous appeal:

> *Queen.* O Hamlet! thou hast cleft my heart in twain.
> *Hamlet.* O! throw away the worser part of it,
> And live the purer with the other half.

It is right that at the close of this movement there should be a return
of the Ghost. He returns to save the soul of the wife he loved and to
prevent Hamlet revealing to her that her husband is a murderer.
He overcomes the spirit of Nero with which his son is struggling.
The Ghost is no longer an awful and majestic figure clad in complete
steel, but pale and faint and pitiful:

> Look, how it steals away;
> My father, in his habit as he liv'd.

Father, mother, and son are re-united. The personal tragedy is
accomplished. Hamlet's public duty remains.

3. **your Grace hath screen'd and stood between.** 'A significant
   glimpse of the Council of war after the Play-scene and of the
   Queen's part therein' (Dover Wilson).

4. **I'll silence me.** Modern editors often follow Hanmer's emendation, 'I'll sconce me', which destroys the irony. Polonius, 'the
   foolish prating knave', can be 'grave and still' only in death.

30. **As kill a king!** Gertrude's amazement shows that she is inno-
    cent of the murder of her husband.

43. **fair forehead.** Malefactors and harlots were branded upon the
    forehead.

52. **index:** i.e. the Table of Contents at the beginning of a book.

53. **this picture, and on this.** Perhaps Gertrude wears a miniature
    of Claudius round her neck and Hamlet one of his father; or

perhaps the portraits (or one of them) may be hanging on the walls of the bedchamber.

58. Mercury. The winged messenger of Olympus, symbol of grace and (in some contexts) of wit and cunning.

89–94. 'It is one of the most passionate passages in the most passionate scene of the play; and yet it is threaded on a string of images almost banal in character. For "grained" and "tinct" being terms of wool-dyeing, have suggested "enseamed", another technical term from the woollen industry meaning "loaded with grease", and that in turn, because the "seam" employed in the greasing process was hog's-lard, has suggested the "nasty sty". It is very unlikely that Shakespeare himself was aware of this train of ideas; the son of the wool merchant of Stratford was unwittingly drawing from the well of early memories, that is all' (Dover Wilson).

98. vice of kings. The Vice with his dagger of lath, ass's ears, and parti-coloured Fool's coat was, like the Devil whose nails he would try to pair, a traditional figure of the Morality plays from which the Fool of Shakespearian and other drama was derived.

109–10. As A. C. Bradley noted, criticism of the Prince's 'delay', of his failure to act, is founded on two things in the text, namely, the Ghost's reminder, 'I come to whet thy almost *blunted* purpose', and Hamlet's own self-condemnation in the soliloquy which closes the second movement (IV. iv. 43):

> I do not know
> Why yet I live to say 'This thing's to do;'
> Sith I have cause and will and strength and means
> To do 't.

An absorbed spectator will not pick these out of their context and put them together as a reader may. Hamlet's words are provoked by the glimpse of Fortinbras and his army, a delicate and tender prince, a soldier, the Hamlet who might have been. They are closely linked with a piece of self-questioning which is the essence of his dramatic role—'whether it be bestial oblivion or the craven scruple of thinking too precisely on th' event'. By himself asking why the deed is still undone, Hamlet forestalls the critics who make so much of his 'delay'—a delay which passes unnoticed in the theatre although a reader may condemn it.

130. To whom do you speak this? Bradley suggests that the Ghost is invisible to Gertrude because he wishes to spare her, but a more

effective reason is supplied by *Der bestrafte Brudermord*, namely,
that she is unworthy to look upon him, a notion which is found
elsewhere. Hence the Ghost's agitation and agony of mind.

169. **And exorcise the devil.** The text reads 'And either the devil
or throw him out', showing that a word has been dropped. Dover
Wilson suggests that 'either' is a misprint by the compositor for
'exorcise' which would give the necessary sense.

178. **I must be cruel.** This couplet completes the secondary theme,
and Hamlet is about to leave her, but he returns with fresh
injunctions and the plot goes forward with his 'I must to England'
and his warning that he will hoist his schoolfellows with their own
petard.

194. **the famous ape.** The story is unknown.

ACT IV, Scene I

This act division introduced by Nicholas Rowe in 1709, following the
Quarto of 1676, is, as Dr. Johnson noted, not very happy and it should
be disregarded. The first three scenes of this Act are really one scene,
and are the aftermath of what has gone before, no change of scene
being required on the unlocalized Elizabethan stage. The murder of
Polonius strengthens Claudius's determination to banish Hamlet.
Claudius's first thought is of his own escape. He is no coward but
his nerve is shaken and he hurries on the action.

40. **so, haply, slander.** The words are supplied by editors. Both
F and Q 2 have dropped half a line.

ACT IV, Scene II

'It is a macabre business, this torchlight hue and cry through the
darkened castle after a lunatic homicide, and the search for the body
—which he has ignominiously bundled beneath a staircase' (Granville-
Barker).

15. **Take you me for a sponge.** 'The notion of sycophants and
extortioners as a monarch's sponges is a commonplace of the time
which derives from Suetonius (*Vespasian*, c. 16). Vespasian
deliberately bestowed high offices upon rapacious persons "so that
the common talk was he used them as sponges, letting them soak
when they were dry and squeezing them out when they were wet"'
(Dover Wilson).

18. **like an ape.** F reading. Q 2 reads 'like an apple', which also makes good sense.

27. **The body is with the king**: i.e. with the late King. But the present King has not joined him—as yet.

30. **Hide fox**: a cry from such a game as Fox and Hounds.

ACT IV, SCENE III

21. **convocation of politic worms.** A punning reference to the Diet of Worms, or congress of the states of the (German) Roman Empire. Cf. 'emperor for diet'. Brandes compares Florio's *Montaigne*, ii. 12: 'The heart and life of a mighty and triumphant Emperor, is but the break-fast of a Seely little Worm.'

47. **I see a cherub.** The Cherubim were the sentinels of Heaven.

ACT IV, SCENE IV

This scene provides the epilogue to the second movement. After it Hamlet is removed from the stage, and when we see him again watching the grave-diggers at their work he is a changed man, older, sadder, wiser. Fortinbras, a delicate and tender prince but a leader of men and man of action, serves as a spiritual and moral contrast to the Prince of Denmark at this turning-point in his fate; and Hamlet weighs himself in the balance and finds himself wanting. With a new and determined resolve to carry out his duty he puts off the old Hamlet and leaves Denmark, an exile under guard. Again, this scene, with its diversion of interest away from the intrigue and wickedness of the court to a world of soldiership and national honour, separates in the main design the murder of Polonius and the madness of Ophelia; it separates her madness from the Prince's antic disposition. Hamlet's departure, thus emphasized, isolates Ophelia and suggests a passing of time necessary for the return of Laertes. F omits the soliloquy and Hamlet's share in the scene, and most stage productions feel obliged to sacrifice it so as to save time and allow an interval.

18. **a little patch of ground.** 'From July 2, 1601 till the spring of 1602 the sand-dunes of Ostend were valiantly defended against the Spaniards in many battles and with great loss of life by an English force under Sir Francis Vere which returned home on March 18. There can be little doubt that Shakespeare is here alluding to these events' (Dover Wilson).

32. How all occasions. 'From opposite types—from the soldiers as from the players—comes the same reproach to Hamlet, the same instigation to act' (Verity).

ACT IV, SCENE V

Here begins the third and final movement. Ophelia's madness and the devotion of Laertes to his dead father and to his sister correspond to Hamlet's melancholy disillusionment and loss of a father at the beginning of the play. The lyric interlude of Ophelia's sad distraction bridges the space between the dramatic crisis at the centre of the play and the counter-movement leading to the ultimate catastrophe. We find a similar effect in the Willow scene in *Othello* of interlude and relief; and in *King Lear* Gloster 'blindly lead' by an old tenant, his meeting with Edgar, the description of the imagined Dover cliff, and the King fantastically dressed with flowers fill in and enrich a similar section of the dramatic design. The effect here is brief. Into Ophelia's snatches of love song break the clamour of the rabble and the cry 'Laertes shall be King!' It is he and not the Prince who is now to be reckoned with by the usurper and we cannot but admire the strength and skill with which Claudius stands up to him. The re-entry of Ophelia changes Laertes' mood and gives the King breathing space. He takes him aside to commune with his grief and exploit the young man's revengeful anger for his own purposes. How ironical is the contrast with Hamlet, who so far from sweeping to his revenge 'with wings as swift as meditation or the thoughts of love', had shown himself 'duller than the fat weed on Lethe wharf'.

21. *Enter* Ophelia. Q 1 gives the direction, 'Enter Ofelia playing on a Lute, and her haire downe singing.'

38. Larded all with sweet flowers. (Q 2.) F omits 'all' and editors wrongly follow it. They also follow Pope in omitting 'not' in the next line although it is in F and both Quartos. But Ophelia is thinking of her father's 'obscure burial', and the broken metre in each line expresses her distraction.

42. They say the owl. The allusion is to a folk-tale of a baker's daughter who gave short measure when Jesus asked for bread to eat. She took away some of the dough put to bake in the oven for Him, but the dough miraculously swelled to enormous size. She cried out 'heugh, heugh, heugh' and was transformed into an owl (Douce). Ophelia's next sentence comments on the tale and refers at the same time to her father's fate and her own.

48. Saint Valentine's day. The first girl seen by a man on St. Valentine's Day (February 14th) was said to be his true love.

48-66. Ophelia's wandering fancy turns to the lover she has lost and to his bitter words and treatment of her.

94. Like to a murdering-piece: a small piece of artillery loaded with bullets, scrap iron, and the like.

96. Switzers: i.e. the body-guard. Swiss mercenaries were thus employed at several courts in Europe and are still found at the Vatican.

109. false Danish dogs. 'Note the implication that she is, by birth, a foreigner to Denmark; such things slip out at such a moment' (Granville Barker).

122. There's such divinity. The idea of the Divine Right of Kings, which Shakespeare makes much of in *Richard II*, was encouraged by Queen Elizabeth and strongly held under the Stuarts.

159. Nature is fine in love. 'Nature' as elsewhere (particularly in *King Lear*) implies family affections. Dover Wilson paraphrases thus: 'Filial love is exquisite in its working, and will sacrifice its most precious possession as a proof of its affection for the dear departed.' The 'precious token' in this case is Ophelia's sanity.

170. O how the wheel. Perhaps the spinning-wheel which turns with the song, as in *Twelfth Night* (the spinsters and the knitters in the sun do use to chant it); or, some say, 'wheel' is a technical term for a 'stanza' and is here used loosely to mean a refrain.
    the false steward: the allusion is unknown.

173. There's rosemary. The flowers have their own language and are given by Ophelia to the appropriate characters. Rosemary for remembrance to Laertes, just as the Ghost had laid his command upon Hamlet, 'Remember me'; pansies for thoughts or love-thoughts to him or to herself; fennel and columbines for the King, signifying flattery and ingratitude; rue for sorrow for herself and the rue of repentance for the Queen. The daisy is the emblem of dissembling and might be given to one who can 'smile and be a villain' or to herself as a warning 'not to trust every fair promise that amorous bachelors make' (Greene, *Quip for an upstart courtier*), the very warning which Laertes had given her so long

ago, or to the Queen seduced by Claudius. Violets are the emblem
of faithfulness. The distribution of herbs and flowers was an old
funeral custom, and Ophelia imagines herself giving her father
proper burial.

181. **with a difference:** an heraldic term which signified an alteration
in a coat of arms to distinguish a particular member or branch of
the line.

ACT IV, Scene VI

This little intervening scene allows us to imagine Claudius and
Laertes in close conference. He has to explain to him what we know
already and to excuse it before proceeding to his own intrigue. The
news of Hamlet's return raises the pitch. The opposing forces begin
to draw together again. Hamlet's letter excites our expectation.
What words has he to speak in Horatio's ear which will strike him
dumb? The pursuit by the pirate ship, the short grapple, the Prince
the sole prisoner—these add a touch of romance. When the scene is
over we feel that fate is working with Hamlet and no longer against
him; as he says himself later of the adventure:

> There's a divinity that shapes our ends
> Rough-hew them how we will.

9. **the ambassador.** The pirates avoid naming Hamlet who has
doubtless warned them to be secret.

19. *but they knew what they did:* i.e. they knew that I was the
Prince and that it was worth their while.

24–5. The words 'will bring thee where I am' suggest a hiding-place.

30. **for these your letters.** But they do not run the risk of deliver-
ing them to the King himself; they give them to 'one Claudio' who
passes them on to a messenger.

ACT IV, Scene VII

A long and carefully wrought scene which fully establishes for us
Hamlet's two adversaries. Just as the first Act laid the foundations
for the action of the second movement, so this scene lays the foundations for the fight in the grave, the duel, and the murder of the King.
We see again the Claudius we saw in the first Council scene; diplo-
matic, cunning, ruthless, and bland. We see Laertes divided between

his desire for revenge and his better nature. Ophelia's death is decisive as regards his intention to kill Hamlet by fair means or foul, but it also reveals his truth and tenderness. Shakespeare is fond of presenting two different characters working upon one another. We find it in the Cassius and Brutus scene in the first Act of *Julius Caesar*, and again in the long temptation scene between Iago and Othello, and (more briefly done) between Macbeth and his wife. It is a common effect in classical drama; the conflict of two wills. One of the advantages here is the great solidity which the scene gives to the latter part of the play.

1. Now must your conscience. They are still in talk. We are ready to believe that part of Claudius's difficult task has been accomplished. He now flatters the youth with confidences.

20. the spring that turneth wood to stone. The baths of King's Newnham in Warwickshire were supposed to have this property.

52. Can you advise me? Claudius is taken by surprise, but after a moment's hesitation he sees his way clear.

91. Lamord. (Q 2.) F reads Lamound. Some particular allusion seems to be intended as fencing and not horsemanship is the business in hand. If it was only a matter of topical interest Shakespeare puts it to good use. For the praise of Laertes as a swordsman sounds all the sweeter from his lips.

117. That we would do. 'These words point the whole moral of *Hamlet*, and are a comment (unconscious on Claudius's part, but intentional on Shakespeare's) upon Hamlet's character' (Dover Wilson).

121. spendthrift sigh. Every sigh was supposed to cost a drop of blood.

128. keep close. 'The King has but one anxiety—to prevent the young men meeting before the fencing match' (Bradley). Ironically enough they do meet—in Ophelia's grave—to the advantage of Claudius.

162. How now, sweet queen! 'She comes with the tale of Ophelia's death, its candid beauty in sharp contrast to the secret wickedness brewing. The "fantastic garlands" themselves seem an innocent reproach to the unction which "no cataplasm so rare collected from all simples" can counteract. The speech fulfils divers ends. It gives actuality to Ophelia's unseen death. . . . And the beauty and pity of it incidentally help to rescue Gertrude in our eyes from the degradation of Hamlet's painting of her in the closet scene. We shall remember her as well as Ophelia by this' (Granville-Barker).

177. **lauds.** (Q 2.) F and Q 1 give 'tunes', which most editions follow. 'Shakespeare seems to refer to the *laude* or hymns of praise sung by wandering bands or guilds of singers in Italy from 13th to 16th century' (Dover Wilson).

189. **The woman will be out.** Cf. *Henry V*, IV. vi. 31: 'all my mother came into my eyes'.

ACT V, SCENE I

The two Clowns at their grave-digging, like the drunken Porter in *Macbeth* and the simple rustic who brings the asps to Cleopatra in a basket of figs, are constantly cited as an example of 'comic relief'. So of course they are, and their perversion of the hair-splitting obscurities of the law will make the audience laugh and heighten what has gone before and what is to come. Here is a further contrast to the dark intrigues and to Ophelia's elegy in the previous scene. But for 'the judicious' the scene gives something more. The leisurely prose lowers the tension and lulls us into rest; and on that ground-work is portrayed a new Hamlet: controlled, speculative, philo-sophical, wise; a melancholy Hamlet, but he wears his melancholy with a difference. He enters with Horatio 'afarre off'—it is F's unusual stage direction—and as he thus steals back into Denmark he is (as Granville-Barker notes) spiritually far off too. Then, again, these homely folk jesting and singing at their work make us feel that the ordinary business of life goes on untroubled despite broken hearts and murderous treachery and the deaths of princes. Thomas Hardy's poem 'In the time of the Breaking of Nations' expresses the same theme. The Clowns serve both to expand the whole play and to give it proportion. Moreover, they have a hold on realities. 'Will you ha' the truth on 't? If this had not been a gentle-woman, she should have been buried out o' Christian burial.' And the other answers, 'Why, there thou sayest; and the more pity that great folk should have countenance in this world to drown or hang themselves more than their even Christian.' And Hamlet also learns to see things as they are as he holds the skull of Yorick in his hands. Yorick the jester and Alexander the Great are as one, and Caesar's dust may stop a hole to keep the wind away. He can learn a lesson from the Grave-diggers as he learned one from the Players.

9. se offendendo. The Clown means *se defendendo*.

10. if I drown myself. Sir John Hawkins, friend of Dr. Johnson, was the first to note that the Grave-digger bases his argument on a famous case of *Hales* v. *Petit*, 1554, of which reports were published in 1571 and 1578, and which settled the law as regards suicide. Sir James Hales, a Common Law Judge, committed suicide by walking into a river at Canterbury. The lawyers disputed as to whether he went to the water or the water came to him.

59. Yaughan. Presumably an innkeeper. Perhaps Shakespeare wrote Iohan—Danish for John.

60. In youth, when I did love. The Grave-digger sings a few verses from 'The Aged Lover renounceth his Love' by Lord Vaux, which was published in Tottel's Miscellany, the first of many sixteenth-century collections of songs and sonnets. Another verse shows the aptness of the song to the context:

> Loe here the bared scull,
> By whose bald signe I know:
> That stoupyng age away shall pull
> What youthfull yeres did sowe.

The Grave-digger mixes up different lines and makes nonsense of them.

64. Has this fellow no feeling. It is dramatic irony that Hamlet reproaches the sexton for indifference when he is himself unaware that this grave is the grave of the girl whose heart his own indifference broke.

76. jaw-bone. The jawbone with which Cain murdered Abel was traditionally that of an ass.

142. the very day that young Hamlet was born. Since the Clown tells us that he has been a grave-maker man and boy for thirty years, and that Yorick who took Hamlet on his knee has been dead twenty-three years, and since the Player King and Player Queen are represented as having been married thirty years, it would seem to fix the Prince's age and to fix it as older than we should expect, particularly as to an Elizabethan thirty was a more mature age than it is to us. We feel, in at any rate the early part of the play, that Hamlet is little more than twenty. Shakespeare may have revised the text to suit a particular actor and, as Bradley says, 'the moment Burbage entered it must have been clear whether the hero was twenty or thirty.' The most convincing performances of the part, be it noted, are often given by schoolboys and undergraduates rather than by professional actors of middle age and long experience.

210. **here comes the king.** Q 2 reads simply 'Enter K. Q. Laertes and the corse'. Modern editions and productions with their priests and processions and mourners and candles are misleading. Hamlet remarks on the 'maimed rites' which show that the dead took his or her life. The priest says that had not royal command overswayed the order of the Church she would have been buried in unsanctified ground. Although Ophelia is allowed her virgin garlands and the passing-bell, her burial is only less 'obscure' than that of her father, interred 'in hugger-mugger'. Q 2 also heads the Priest's speeches 'Doct.', i.e. a Doctor of Divinity in a black gown.

246. **old Pelion.** The giants when they made war upon the gods tried to scale heaven by piling Pelion on Ossa (l. 276). They were mountains in Thessaly.

269. **eisel.** F gives 'Esile', Q 1 'vessels', Q 2 'Esill'. The emendation was made by Theobald. Vinegar was thought to moderate rage or to induce melancholy. Cf. Sonnet 111, 'Potions of Eysell'.

276. **Nay, an thou'lt mouth.** There was a time when Hamlet had to rebuke himself for his ranting protestations and curses, while the player 'but in a fiction' could shed genuine tears:

> Why what an ass am I! This is most brave,
> That I, the son of a dear father murdered,
> Must, like a shrew, unpack my heart with words,
> And fall a-cursing, like a very drab. . . .

284. **Hercules:** in scornful reference to Laertes' bragging. 'My turn will come.'

ACT V, SCENE II

Hamlet re-enters at once in eager talk with Horatio. His rapid and excited narrative, told with a sense of power which is unusual with him, leads us on to the entry of Osric the fop. The verbal fencing match, the flourishes of court dialect and fashionable etiquette are an ironical preparation for the realities of the encounter to come, and

the pause tightens up the suspense. But it changes Hamlet's mood
to foreboding and fatalism and something of the old melancholy. In
this gentler, sadder mood he makes the generous boyish apology to
Laertes which Laertes pretends to accept but stands upon his honour.
The Prince wins the first bout. The King pledges his nephew, the
trumpets sound, the cannon is discharged. The second bout is also
Hamlet's. The third is a draw, and the judges part them with a
'Nothing neither way'. Laertes is desperate and resorts to foul play,
lunging suddenly at the Prince when off his guard between the bouts.
They close again. Hamlet's blood is up. He drops his foil and wrests
from Laertes his 'venomed stuck'. Claudius bids the judges part
them, but he is too late. Laertes falls back dying into the arms of
Osric. And now the Queen falls poisoned by the cup prepared for
her son; Laertes betrays his royal accomplice; and with a last effort
Hamlet stabs Claudius and forces the dregs of poison down his throat.
After the violent rush of the long-delayed action the tension relaxes,
the pace slows up, the verse becomes at once more formal and
musical, a warlike march is heard afar. Hamlet gives his dying voice
to young Fortinbras who has 'some rights of memory in the kingdom'.
Shakespeare, as is his custom, gives us the quiet close of classical
tragedy, and Hamlet is born off like a soldier to the sound of fife and
drum and a peal of ordnance.

1–2. Hamlet enters talking and already in the middle of his story.

22. **bugs and goblins.** Johnson suggests that these are crimes
imputed to Hamlet rather than punishments threatened to the
bearers.

32. **wrote it fair:** i.e. the elaborate Italian calligraphy of State
papers.

42. **comma.** 'Though a truce may give a comma or colon to the
war, nothing under a peace can give a perfect period' (i.e. full
stop) (Fuller's *Worthies*, 1662).

43. **As'es:** a pun on asses.

74. **to say 'One':** the single thrust of a rapier.

93. **to his right use.** The Elizabethans wore their hats indoors.

111–19. Hamlet bewilders and disconcerts Osric with court jargon
equal to his own.

138. **to know himself:** i.e. oneself. Cf. 'No man can judge another
because no man knows himself' (Sir Thomas Browne, *Religio
Medici*).

162. **The king, sir, hath laid.** 'The conditions are: on the King's side that Laertes must win by at least three up; and on Laertes's, that the match must be one of twelve bouts instead of the usual nine in order to give him more elbow room, since to win "three up" in a match of nine would mean winning six bouts to Hamlet's three, with no allowance for "draws" which would be fearful odds to give' (Dover Wilson).

181. **This lapwing.** The newly hatched lapwing was supposed to run about with its shell on its head. The unfledged courtier Osric departs in his bonnet.

187. **most fond and winnowed** (F). Q 2 reads 'prophane and trennowed'. The best emendations are 'fanned and winnowed', meaning 'sifted and considered', or 'profound and winnowed'.

212. **If it be now.** The speech is suggested by a passage in Montaigne, 'That to Philosophie is to learne how to die.'

214. **the readiness is all**: cf. King Lear, 'Ripeness is all.'

214–15. **no man has aught of what he leaves.** 'I think . . . that Shakespeare had come across Seneca's *Nihil perdis ex tuo tempore, nam quod relinquis alienum est* (Epist. lxix)' (C. S. Lewis).

217. *Enter* King. This is the stage direction of F; but that of Q 2 shows that the curtains of the inner stage parted discovering 'a table prepared', the King and Queen 'and all the state', and Laertes. Q 2 gives 'Foiles, daggers' and F 'Foyles and Gauntlets', which points to a change of fashion between 1601 and 1623. At the end of the sixteenth and the beginning of the seventeenth centuries the dagger was held in the left hand and used to ward off the rapier thrust (Dover Wilson).

236. **And hurt my brother. . . .** 'In the sad cadence of that "brother" is the last echo of Ophelia's story' (Granville-Barker).

242–4. Hamlet appeals to the generosity of Laertes and Laertes responds with affected sincerity and a quibble about his honour. It is only when all is over that Laertes recovers his truth and manhood (ll. 320–3).

256. **let me see another.** At this moment, while Osric turns to answer Hamlet's question, we may suppose Laertes selects in exchange the unbated weapon. While Claudius gives commands to the attentive court about the wine and the healths Laertes can anoint the sword-tip unnoticed. There is no need to make the butterfly, Osric, a party to the plot.

260. i.e. if Hamlet wins the first or second bout; or draws the third
after winning the first or the second.

264. The idea, it would seem, was to make the drink more precious—
therefore the pledge more flattering. Cleopatra is said by Pliny to
have dissolved a pearl in vinegar. Claudius is thus able to conceal
his insertion of the poison.

279. **fat, and scant of breath.** It is ludicrous to suppose that
Shakespeare is referring to the increasing corpulence of his tragic
actor Richard Burbage. 'Fat' means no more than puffed or over-
heated, out of condition.

318. **union:** a last quibble. Claudius and Gertrude are united by the
poison.

348. **my dying voice.** Hamlet is now *de facto* King. A King without an heir could by his dying voice secure to some degree the
rights of his successor. The Privy Council were concerned to
obtain the voice of the dying Elizabeth in favour of James I
(Dover Wilson).

388. **Bear Hamlet, like a soldier.** 'It is not by mere convention
that Shakespeare allots him a hero's end' (Granville-Barker).

SELECT LITERARY CRITICISM

IF the dramas of Shakespeare were to be characterized, each by the particular excellence which distinguishes it from the rest, we must allow to the tragedy of *Hamlet* the praise of variety. The incidents are so numerous that the argument of the play would make a long tale. The scenes are interchangeably diversified with merriment and solemnity; with merriment that includes judicious and instructive observations; and solemnity not strained by poetical violence above the natural sentiments of man. New characters appear from time to time in continual succession, exhibiting various forms of life and particular modes of conversation. The pretended madness of Hamlet causes much mirth, the mournful distraction of Ophelia fills the heart with tenderness, and every personage produces the effect intended, from the Apparition, that in the First Act chills the blood with horror, to the Fop in the last, that exposes affectation to just contempt. . . .

Hamlet is, through the whole piece, rather an instrument than an agent. After he has, by the stratagem of the play, convicted the King, he makes no attempt to punish him; and his death is at last effected by an incident which Hamlet had no part in producing.

SAMUEL JOHNSON (1765).

THE grief of Hamlet is for the death of a father: he entertains aversion against an incestuous uncle, and indignation at the ingratitude and guilt of a mother. . . . The death of his father was a natural evil, and as such he endures it. That he is excluded from succeeding immediately to the royalty that belongs to him, seems to affect him slightly; for to vehement and vain ambition he appears superior. He is moved by finer principles, by an exquisite sense of virtue, of moral beauty and turpitude. The impropriety of Gertrude's behaviour, her ingratitude to the memory of her former husband, and the depravity she discovers in the choice of a successor, afflict his soul, and cast him into utter agony. Here then is the principle and spring of all his actions.

WILLIAM RICHARDSON (1784).

AROUND the main action the play gathers a varied and attractive world within which the whole Renaissance atmosphere in its humours, its intrigue, its interest in art, language and superstition, gains ample illustration. At the centre is Hamlet himself, melancholic, introspective, witty, incomprehensible and gracious, that strange, unaccountable Renaissance prince in whom, by some unfathomable miracle, Everyman not only in England but wherever the play is enacted, finds the image of his own art.

B. IFOR EVANS, *English Literature* (1944).

The Character of Hamlet

THE character of Hamlet has been many times discussed, and the opinions expressed may, for the most part, be ranged in two opposing camps. Some critics have held, with Goethe and Coleridge, that Hamlet is Shakespeare's study of the unpractical temperament; the portrait of a dreamer. Others, denying this, have called attention to his extraordinary courage and promptitude in action. He follows the Ghost without a moment's misgiving, in spite of his companions' warnings. He kills Polonius out of hand, and, when he finds his mistake, brushes it aside like a fly, to return to the main business. He sends Rosencrantz and Guildenstern to their death with cool despatch, and gives them a hasty epitaph:

> 'Tis dangerous when the baser nature comes
> Between the pass and fell incensed points
> Of mighty opposites.

In the sea-fight, we are told, he was the first to board the pirate vessel. And nothing in speech could be more pointed, practical, and searching, than his rapid cross-examination of Horatio concerning the appearance of the Ghost. Some of those who lay stress on these things go further, and maintain that Hamlet succeeds in his designs. His business was to convince himself of the King's guilt, and to make open demonstration of it before all Denmark. When these things are done, he stabs the King, and though his own life is taken by treachery, his task is accomplished, now that the story of the murder cannot be buried in his grave.

Yet when we read this or any other summary of the events narrated, we feel that it takes us far from the real theme of the play. A play is not a collection of the biographies of those that appear in it. It is a grouping of certain facts and events round a single centre, so that they may be seen at a glance. In this play that centre is the mind of Hamlet. We see with his eyes, and think his thoughts. When once we are caught in the rush of events we judge him no more than we judge ourselves. Almost all that has ever been said of his character is true; his character is so live and versatile that it presents many aspects.

It is observed by Coleridge that in Hamlet the equilibrium between the real and the imaginary worlds is disturbed. Just such a disturbance, so to call it, is produced by any great shock given to feeling, by bereavement or crime breaking in upon the walled serenity of daily life and opening vistas into the infinite expanse, where only the imagination can travel. The horizon is widened far beyond the narrow range of possible action; the old woes of the world are revived, and pass like shadows before the spellbound watcher. What Hamlet does is of little importance; nothing that he can do would avert the tragedy, or lessen his own agony. It is not by what he does that he appeals to us, but by what he sees and feels.

WALTER RALEIGH, Shakespeare (1907).

IN Hamlet, what Shakespeare values and makes us value is an extreme of experiencing power which, while it may produce the symptoms of irresolution, is not irresolution. In Hamlet there is neither uncertainty nor poverty of values; it is because his values are so rich and strong that he experiences all things so fully; and because he experiences them fully, he is more hurt by the calamity that befalls him than the common hero would be. But his hurt is also of a peculiar kind; the very calamity, beginning as external, becomes internal; his mind cannot adjust itself to the world of the court, as he finds it, or to life itself, since the world of the court is part of life. It is not merely conscience but his sovereign reason that rebels and is shaken by its own rebellion. The common hero, in such a case, would do something effective; in a tragedy he would be killed doing it, and the tragedy would consist of his death. But Hamlet's tragedy is his life after he has learned the truth from the Ghost; and it consists in the fact that, by his very virtues, moral, intellectual, and aesthetic, he is prevented from doing anything effective. It is the tragedy of 'Captive good attending captain ill'; and yet we are sure that this very capacity for suffering is more to be valued than the common hero's effectiveness. We may not be able to say why; we may, when the spell of Hamlet is no longer upon us, even ask why he does not act like the common hero; but, so long as we are under his spell, we do value him, not in terms of what he does, but in terms of himself.

A. CLUTTON BROCK, *Hamlet* (1922).

IT should be plain to any reader that the signal characteristic of Hamlet's inmost nature is by no means irresolution or hesitation or any form of weakness, but rather the strong conflux of contending forces. That during four whole acts Hamlet cannot or does not make up his mind to any direct and deliberate action against his uncle is true enough; true, also, we may say, that Hamlet had somewhat more of mind than another man to make up, and might properly want somewhat more time than might another man to do it in; but not, I venture to say in spite of Goethe, through innate inadequacy to his task and unconquerable weakness of will; not, I venture to think in spite of Hugo, through immedicable scepticism of the spirit and irremediable propensity to nebulous intellectual refinement. One practical point in the action of the play precludes us from accepting so ready a solution of the riddle as is suggested either by the simple theory of half-heartedness or by the simple hypothesis of doubt. There is absolutely no other reason, we might say there was no other excuse, for the introduction or intrusion of an else superfluous episode into a play which was already, and which remains even after all possible excisions, one of the longest plays upon record. The compulsory expedition of Hamlet to England, his discovery by the way of the plot laid against his life, his interception of the King's letter and his forgery of a substitute for it against the lives of the King's agents, the ensuing adventure of the sea-fight, with Hamlet's daring act of hot-headed personal intrepidity, his capture and subsequent release on terms giving no less patent proof of his cool-headed and ready-witted courage and resource than the attack had afforded of his physically impulsive and even impetuous hardihood—all this serves no purpose whatever but that of exhibiting the instant and almost unscrupulous resolution of Hamlet's character in time of practical need. But for all that he or Hamlet has got by it, Shakespeare might too evidently have spared his pains; and for all this voice as of one crying in the wilderness, Hamlet will too surely remain to the majority of students, not less than to all actors and all editors and all critics, the standing type and embodied emblem of irresolution, half-heartedness, and doubt.

A. C. SWINBURNE, *A Study of Shakespeare* (1879).

His troubles apart, what sort of a man is Hamlet? The course of the action gives us three different views of him: in his disillusioned grief; under the strain of his madness; and returning, hardened, to quit his account with the King. But they are all abnormal views. And, while we discount without much difficulty the antic disposition and even the moments of sore distraction, there would be no measuring the depth of the moral tragedy did not Shakespeare contrive to give us also some refracted glimpses of a more normal man.

The players are put to this use. The imaginative Hamlet finds forgetfulness in that unreal world, and in the noble music of Aeneas' tale to Dido, though his thoughts soon drift back.

Here is the man of fastidious taste, who prefers a play that 'pleased not the million' and had 'no sallets in the lines to make the matter savoury'—upon which small point alone he will be at odds with his surroundings, with the revelling Claudius, and with that man of the world Polonius, who is

for a jig, or a tale of bawdry, or he sleeps.

Here is a Hamlet, too, as princely in welcoming a common player as his friend, as (from another standpoint) in his frank mockery of Polonius, and (from yet another) in his curt warning to the favoured player not to follow his example. The famous advice to the players throws light on the intrinsic Hamlet too.

It is like him, at such a crisis, to trouble with it at all. Upon *what* he has written for them to act his whole project may depend; but that they might mouth it, or saw the air with their hands, or o'erstep the modesty of nature cannot matter in the least. But this is Hamlet ingrain; delighting in the thing that does not matter, and delighting in it for its own sake; and only the more because it is a fictive thing. The imaginative man prefers the unreal to the real; he can have his will of it.

But the chief use of these glimpses of a sounder Hamlet is for a counterpoise to the soliloquies—where, at first blush, we might expect to see him as he most unfeignedly is. But we do not. In a tragedy of spiritual struggle, discord will be at its worst when a man is left alone with his thoughts. When we see Hamlet alone he is either lapsed in self-conscious grief, or savagely self-reproachful, wrought to murderous excitement, or in suicidal despair. And when, in the calm of defeat, he deliberately questions himself, he has to admit that he knows nothing of himself at all.

But, this moral turmoil apart, it is not from his self-communings that we should best learn the simple truth about him. He is too imaginative a man for that. When he says to his mother:

> you shall not budge;
> You go not till I set you up a glass
> Where you may see the inmost part of you . . .

it is his own disposition that prompts the image. He is always looking at himself in the glass of his conscience. He tells the players 'to hold, as 'twere, the mirror up to nature'; and there is, indeed, more than a little of the actor in him.

It is not that he is crudely self-conscious. But he is ever trying to see himself, with his mind's eye, as he is; never, in the nature of things, succeeding; never satisfied of the truth of what he sees. Before such a mirror so constantly and provokingly held up a man inevitably falls to attitudinising, and to distorting the truth about himself. Till suffering has flogged all self-consciousness out of him, Hamlet is ever a little apt to be striking spiritual attitudes.

HARLEY GRANVILLE-BARKER,
Prefaces to Shakespeare: Third Series (1937)

THE character of Hamlet is itself a pure effusion of genius. It is not a character marked by strength of passion or will, but by refinement of thought and feeling. Hamlet is as little of the hero as a man can well be: but he is a young and princely novice, full of high enthusiasm and quick sensibility—the sport of circumstances, questioning with fortune, and refining on his own feelings, and forced from the natural bias of his character by the strangeness of his situation. He seems incapable of deliberate action, and is only hurried into extremities on the spur of the occasion, when he has no time to reflect, as in the scene where he kills Polonius, and again, where he alters the letters which Rosencrantz and Guildenstern are taking with them to England, purporting his death. At other times, when he is most bound to act, he remains puzzled, undecided and sceptical, dallies with his purposes, till the occasion is lost, and always finds some pretence to relapse into indolence and thoughtfulness again. For this reason he refuses to kill the King when he is at his prayers, and by a refinement in malice, which is in truth only an excuse for his own want of resolution, defers his revenge to some more fatal opportunity, when its object shall be engaged in some act 'that has no relish of salvation in it'.

He is the prince of philosophical speculators, and because he cannot have his revenge perfect, according to the most refined idea his wish can form, he misses it altogether. So he scruples to trust the suggestions of the Ghost, contrives the scene of the play to have surer proof of his uncle's guilt, and then rests satisfied with this confirmation of his suspicions, and the success of his experiment, instead of acting upon it. Yet he is sensible of his own weakness, taxes himself with it, and tries to reason himself out of it. . . . It is not for any want of attachment to his father or abhorrence of his murder that Hamlet is thus dilatory, but it is more to his taste to indulge his imagination in reflecting upon the enormity of the crime and refining on his schemes of vengeance, than to put them into immediate practice. His ruling passion is to think, not to act: and any vague pretence that flatters this propensity instantly diverts him from his previous purposes. . . .

Hamlet is probably, of all other of Shakespeare's characters, the most difficult to personate on the stage. It is like the attempt to embody a shadow. . . . The character is spun to the finest thread, yet never loses its continuity. It has the yielding flexibility of a wave of the sea! It is made up of undulating lines, without a single sharp angle. There is no set purpose, no straining at a point. The observations are suggested by the passing scene—the gusts of passion come and go, like the sounds of music borne on the wind. The interest depends not on the action, but on the thoughts.

WILLIAM HAZLITT, *Characters of Shakespeare's Plays* (1818).

Hamlet himself would never hav been aught to us, or we
to Hamlet, wer't not for the artful balance whereby
Shakespeare so gingerly put his sanity in doubt
without the while confounding his Reason.

BRIDGES, *The Testament of Beauty* (1929).

PEOPLE indeed reflect so little in the theatre. What has just passed is scarcely remembered, yet judgement is pronounced upon what is directly before their eyes; the public depends upon what it sees, and is so engrossed with that, that it is led without thought into the greatest violations of logic. To consider Hamlet insane, then again immediately to believe that it is mere feigning, and then to return to the first impression, and to continue changing thus backwards and forwards, is nothing that a poet like Shakespeare might not count upon in a susceptible public. He commands, and his audience follow him obediently like children, to whom he tells a story, making them laugh and cry by turns.

HERMAN GRIMM (1875).

ONE very manifest purpose of adopting the disguise of feigned madness was to obtain access to the King in some moment of unguarded privacy. . . . The ordinary tone of social intercourse would be the last he would willingly or successfully support. This feint of madness offered a disguise to him the more welcome, and which called for less constraint, than the laboured support of an ordinary, unnoticeable demeanor. The mimicry of madness was but the excess of that levity and wildness which naturally sprang from his impatient and overwrought spirit. It afforded some scope to those disquieted feelings which it served to conceal. The feint of madness covered all,—even the sarcasm, and disgust, and turbulence, which it freed in some measure from an intolerable restraint. Nor was it a disguise ungrateful to a moody spirit, grown careless of the respect of men, and indifferent to all the ordinary projects and desires of life. The masquerade brought with it no sense of humiliation—it pleased a misanthropic humor,—it gave him shelter and a sort of escape from society, and it cost him little effort. That mingled bitterness and levity, which served for the representation of insanity, was often the most faithful expression of his feelings.

Blackwood's Magazine (1839).

HAMLET, among all the characters of Shakespeare, is the most eminently a metaphysician and psychologist. He is a close observer, continually analysing his own nature and that of others, letting fall his little drops of acid irony on all who come near him, to make them show what they are made of. Even Ophelia is not too sacred, Osric not too contemptible for experiment. If such a man assumed madness, he would play his part perfectly. . . . If you deprive Hamlet of reason, there is no truly tragic motive left. He would be a fit subject for Bedlam, but not for the stage. We might have pathology enough, but no pathos. Ajax first becomes tragic when he recovers his wits. If Hamlet is irresponsible, the whole play is a chaos.

This feigned madness of Hamlet's is one of the few points in which Shakespeare has kept close to the old story on which he founded his play ; and as he never decided without deliberation, so he never acted without unerring judgement. Hamlet *drifts* through the whole play. . . . The scheme of simulated insanity is precisely the one he would have been likely to hit upon, because it enabled him to follow his own bent, and to drift with an apparent purpose, postponing decisive action by the very means he adopts to arrive at its accomplishment, and satisfying

himself with the show of doing something that he may escape
so much the longer the dreaded necessity of really doing anything at all.

J. R. LOWELL (1870).

Claudius

OF the circumstances and method of the murder of Hamlet's
father, upon which so much hangs, and which are twice detailed,
first in the account the Ghost renders of his own death, and
again in the Gonzago play, or rather in the dumb-show that
precedes it, there is no hint in either Saxo or Belleforest. The
Danish story does not mention poison, sleep or orchard. On
the contrary Belleforest expressly states that the deed was
done by bloody violence in the banqueting-hall of the palace,
while Amleth's father sat at meat. On the other hand, *The
Murder of Gonzago* bears all the marks of being founded upon
an Italian original; and I see no reason for doubting that
Hamlet's words at III. ii. 262, 'The story is extant and written
in very choice Italian', were substantially correct. Indeed,
there are even indications of a historical foundation for the
tale, since according to Dowden, 'In 1538 the Duke of Urbino,
married to a Gonzaga, was murdered by Luigi Gonzaga, who
dropped poison into his ear'. What more likely than that
Shakespeare, or Kyd, used a scene from a contemporary play
upon this subject for his Play-scene, and in order to make the
resemblance exact, altered the Hamlet-story to suit the story
of Gonzago?

And if something like this happened, it follows that the
character of Claudius was also in large measure derived from,
or suggested by, the Gonzago-tale. The murderer in the Danish
legend was crafty, it is true: 'The man', Saxo tells us, 'veiled
the monstrosity of his deed with such hardihood of cunning,
that he made up a mock pretence of goodwill to excuse his
crime, and glossed over fratricide with a show of righteousness.'
But he was essentially a man of violence. The Claudius of
Hamlet is effeminate and Italianate. Not without courage and
possessed of considerable intellectual powers, he presents never-
theless a mean and contemptible figure. He is a prey to lust,

works by spying, and listens behind hangings; if murder is to
be done, he eggs on others, when he can, to do it for him; and
his trump card, when all else fails, is poison—poison in a 'vial',
a drinking-cup, or on the point of an unbated foil. It is in
keeping with all this that he should put his brother out of the
world by an act which could only have originated in decadent
Italy, an act which revolts us less by its base treachery than
by its hideous and unnatural character. Claudius was a 'politician' in the sixteenth century meaning of that word, a man
who lived by dropping poison into other people's ears, and his
supreme crime is but the symbol of his personality. Such a
being was bred not at Elsinore, but at some petty Italian court.
Yet his insertion into the *Hamlet* frame was a masterly stroke.
The man of violence, the Laertes type, is useful as a foil to
Hamlet; but for his antagonist it was essential to have a man
of great cunning, since one of the main interests of the play is
the spectacle of two extraordinarily subtle men engaged in a
deadly duel of wits.

JOHN DOVER WILSON, *Hamlet* (The New Shakespeare) (1936).

Polonius

POLONIUS is a man, bred in courts, exercised in business, stored
with observation, confident of his knowledge, proud of his
eloquence, and declining into dotage. His mode of oratory is
truly represented as designed to ridicule the practice of those
times, of prefaces that made no introduction, and of method
that embarrassed rather than explained. This part of his
character is accidental, the rest is natural. Such a man is
positive and confident, because he knows that his mind was
once strong, and knows not that it is become weak. Such a
man excels in general principles, but fails in the particular
application. He is knowing in retrospect, and ignorant in foresight. While he depends upon his memory, and can draw from
his repositories of knowledge, he utters weighty sentences, and
gives useful counsel; but as the mind in its enfeebled state
cannot be kept long busy and intent, the old man is subject to
sudden dereliction of his faculties, he loses the order of his ideas,

and entangles himself in his own thoughts, till he recovers the leading principle and falls again into his former train. This idea of dotage encroaching upon wisdom will solve all the phenomena of the character of Polonius.

SAMUEL JOHNSON (1765).

WE can, I think, see Shakespeare changing his mind a little about Polonius. In his first scene (not to count the single speech at the Council) he is far from being a 'tedious old fool'. His injunctions to Laertes and Ophelia are clear and terse, and contain sound worldly wisdom. The change comes with the charge to Reynaldo; and hence, perhaps, the seemingly undue length allowed to that minor matter; our first impressions of the character must be corrected. After the resolution into the more comic key we have him more spontaneously and abundantly himself; though the mere abundance is gradually pruned, for once the garrulity has been demonstrated, the effect of it can be gained without much indulgence in the thing itself.

His adjusted place in the play's character scheme soon becomes plain. Hamlet doubts and delays, questions and suffers. Claudius, all outward candour, keeps his secret close and moves surely to his ends. Polonius is the complacent wiseacre, infatuate in opinion, precipitate in action—and usually wrong. He is not wholly or obviously a fool, nor externally ridiculous at all. He can occupy his high place with dignity enough—only now and then calling pomposity to his aid—so long as everybody will keep theirs.

HARLEY GRANVILLE-BARKER,
Prefaces to Shakespeare: Third Series (1937).

The Queen

THE Queen was not a bad-hearted woman, not at all the woman to think little of murder. But she had a soft animal nature, and was very dull and very shallow. She loved to be happy, like a sheep in the sun; and, to do her justice, it pleased her to see others happy, like more sheep in the sun. She never saw that drunkenness is disgusting till Hamlet told her so; and, though she knew that he considered her marriage 'o'er-hasty'

(II. ii. 57), she was untroubled by any shame at the feelings that had led to it. It was pleasant to sit upon her throne and see smiling faces round her, and foolish and unkind in Hamlet to persist in grieving for his father instead of marrying Ophelia and making everything comfortable. She was fond of Ophelia and genuinely attached to her son (though willing to see her lover exclude him from the throne); and, no doubt, she considered equality of rank a mere trifle compared with the claims of love. The belief at the bottom of her heart was that the world is a place constructed simply that people may be happy in it in a good-humoured sensual fashion.

Her only chance was to be made unhappy. When affliction comes to her, the good in her nature struggles to the surface through the heavy mass of sloth. Like other faulty characters in Shakespeare's tragedies, she dies a better woman than she had lived. When Hamlet shows her what she has done she feels genuine remorse. It is true, Hamlet fears it will not last, and so at the end of the interview (III. iv. 180 ff.) he adds a warning that, if she betrays him, she will ruin herself as well. It is true too that there is no sign of her obeying Hamlet in breaking off her most intimate connexion with the King. Still she does feel remorse; and she loves her son, and does not betray him. She gives her husband a false account of Polonius's death, and is silent about the appearance of the Ghost. She becomes miserable;

> To her sick soul, as sin's true nature is,
> Each toy seems prologue to some great amiss.

She shows spirit when Laertes raises the mob, and one respects her for standing up for her husband when she can do nothing to save her son. If she had sense to realise Hamlet's purpose, or the probability of the King's taking some desperate step to foil it, she must have suffered torture in those days. But perhaps she was too dull.

The last we see of her, at the fencing match, is most characteristic. She is perfectly serene. Things have slipped back into their groove, and she has no apprehensions. She is, however, disturbed and full of sympathy for her son, who is out of condition and pants and perspires. These are afflictions she can thoroughly feel for, though they are even more common than the death of a father. But then she meets her death because she cannot resist the wish to please her son by drinking to his success. And more: when she falls dying, and the King tries to make out that she is merely swooning at the sight of blood, she collects her energies to deny it and to warn Hamlet:

> No, no, the drink, the drink,—O my dear Hamlet,—
> The drink, the drink! I am poison'd.   [*Dies.*

Was ever any other writer at once so pitiless and so just as Shakespeare? Did ever any other mingle the grotesque and the pathetic with a realism so daring and yet so true to 'the modesty of nature'?

A. C. BRADLEY, Shakesperean Tragedy (1904).

Osric

PERHAPS the vitalising power of Shakespeare is best seen in the loving care that he sometimes spends on subsidiary characters, whose connection with the plot is but slight. The young Osric, in *Hamlet*, has no business in the play except to carry Laertes' challenge to Hamlet. Shakespeare draws his portrait; we learn that he is a landowner, and perceive that he is an accomplished courtier. Hamlet and Horatio discuss him at some length, and his own speech shows how seriously he is preoccupied with all the etiquette and formality of Court life. He exists, it cannot be doubted, merely as a foil for Hamlet's wit and melancholy. When the mind is wholly taken up with tragic issues, when it is brooding on a great sorrow, or foreboding a hopeless event, the little daily affairs of life continue unaltered; tables are served, courtesies interchanged, and the wheels of society revolve at their accustomed pace. Osric is the representative of society; his talk is of gentility, skill in fencing, and the elegance of the proffered wager. How distant and dream-like it all seems to Hamlet, and to those who are in his secret! But this trivial society is real and necessary, and strong with the giant strength of custom and institution. Shakespeare demonstrates its reality by showing us a live

inhabitant. He might have entrusted the challenge to a
walking-gentleman, and concluded the business in a few lines.
By making a scene of it, he adds a last touch of pathos to the
loneliness of Hamlet, and gives a last opportunity for the
display of that incomparable vein of irony.

WALTER RALEIGH, Shakespeare (1907).

The Place of the Action

THE action of *Hamlet* is concentrated at Elsinore; and this
though there is much external interest, and the story abounds
in journeys. As a rule in such a case, unless they are mere
messengers, we travel with the travellers. But we do not see
Laertes in Paris, nor, more surprisingly, Hamlet among the
pirates; and the Norwegian affair is dealt with by hearsay till
the play is two-thirds over. This is not done to economise
time, or to leave space for more capital events. Scenes in
Norway or Paris or aboard ship need be no longer than the
talk of them, and Hamlet's discovery of the King's plot against
him is a capital event. Shakespeare is deliberately concentra-
ting his action at Elsinore. When he does at last introduce
Fortinbras he stretches probability to bring him and his army
seemingly to its very suburbs; and, sooner than that Hamlet
should carry the action abroad with him, Horatio is left behind
there to keep him in our minds. On the other hand he still,
by allusion, makes the most of this movement abroad which
he does not represent; he even adds to our sense of it by such
seemingly superfluous touches as tell us that Horatio has jour-
neyed from Wittenberg, that Rosencrantz and Guildenstern
have been 'sent for'—and even the Players are travelling.

The double dramatic purpose is plain. Here is a tragedy of
inaction; the centre of it is Hamlet, who is physically inactive
too, has 'foregone all custom of exercises', will not 'walk out
of the air', but only, book in hand, for 'four hours together,
here in the lobby'. The concentration at Elsinore of all that
happens enhances the impression of this inactivity, which is
enhanced again by the sense also given us of the constant
coming and going around Hamlet of the busier world without.

The place itself, moreover, thus acquires a personality, and even develops a sort of sinister power; so that when at last Hamlet does depart from it (his duty still unfulfilled) and we are left with the conscience-sick Gertrude and the guilty King, the mad Ophelia, a Laertes set on his own revenge, among a

> peopled muddied
> Thick and unwholesome in their thoughts and whispers ...

we almost seem to feel it, and the unpurged sin of it, summoning him back to his duty and his doom. Shakespeare has, in fact, here adopted something very like unity of place; upon no principle, but to gain a specific dramatic end.

He turns time to dramatic use also, ignores or remarks its passing, and uses clock or calendar or falsifies or neglects them just as it suits him.

HARLEY GRANVILLE-BARKER,
Prefaces to Shakespeare: Third Series (1937).

'Hamlet' and 'Macbeth'

IN *Macbeth* and *Hamlet* not only is the feeling of a supreme power or destiny peculiarly marked, but it has also at times a peculiar tone, which may be called, in a sense, religious. I cannot make my meaning clear without using language too definite to describe truly the imaginative impression produced; but it is roughly true that, while we do not imagine the supreme power as a divine being who avenges crime, or as a providence which supernaturally interferes, our sense of it is influenced by the fact that Shakespeare uses current religious ideas here much more decidedly than in *Othello* or *King Lear*. The horror in Macbeth's soul is more than once represented as desperation at the thought that he is eternally 'lost'; the same idea appears in the attempt of Claudius at repentance; and as *Hamlet* nears its close the 'religious' tone of the tragedy is deepened in two ways. In the first place, 'accident' is introduced into the plot in its barest and least dramatic form, when Hamlet is brought back to Denmark by the chance of the meeting with the pirate ship. ... It appears probable that the 'accident' is meant to impress the imagination as the very reverse of 'accidental', and with many readers it certainly does so. And that this was the intention is made the more likely by a second fact, the fact that in connection with the events of the voyage Shakespeare introduces that feeling on Hamlet's part of his being in the hands of Providence. . . .

We may remember another significant point of resemblance between *Hamlet* and *Macbeth*, the appearance in each play of a Ghost,—a figure which seems quite in place in either, whereas it would seem utterly out of place in *Othello* or *King Lear*. Much might be said of the Ghost in *Hamlet*, but I confine myself to the matter which we are now considering. What is the effect of the appearance of the Ghost? And, in particular, why does Shakespeare make this Ghost so *majestical* a phantom, giving it that measured and solemn utterance, and that air of impersonal abstraction which forbids, for example, all expression of affection for Hamlet and checks in Hamlet the outburst of pity for his father? Whatever the intention may have been, the result is that the Ghost affects imagination not simply as the apparition of a dead king who desires the accomplishment of *his* purposes, but also as the representative of that hidden ultimate power, the messenger of divine justice set upon the expiation of offences which it appeared impossible for man to discover and avenge, a reminder or a symbol of the connection of the limited world of ordinary experience with the vaster life of which it is but a partial appearance. And as, at the beginning of the play, we have this intimation, conveyed through the medium of the received religious idea of a soul come from purgatory, so at the end, conveyed through the similar idea of a soul carried by angels to its rest, we have an intimation of the same character, and a reminder that the apparent failure of Hamlet's life is not the ultimate truth concerning him.

A. C. BRADLEY, Shakesperean Tragedy (1904).

The Imagery of the Play

IN *Hamlet*, naturally, we find ourselves in an entirely different atmosphere. If we look closely we see this is partly due to the number of images of sickness, disease or blemish of the body, in the play, and we discover that the idea of an ulcer or tumour,

as descriptive of the unwholesome condition of Denmark
morally, is, on the whole, the dominating one.

Hamlet speaks of his mother's sin as a blister on the 'fair
forehead of an innocent love', she speaks of her 'sick soul',
and as in *King Lear* the emotion is so strong and the picture
so vivid, that the metaphor overflows into the verbs and
adjectives: heaven's face, he tells her, is *thought-sick* at the act;
her husband is a *mildew'd ear*, *blasting* his *wholesome* brother;
to have married him, her sense must be not only *sickly*, but
apoplex'd. Finally, at the end of that terrific scene (III. iv.), he
implores her not to soothe herself with the belief that his
father's apparition is due to her son's madness, and not to her
guilt, for that

> will but skin and film the ulcerous place,
> Whiles rank corruption, mining all within,
> Infects unseen.

So also, later, he compares the unnecessary fighting between
Norway and Poland to a kind of tumour which grows out of
too much prosperity. He sees the country and the people in it
alike in terms of a sick body needing medicine or the surgeon's
knife. When he surprises Claudius at his prayers, he exclaims,

> This physic but prolongs thy sickly days;

and he describes the action of conscience in the unforgettable
picture of the healthy, ruddy countenance turning pale with
sickness. A mote in the eye, a vicious mole, a galled chilblain,
a probed wound and purgation, are also among Hamlet's
images; and the mind of Claudius runs equally on the same
theme.

When he hears of the murder of Polonius, he declares that
his weakness in not sooner having had Hamlet shut up was
comparable to the cowardly action of a man with a 'foul
disease' who

> To keep it from divulging, let it feed
> Even on the pith of life;

and later, when arranging to send Hamlet to England and to
his death, he justifies it by the proverbial tag:

> diseases desperate grown
> By desperate appliance are relieved,
> Or not at all;

and adjures the English King to carry out his behest, in the words of a fever patient seeking a sedative:

> For like the hectic in my blood he rages,
> And thou must cure me.

When working on Laertes, so that he will easily fall in with the design for the fencing match, his speech is full of the same underlying thought of a body sick, or ill at ease:

> goodness, growing to a plurisy,
> Dies in his own too much;

and finally, he sums up the essence of the position and its urgency with lightning vividness in a short medical phrase:

> But, to the quick o' the ulcer:
> Hamlet comes back.

. . . In *Hamlet*, . . . *anguish* is not the dominating thought, but *rottenness*, disease, corruption, the result of *dirt*; the people are 'muddied',

> Thick and unwholesome in their thoughts and whispers;

and this corruption is, in the words of Claudius, 'rank' and 'smells to heaven', so that the state of things in Denmark which shocks, paralyses and finally overwhelms Hamlet, is as the foul tumour breaking inwardly and poisoning the whole body, while showing

> no cause without
> Why the man dies.

This image pictures and reflects not only the outward condition which causes Hamlet's spiritual illness, but also his own state.

CAROLINE SPURGEON, *Shakespeare's Imagery* (1935).

APPENDIX I

THE LIFE OF WILLIAM SHAKESPEARE

(condensed from Sir Edmund Chamber's *William Shakespeare*)

WILLIAM SHAKESPEARE was born of middle-class parents at Stratford-on-Avon, a provincial market town of some importance, at an uncertain date between April 24, 1563, and April 23, 1564. His parents were natives of Warwickshire. His father, John Shakespeare, whose principal business was that of glover, rose high in civic life, becoming alderman in 1565 and bailiff in 1568, but later fell on evil days. His mother was Mary Arden. Shakespeare was educated at King Edward VI's Grammar School, Stratford, where he must have learnt a fair amount of Latin, if little or no Greek. He married in 1582 Anne Hathaway, and his first child, Susanna, was baptized in May 1583, to be followed in February 1585 by twins, Hamnet and Judith. Susanna's daughter, Elizabeth (died 1670), was the poet's last direct descendant.

We have no certain information as to Shakespeare's life between 1584 and 1592. There is an early tradition that he stole deer from Sir T. Lucy of Charlecote. We know Shakespeare was in London by 1592 but not when he went there. During these years Shakespeare must have acquired the varied knowledge and experience of life shown in his plays.

The mention of Shakespeare in a death-bed letter of the playwright Greene in September 1592 shows that as a writer for the stage Shakespeare was just becoming a serious rival to the university wits—Marlowe, Peele, Nashe, and Lodge. The years when the theatres were closed on account of plague gave time for the poems *Venus and Adonis* (1593) and *Lucrece* (1594), both dedicated to the Earl of Southampton. By March 1595 Shakespeare was a shareholder in the acting company of the Lord Chamberlain's men, who divided with the Admiral's men the command of the London stage from about 1594 to 1603. For this company, which later became the King's men, Shakespeare seems to have written during the rest of his career. After

1599 most of his plays were performed at the Globe Theatre. Shakespeare probably wrote his *Sonnets* between 1595 and 1600, but they were not printed till 1609.

In 1596 Shakespeare obtained a grant of arms; in 1597 he bought New Place, a substantial house and garden at Stratford, but he is still found living in London in 1597, 1599, and 1604. Shakespeare occasionally appeared as an actor himself, chiefly before 1598.

About 1610 Shakespeare retired to Stratford, and he wrote no more after 1613. He took no part in civic life, and died on 23 April 1616. There is no reason to reject the report that he died of fever contracted from drinking too hard at a merry meeting with Drayton and Ben Jonson.

APPENDIX II

A NOTE ON SHAKESPEARE'S LANGUAGE

By C. T. ONIONS

VOCABULARY. As the *Oxford Shakespeare Glossary* shows, there are some ten thousand words in the whole of the works attributed to Shakespeare which require explanation for the general reader, either because they are no longer in ordinary use or because they are used by him in some way that is not now familiar. Among the former are such words as *ballow* cudgel, *phill-horse* shaft-horse, and *neaf* fist, which are now only provincial, and such others as *benison* blessing, *foison* abundance, *mow* grimace, *parlous* dangerous, *puissant* powerful, *teen* grief, which may be found still in literary diction, as well as a considerable number that have been used, so far as we know, by Shakespeare alone. With such as these we become acquainted by reference to glossaries and notes. But it is possible to continue to read Shakespeare without properly understanding him because we are unaware of, and sometimes do not even suspect, differences in the meaning of words that are in general use to-day. The following selection of such words will serve to indicate the nature of the differences that may be looked for:

allow approve
argument proof, subject of discourse
brave fine, splendid
churchman clergyman
close secret
complexion habit or constitution of body or mind, look, aspect, appearance
conceit idea, thought, invention
condition covenant, rank character
difference disagreement, dispute
evil disease
fashion sort
favour appearance, face
feature bodily form
gear affair, business
grudge complain
hint opportunity
hope expect, suppose
infer allege
instance cause, evidence, proof
level aim
lewd bad, vile

liberal unrestrained, licentious
mere absolute, downright
merely entirely
miss do without
note sign, stigma, information
obsequious dutiful
owe own
painful laborious
passion painful disease, strong emotion
peevish silly, perverse
present immediate
presently at once
prevent anticipate
quality rank, profession
rate estimation
respect consideration
sad grave, serious
shrewd mischievous, bad
sort rank, class, way, manner
still always, continually
stomach inclination, angry or proud temper
sudden swift, violent
tall fine, valiant
type mark, badge
very true, complete

Among words having a very wide range of meaning the following may be noted:

humour (1) moisture, (2) any of the four fluids of the human body recognized by the old physiologists, (3) temperament, (4) mood, temper, fancy, caprice, inclination;

nice (1) delicate, (2) shy, coy, (3) fastidious, (4) subtle, minute, (5) trivial, (6) critical, precarious, (7) exact, precise;

quaint (1) skilled, clever, (2) pretty, dainty, (3) handsome, elegant, (4) carefully elaborated;

sensible (1) sensitive, (2) of the senses, (3) capable of emotion, (4) rational, (5) tangible, substantial, (6) full of good sense;

wit (1) mental powers, mind, faculty of perception, as in *the five wits*, (2) inventive power, (3) understanding, intelligence, (4) wisdom, good sense, as in *brevity is the soul of wit*, (5) lively fancy producing brilliant talk.

A second adjective **dear** grievous, severe, dire (distinct from *dear* beloved, precious) is seen in *my dear offence, thy dear exile*.

Many adjectives and participial words show the application of a suffix with a force different from that which is now usual:

deceivable deceitful	**questionable** inviting question
tuneable tuneful	**careless** uncared for
unmeritable undeserving	**unexpressive** inexpressible
cureless incurable	**plausive** plausible
grac'd gracious	**unavoided** inevitable
guiled treacherous	**beholding** obliged, beholden
disdain'd disdainful	**timeless** untimely, premature

Note also the double meaning, active and passive, of **artificial** (1) constructive, creative, (2) produced by art.

Shakespeare uses a multitude of technical terms of the arts and sciences; these are treated in their historical setting in *Shakespeare's England* (O.U.P.); note especially the glossary of musical terms in vol. ii, pp. 32 ff. Some general aspects of the vocabulary are dealt with in G. S. Gordon's *Shakespeare's English*, Society for Pure English, Tract xxix (O.U.P.).

PRONUNCIATION. In order to understand the scansion of the verse it is necessary to bear in mind certain features of the pronunciation of the time. Many words of French or Latin origin had been variously stressed from early times, and deviation from present usage is to be seen, for example, in Shakespeare's *adver'tizèd, aspect', canon'izèd, chas'tise, compact'* (noun), *exile'*, *instinct'* (noun), *obdu'rate*, *reven'ue*, *sepul'chre*, *solem'nizèd*, *triumph'ing*. The stressing of certain adjectives and participles of two syllables is subject to the rule that immediately before the nouns of one syllable, and before other nouns stressed on the 1st syllable, they themselves are stressed on the 1st syllable, but in other positions on the 2nd; thus: *all' the com'plete ar'mour*, *ev'ery way' complete'*; *the en'tire sum'*, *your' entire' affec'tion*; *the crown' so foul' misplaced'*, *the mis'placed John'*.

In words in *-ian*, *-ience*, *-ient*, *-ion*, these endings may count as two syllables; thus, *Christian*, *patient* may be 3 syllables, *condition*, *impatience* 4, *lamentation* 5. Similarly *marriage* and *soldier* may be three syllables. There is variation in such words as *fire*, *hour*, *power*, *prayer*, which may count as either one or two syllables. *Either* and *neither* may be slurred into one syllable, and *whether* is often so reduced, the form *where* frequently occurring in the old editions, continuing what was a regular early English variant form. *Hither*, *thither*, *whither*, and *having*, *evil*, *devil* are treated in the same way. *Statue* occurs in several passages in the old editions where three syllables are required; many modern editions substitute *statua*, which was a common Tudor and Stuart form.

NOUNS. The genitive singular ending *s* may be replaced by *his*, as *the count* his *galleys*, *Mars* his *armour*. The inflexion is dropped before *sake*, e.g. *for justice sake*, *for heaven sake*. Proper names often occur without inflexion, where the genitive might be expected, or *of*: e.g. *Venice gold*, *Rome gates*, *Tiber banks*. One of the adverbial uses of the genitive is preserved in *come your ways*. Notable examples of the *n*-plural are *shoon* for *shoes*, and *eyne* (eyes), which are used chiefly for rhyme. *Aches* is of two syllables, since the noun *ache* was pronounced *aitch*, as distinct from the verb, which was regularly spelt *ake* in the old editions. Names of measures and periods of time are often uninflected, as *twelve year*, *a thousand pound*: cf. *sennight* (= seven nights) *week*.

ADJECTIVES. Adjectives are converted into nouns with greater freedom than at present: *fair* is used for beauty as well as for lady, *the general* for the public, the multitude, *the subject* for the people of a state. Note the phrases: *in few* in few words, in short; *by small and small* little by little; *the most* (= majority) *of men. Enow* represents the old plural of *enough*, and is so used, always following its noun or pronoun. *Mo, moe* (= more) is also plural: it represents an old comparative adverb, which was used at first with a genitive, but became in time an adjective like *more*. The plural of *other* is either *others* or *other* (e.g. *and then come in the other*).

Peculiarities in the comparison of adjectives are: the use of the suffixes where we prefer *more* and *most*, as *certainer, perfecter, violentest*; the addition of *-er* to a comparative, as *worser*; the use of *more* and *most* with comparatives and superlatives, as *more better, most best, most dearest, more worthier, most worst, most unkindest*. Note the old comparative *near*, as in *ne'er the near*. An absolute superlative may be strengthened by prefixing *one*, e.g. *one the truest-mannered*.

PRONOUNS. The distinction between the familiar or contemptuous *thou* (*thee, thy*) and the respectful *ye* (*you, your*) is in general preserved. The old weak form *a* of *he* occurs in *There was a gaming*. The commonest genitive of *it* is *his*; the present-day *its* and the obsolete *it* (as in *It had it head bit off by it young*) are about equally frequent in the old editions. Pronominal possessive forms are sometimes used as adjectives, but only in company with other possessives, as in *his and* mine *lov'd darling*. Note the position of the possessive in *good* my *liege,* sweet my *coz*.

There is much irregularity in the use of the cases of pronouns. *Thee* is used for *thou*, as with intransitive imperatives, *look thee, stand thee close*; also in *I would not be thee*, and the like. We find also: *between you and* I; *Is she as tall as* me?; *Which, of* he *or Adrian . . . ?; Damn'd* be him *. . .* The functions of the original nominative *ye* and objective *you* are reversed in *I do beseech* ye, *if* you *bear me hard . . .; us* is usual for *we* in the interrogative *Shall*'s. There is no consistency in the use of *who* and *whom*; a common confusion is illustrated in whom *they say is killed*.

The relative pronouns are not discriminated according to present practice, since *which* may refer to persons and *who* to things. *The which* is very frequent; it may be used adjectivally, as in *For the which blessing I am at him upon my knees*. The nominative relative (the subject of the clause) is often absent, as in *There be some sports are painful*. After a negative or an interrogative, *but* is frequently used as a relative = that . . . not; e.g. *No man but prophesied revenge for it; What canst thou say but will perplex them more?*

VERBS. Verbs show many old forms as well as a variety of conjugation which are no longer possible in ordinary language.

Early strong forms are retained in *holp, holp'st*, alongside *helped, helped'st; spake* and *spoke* are both in use; old strong forms are replaced by weak in *becomed, shaked;* the past tenses *drunk* and *sprung* are more frequent than *drank* and *sprang;* the clipped *broke, spoke* occur beside the original participial forms *broken, spoken; catched* and *caught* are both found; many past tense forms are used for the past participle, as *eat, holp, forsook, rode, shook, swam*. Remarkable instances of the great variety of usage may be seen in *struck, strucken, stricken*, for the past participle of *strike*, and in the conjugation *write*, past tense *writ*, occasionally *wrote*, past participle *written, writ*, less frequently *wrote*. Weak verbs of which the stem ends in *d* or *t* often have shortened past participles, as *betid, heat, wed, wet*. Observe that *graft* and *hoist* are rather participles of the older verbs *graff* and *hoise* than of *graft* and *hoist*.

Present tense forms in *s* (including *is*) are not uncommonly used with plural subjects, especially where the verb precedes the subject; e.g. *What cares these roarers for the name of king?; There is no more such masters*.

There are many survivals of impersonal uses, some of them in disguise. The older forms of *I were better, Thou'rt best* were *Me were better* It would be better for me, *Thee were best* It would be best for thee; but in *You were better* the case of the pronoun became ambiguous, *you* was in time felt as a nominative, and other pronouns fell into line. The history of the development of *I am woe* (in which *woe* is felt as an adjective) from the original *Me is woe* is somewhat similar. In *Fair befall thee* the verb is impersonal and *fair* an adverb.

The uses of the subjunctive are many and various. An exceptional construction is seen in *Live thou* (= if thou live), *I live*.

An old use of the past subjunctive is exemplified in *If you would put me to verses, Kate, why, you* **undid** (= would undo) *me.*

The infinitive of a verb of motion is often to be supplied in thought with an auxiliary verb; e.g. *I must to England;* **Shall we** *to this gear?*

ADVERBS. Adverbs, especially those of one syllable, may have the same form as their corresponding adjectives, as *dear, full, fair, near, true*; such words as *excellent, equal, instant, prodigal* are also used adverbially. When two adverbs are coupled together which would both normally have the suffix *-ly,* one of them may lack it, as in *sprightfully and bold, so lamely and unfashionable.* A rare formation is *chirurgeonly* like a surgeon. Comparative forms with the suffix are used more freely than at present; e.g. *earthlier happy, wiselier.*

The use of *but* in the sense of 'only' needs to be specially noticed: *but now* just now, only this moment; similarly, *but while-ere* only a short time ago, *but late* only lately. It is coupled redundantly with *only* in *He only lived but till he was a man.*

Normally, *only* should stand immediately before the words it modifies; but it is often loosely placed, as in *He only loves the world for him* (i.e. only for him).

A negative adverb (or conjunction) may be used with another negative word, superfluously from our point of view (the use was originally emphatic): *You know my father hath no child but I,* **nor none** *is like to have.* The negative may even be tripled: *Love no man in good earnest;* **nor no** *further in sport* **neither.** In the following a redundant negative occurs in a dependent clause after a verb of negative meaning: *You may deny that you were* **not** *the cause.*

PREPOSITIONS. Prepositions have many uses that differ from their present ones; for example, *for, of,* and *to* have each some ten meanings that are not current now. *Of* and *with* are both used to express the agent, as in *seen* of *us, torn to pieces* with *a bear,* or the instrument, as in *provided* of *a torch-bearer,* *killed* with *a thunderstroke.* With abstract nouns, *of* forms equivalents of the corresponding adjectives; e.g. *of desperation* desperate, *of nature* natural. Both *for* and *to* may be used, though in different kinds of context, = in the character of, as:

e.g. *turned out of all towns and cities* for *a dangerous thing; I have a king here* to *my flatterer*. A preposition is used freely at the end of the sentence or clause, e.g. *he I am before* = he in whose presence I am; sometimes it is redundant, as in *the scene wherein we play* in; or again, it may be dropped, as in *I see thou lovest me not with the full weight that I love thee* (i.e. *with*).

At in *at door, at gate*, and the like, is descended from the earlier *atte* (two syllables), which is for *at the*.

CONJUNCTIONS. The following should be noted: *an* or *an if* if; *as* as if; *for* because; *but* if . . . not, unless; *nor . . . nor . . .* neither . . . nor . . ., *or . . . or . . .* either . . . or . . .; *or ere* before ever; *so* provided that; *that* (in much wider use than at present) for the reason that, because, in order that, so that; *whiles* while.

The full exposition of the language of Shakespeare requires a book to itself, and such will be found in E. A. Abbot's *Shakespearian Grammar* and W. Franz's *Shakespeare-Grammatik*. An illuminating sketch is Henry Bradley's essay 'Shakespeare's English' in *Shakespeare's England*, vol. ii, pp. 539–74. Selected points are treated with some fullness in *Nine Plays of Shakespeare* (O.U.P.), pp. xix–xxvi.